W9-DAU-732

HOLY SPIRIT LIBRARY
CABRINI COLLEGE, RADNOR, PA.

Democracy
at the
Point of Bayonets

Democracy
at the
Point of Bayonets

Mark Peceny

HOLY SPIRIT LIBRARY
GWYNEDD COLLEGE, GWYNEDD, PA.

The Pennsylvania State University Press
University Park, Pennsylvania

E
744
.P33
1999

#39765265

Library of Congress Cataloging-in-Publication Data

Peceny, Mark, 1961–
    Democracy at the point of bayonets / Mark Peceny.
        p.   cm.
    Includes bibliographical references and index.
    ISBN 0-271-01882-8 (cloth : alk. paper)
    ISBN 0-271-01883-6 (pbk. : alk. paper)
    1. United States—Foreign relations—20th century.   2. United States—Military
policy—History—20th century.   3. Democracy—History—20th century.
4. Intervention (International law)—History—20th century.   5. Military
assistance, American—History—20th century.   6. National security—United
States—History—20th century.   I. Title
    E744.P33   1999
    327.73'009—dc21   98-37146
                                                                                          CIP

Copyright © 1999 The Pennsylvania State University
All rights reserved
Printed in the United States of America
Published by The Pennsylvania State University Press,
University Park, PA 16802–1003

It is the policy of The Pennsylvania State University Press to use acid-free paper for
the first printing of all clothbound books. Publications on uncoated stock satisfy the
minimum requirements of American National Standard for Information Sciences—
Permanence of Paper for Printed Library Materials, ANSI Z39.48–1992.

To Connie, Sarah, and Hannah

Contents

List of Tables

Acknowledgments

It is customary to conclude acknowledgments by thanking one's family. I begin mine by thanking my wife, Connie, and my two daughters, Sarah and Hannah, because I could not have completed this work without their constant love, support, and patience. No one played more crucial roles in helping me successfully finish this project than they. I dedicate this book to them.

This book began as a dissertation at Stanford University, where I was able to work with an outstanding committee. Stephen Krasner, Terry Lynn Karl, and Richard Fagen were an unfailing source of inspiration, support, and direction through my graduate school years. Their perceptive comments and criticisms are responsible for many of the insights that have guided my work. I also thank John Ferejohn, Kurt Taylor Gaubatz, Alexander George, Judith Goldstein, Stephen Haber, and Scott Sagan of the Stanford faculty for their helpful comments on parts of the dissertation. Kurt later read the manuscript in its entirety.

I am also deeply indebted to my colleagues in the graduate program at Stanford, especially Alison Brysk, Scott Johnson, Jeff Knopf, and Lee Metcalf of my dissertation writer's group, who read endless drafts of most of the chapters and provided great suggestions and the moral support to help me finish. Thanks also to Cheryl Boyer, Shelley McConnell, Catherine Shapiro, and Chuck Shipan for their helpful comments on early chapters.

At the University of New Mexico, I have found that rarest of things in academia, a real scholarly community where faculty and students who share similar interests but diverse talents and perspectives can learn from one another and work together on a variety of collaborative projects. My colleagues at UNM have enriched this book in countless ways. Bill Stanley and Ken Roberts provided detailed comments on the entire manuscript. I cannot thank them enough for their excellent suggestions and their friendship. Karen Remmer has been an outstanding mentor and has helped me in innumerable ways. Other UNM colleagues, Andrew Enterline, Wendy Hansen, Neil Mitchell, and Rick Waterman, commented on draft chapters. Away from UNM, Margaret Hermann, Tony Smith, Kathryn Sikkink, and Robert Pastor also read draft chapters and provided excellent comments.

I have also been blessed to work with many outstanding students at UNM who have helped with this book. Shannon Sanchez-Terry has done a fantastic job as a research assistant over the course of two summers, joining me as a co-author on a related article. Erin Ferreira and Betts Putnam provided valuable research assistance at other times. Caroline Beer, Lori Blair, Anna Hadley, Randall Parish, and Shawn Sullivan commented in detail on draft chapters and/or joined me as co-authors on related projects. The students in my Graduate Seminars in International Relations Theory and Democracy and the International System helped me develop the argument of the book in numerous ways. I thank them all.

Much of the material included in this book is related to articles that have appeared in print elsewhere. "Two Paths to the Promotion of Democracy During U.S. Military Interventions," *International Studies Quarterly* 39, no. 3 (fall 1995): 371–401, presents an early version of the analysis presented in Chapter 2. "A Constructivist Interpretation of the Liberal Peace: The Ambiguous Case of the Spanish-American War," *Journal of Peace Research* 34, no. 4 (November 1997): 415–30, draws on some of the material in Chapter 3 to make an argument which moves beyond that made in this book. An early version of Chapter 4 appeared as "Culture, Congress, and the Promotion of Democracy in Reagan's Policy Toward El Salvador," *Low-Intensity Conflict and Law Enforcement* 3, no. 1 (summer 1994): 80–103. "Liberal Interventionism in Bosnia," *Journal of Conflict Studies* (spring 1998), a piece co-authored with Shannon Sanchez-Terry, examines the Bosnian case in greater depth than in Chapter 6 of the book. Finally, "Forcing Them to Be Free," forthcoming in *Political Research Quarterly*, draws upon material in Chapters 2 and 7. I thank each of these journals for allowing me to reproduce parts of these articles in the book.

I thank the Institute for the Study of World Politics, the MacArthur Foundation, Center for International Security and Arms Control at Stanford, and the Center for Latin American Studies at Stanford for their generous financial support of my dissertation research. The Institute's grant funded a research trip to the National Security Archives in Washington, D.C., where the excellent staff helped me find my way through their collection of declassified documents on U.S. policy toward El Salvador. The Eugene Gallegos Regents' Lectureship and the Research Opportunities Program provided additional financial support at the University of New Mexico. I thank all of these supporters and the taxpayers of the state of New Mexico for helping me to complete this work.

Finally, I thank Penn State Press. Yale Ferguson and James Lee Ray read the manuscript for the Press and made many perceptive suggestions. I thank Ray especially for his recommendations for improving the quantitative analysis in Chapters 2 and 7. I thank Cherene Holland for her assistance throughout the production process and Dana Bell for preparing the index. It has been a pleasure to work with Sandy Thatcher. He showed an early and enthusiastic interest in the project and has done everything he could to help me succeed in this endeavor.

1

The Promotion of Democracy and the Liberal Peace

To the extent that democracy and market economics hold sway in other nations, our own nation will be more secure, prosperous and influential while the broader world will be more humane and peaceful. . . . [D]emocracies tend not to wage war on each other or sponsor terrorism. They are more trustworthy in diplomacy and do a better job of respecting the human rights of their people. . . . [Therefore,] the successor to a doctrine of containment must be a strategy of enlargement—enlargement of the world's free community of market democracies. (Lake 1993:660)

No state has more consistently proclaimed its adherence to this liberal vision of the international system than the United States (Smith 1994). No state has worked harder to promote this vision by coercing others to adopt liberal institutions "at the point of bayonets."[1] The United States concluded the nineteenth century with a war to "liberate" Cuban "freedom fighters" from Spanish "tyranny." For the next two and a half decades, U.S. Marines tried to teach a variety of Caribbean Basin nations how to "elect good men." In the immediate aftermath of World War II, the United States mobilized extraordinary resources to transform Germany and Japan into liberal democracies during its military occupations of the Axis powers. During the Cold

---

1. The phrase "at the point of bayonets" was used by Warren Harding during the 1920 presidential election campaign to criticize Woodrow Wilson's Haitian policies. The full quotation represented an attack on the Democrats' vice presidential candidate in the 1920 elections, Franklin Delano Roosevelt, who had boasted that he had written the Haitian constitution while serving as assistant secretary of the Navy under Wilson. Harding replied that he "would not empower an Assistant Secretary of the Navy to draft a Constitution for helpless neighbors in the West Indies and jam it down their throats at the point of bayonets borne by U.S. Marines" (Schmidt 1971:118).

War, the United States promoted democracy during military interventions in Greece, South Korea, South Vietnam, Lebanon, the Dominican Republic, El Salvador, and a variety of other nations.

Thus, the Clinton administration follows a century-long American tradition in its paradoxical practice of imposing self-determination through military force. In 1993 Clinton tried to turn the Bush administration's limited humanitarian intervention in Somalia into an attempt to lift that country "from the category of a failed state into that of an emerging democracy" (Albright 1993a). In 1994 Clinton launched an invasion to depose Haiti's dictators and restore the democratically elected government of Jean Bertrand Aristide. In 1995 American troops embarked for Bosnia in support of a U.S.-brokered accord that pinned its hopes for maintaining a single Bosnian state, in part, on the "free and fair" elections held in September 1996.

In all, the United States has attempted to implant liberal institutions in its target states during thirty-three of its ninety-three twentieth-century military interventions. Indeed, policymakers have often pursued "proliberalization" policies even when they expected that U.S. efforts "to impose liberalization and democratization on a government confronted with violent internal opposition [would] not only fail, but actually assist the coming to power of new regimes . . . hostile to American interests and policies" (Kirkpatrick 1979:36).

At the same time, however, this commitment to the promotion of democracy during military interventions has been far from absolute. The United States failed to promote democracy during nearly two-thirds of its interventions. It has often allied itself with brutally repressive authoritarian regimes rather than with the liberal opponents of such regimes. The U.S. has often supported counterinsurgency policies that devastated democratic rights in partially liberal allies. In perhaps half a dozen nations, most prominently in Guatemala in 1954 and Chile in 1973, the United States used covert measures to help overthrow elected governments. The subsequent U.S.-backed governments were consistently less democratic than the regimes they replaced (Forsythe 1992).[2]

What explains this seemingly contradictory practice? Under what conditions does the United States decide to promote democracy during military interventions? More precisely, why has the United States so often adopted

---

2. Russett 1993, pages 120–24, argues that the regimes opposed by the United States were universally short of the standards of full democracy and therefore these cases did not involve warfare among democracies. While this may have been true in cases like Mossadeq's Iraq, it is much more difficult to make this sort of case against countries like Guatemala in 1954 or Chile in 1973.

"proliberalization" policies, defined as the combination of active support for "free and fair" elections with the promotion of at least one of the following: centrist political parties, moderate interest groups, reductions in human rights abuses, and/or formal subordination of the military to civilian authority, during its twentieth-century military interventions? Why have policymakers chosen not to adopt such policies on other occasions? Understanding this puzzle is important in its own terms, given the increasing significance of democracy promotion in American foreign policy. It is also important for shedding new light on the critically important debate between realism and liberalism in the international relations field.

International Security, Ideals, and Institutions

Those who attempt to explain why the United States promotes democracy abroad begin by debating whether U.S. security interests or America's liberalism drives policy. On the one hand, a security-based approach suggests that presidents adopt proliberalization policies in order to build more stable and friendly allied regimes in Third World states (Wright 1964; Ferguson 1972; Pastor 1987; Schoultz 1987; Shafer 1988; MacDonald 1992; Smith 1994; Steinmetz 1994). Presidents will abandon proliberalization policies when the promotion of democracy contradicts U.S. security interests. In general, the greater the international threat faced by the United States, the less flexibility it will have to experiment with liberalizing reforms (Krasner 1978; Walt 1987). The more intense the ongoing war, the less emphasis the United States can place on supporting liberalizing reforms (Kirkpatrick 1979). Finally, the United States will be least likely to adopt proliberalization policies when it opposes the local government in the target state, where purely coercive overt or covert force will predominate.

On the other hand, many analysts have argued that America's liberalism fundamentally shapes its efforts to promote democracy abroad. Some analysts emphasize the power of America's liberal ideals. In this approach, U.S. policymakers adopt proliberalization policies because they are compelled to do so by a universally shared cultural bias in favor of democracy (Hartz 1955; Packenham 1973; Huntington 1981; Quester 1982). Others have emphasized that institutional constraints imposed by Congress or interest groups have pushed the United States to promote democracy abroad (Schoultz 1981; Forsythe 1988; Arnson 1993; Pastor 1992).

The standard synthesis for policymakers and many analysts has been to assume that "all good things go together" (Packenham 1973). Indeed, policymakers have usually argued that proliberalization policies serve both American ideals and interests (Ferguson 1972:351). This synthesis cannot explain either why the United States would often pursue illiberal policies, or why it might at other times pursue liberal reforms even when policymakers believed such reforms could harm U.S. security interests.

This book offers an alternative synthesis of the realist and liberal approaches. It argues that there are two paths to the promotion of democracy during U.S. military interventions. The security argument provides the best explanation of the initial decisions of presidents. At first, presidents choose proliberalization policies when the international system is least threatening, when it has the most leverage over the target government, and the conditions within the target country are most conducive to pursuing such reforms. If the United States faces significant threats in the international environment, there is an ongoing conflict in the target country, or the United States possesses limited leverage over the target regime, presidents are not likely to push for liberalizing reforms.

When presidents fail to adopt proliberalization policies at the outset of an intervention, however, liberal ideological attacks from the Congress often compel them to shift policies, despite the fact that they think that proliberalization policies might harm U.S. security interests. Congressional pressure can also dissuade presidents from abandoning proliberalization policies in response to a changing security environment. Under these circumstances, presidents use the promotion of democracy to build domestic political consensus and "policy legitimacy" for U.S. interventions (George 1980; Herman and Brodhead 1984; Melanson 1991).

Thus, America's liberalism fundamentally shapes the use of force in U.S. policy toward the Third World. One must integrate the cultural and institutional components of the liberal argument, however, to understand why the United States does not pursue a consistent liberal policy. Liberal culture plays a crucial role in guiding policy, but only when political actors in important institutional positions in the democratic political process use liberal appeals in support of or opposition to policy. Furthermore, security considerations are most important when decisions are lodged in the executive branch institutions most insulated from democratic politics.

More broadly, the promotion of democracy is one of the most important tools American leaders use to transcend the potential contradictions involved in being a liberal great power. America's liberal institutions do indeed constrain the country's ability to pursue a vigorous foreign policy abroad. In this context, the promotion of democracy has become a central theme in overcoming institutional inertia by forging a domestic consensus in favor of an expansionist foreign policy. Internationally, America offers an appealing vision of a peaceful union of democratic states, under American leadership, that will bring liberty and prosperity to all like-minded states. When others accept this vision not just because it is being imposed by a more powerful state, but because they find it persuasive and compelling, the United States can avoid creating the balancing coalitions that realists contend inevitably confront dominant powers.

Liberal Peace and Liberal Interventionism

The debate over the promotion of democracy in U.S. foreign policy reflects the broader debate about the "liberal peace" in the international relations field. The primary question in that broader debate has been whether security interests or domestic liberalism play the most important role in shaping the foreign policy behavior of liberal states. Realists expect states to go to war whenever necessary to protect their security and enhance their power. They argue that regime type is irrelevant and that security considerations often compel states to abandon ideological goals. Realists dismiss the rarity of war between democracies, which seems to lend credence to the liberal argument as a mere statistical coincidence (Mearsheimer 1990; Layne 1994; Spiro 1994; Farber and Gowa 1995).

Domestic liberals, on the other hand, believe the near absence of war between democracies to be one of the most profound empirical laws of international relations (Doyle 1983a; Russett 1993; Ray 1995; Thompson and Tucker 1997; Gleditsch and Hegre 1997). As is true of the debate about the promotion of democracy, liberals differ about which aspect of liberalism is most crucial in shaping the democratic peace. Some liberals emphasize that the institutional constraints imposed by republican government limit the ability of liberal states to go to war against any type of potential adversary (Gaubatz 1991; Morgan and Campbell 1991; Lake 1992). Others believe that liberal cultural norms of tolerance for self-determination and support for nonviolent conflict resolution bind liberal states together in a "pacific union" (Doyle 1983a; Russett 1993; Dixon 1994).[3]

3. Many liberals emphasize that liberal states are also more likely to engage in the kind of broad-based, mutually beneficial trade relationships that can build peaceful cooperation between states (Doyle 1983a; Russett and O'Neal 1997). While economic relationships will be an important focus of the case studies, this book focuses more intently on the other components of the domestic liberal argument.

One of the central puzzles surrounding the liberal peace, as emphasized in Doyle's path-breaking two-part article on the subject in 1983, is that while liberal states tend not to war with one another, they participate in wars as often as do illiberal states.[4] Indeed, liberal states have launched wars of aggression against illiberal states. In the often-ignored second part of his article, Doyle points to two factors to explain this puzzling behavior:

> First, outside the pacific union, liberal regimes, like all other states, are caught in the international state of war Hobbes and the Realists describe. Conflict and wars are a natural outcome of struggles for resources, prestige, and security among independent states. . . . Second, these failures are also the natural complement of liberalism's success as an intellectual guide to foreign policy among liberal states. The very constitutional restraint . . . and international respect for individual rights that promote peace among liberal societies can exacerbate conflicts in relations between liberal and non-liberal societies. (Doyle 1983b:324–25)

This book explicitly focuses on the second part of Doyle's puzzle and uses his fundamental insights to frame its central argument. While domestic liberalism might explain the separate peace that has emerged among democracies, one must integrate the realist and liberal perspectives to understand fully the conflict behavior of liberal states in an often illiberal world. Furthermore, an analysis of the promotion of democracy during U.S. military interventions demonstrates that liberal institutions and ideals can generate a variety of contradictory foreign policy behaviors unexpected by the most optimistic advocates of the liberal peace.

Organization of the Book

This book examines the record of U.S. efforts to promote democracy at the point of bayonets using both a broad quantitative analysis of twentieth-century U.S. military interventions and in-depth studies of individual cases based on secondary sources and documentary evidence. Chapter 2 spells out

---

4. Hermann and Kegley (1996) have discovered a similar pattern in their work on democracy and military intervention. While democracies generally intervene as often as nondemocracies, they rarely intervene against other democracies. In an interesting twist on the liberal argument, they have found that democracies are also less likely to be the target of military intervention by any type of state than is true of nondemocracies.

the argument in greater detail and tests the contrasting realist and liberal hypotheses with an examination of the adoption of proliberalization and nonliberalization policies during ninety-three military interventions between 1898 and 1996. The analysis in this chapter demonstrates strong support for the argument that there are two paths to the promotion of democracy, depending on whether the initiative for the adoption of such policies comes from the president or the Congress.

Chapter 3 argues that the McKinley administration's occupation policies in Cuba after the Spanish-American War provide a paradigmatic example of the congressional path to the promotion of democracy. Realist considerations initially led McKinley to pursue a long-term U.S. military occupation of Cuba to prevent political instability on the island. By 1899, however, liberal attacks from the Congress claiming that America's commitment to "liberate" Cuba from Spanish tyranny was being subverted by McKinley's occupation policies, pushed the president to sponsor "free and fair" elections in Cuba. The United States granted independence to a newly elected government of Cuba in 1902. Chapter 3 also investigates the contrasting example of the Philippines where the United States engaged in a brutal counterinsurgency war against Filipino nationalists and erected the framework for long-term colonial rule, despite congressional pressure to pursue more liberal policies.

Chapter 4 examines a case from the presidential path to the promotion of democracy, Kennedy administration policy toward the Diem regime in South Vietnam. In this case, realist concerns rather than congressional pressure led Kennedy first to push Diem to open up his regime to include participation by the noncommunist opposition, and later to support Diem's overthrow in a November 1963 coup. Kennedy's affiliation with the Democratic Party both predisposed him to select proliberalization policies to serve U.S. security interests and limited potential opposition to his policies by liberal Democrats in Congress.

Chapter 5 looks at another case from the congressional path to the promotion of democracy: the Reagan administration's policy toward El Salvador between 1981 and 1984. In 1981 Reagan committed the United States to support the most authoritarian military elements of the governing junta in El Salvador in their effort to achieve a military victory over the leftist guerrillas of the FMLN. Reagan officials were convinced that such policies were essential to avoid a repeat of the debacle of Carter's policies toward Nicaragua. Nevertheless, by 1984 liberal pressure from Congress had compelled the Reagan administration to place itself firmly behind a set of proliberalization policies in El Salvador, including support for elections,

José Napoleón Duarte's Christian Democratic Party, and improvement in the human rights record of the Salvadoran armed forces.

Chapter 6 examines the application of Clinton's policies of democratic enlargement during its military interventions in Haiti and Bosnia and suggests that the present era is likely to involve consistent U.S. support for democracy during interventions because both the realist and liberal arguments are pushing in the same direction. The comparatively low level of international threat to the United States in the global balance of power provides a permissive international environment for the pursuit of liberal goals. In addition, the congressional argument suggests that in a post–Cold War world where anticommunism is no longer available as an ideological tool for forging consensus, liberal internationalism is the most likely alternative tool for building consensus behind an activist foreign policy. Thus, Clinton's emphasis on the policy of democratic enlargement must be conceived of as an essential tool for building a domestic consensus for an activist foreign policy in the context of a Congress with potentially strong opposition to any internationalist foreign policy. As both cases suggest, however, congressional pressure in this era is also more likely to lead to extreme caution in the practice of potentially costly interventions. Nevertheless, in a world in which the United States is the lone superpower, promotion of the idea of the liberal pacific union can be an effective strategy for convincing other liberal powers not to challenge U.S. dominance in the global balance of power.

Chapter 7 asks whether U.S. efforts to promote democracy at the point of bayonets actually leads to successful democratization. A broad examination of twentieth-century U.S. interventions suggests that the promotion of democracy during U.S. military intervention can have a profound and positive impact on the democratization of target states, especially when proliberalization policies are combined with efforts to dismantle or diminish the power of local military institutions in target states. Finally, the concluding chapter speculates about the relationship among American power, the promotion of democracy, and the liberal peace in the decades to come.

2

Presidents, Congress, and the Promotion of Democracy

Teddy Roosevelt's Rough Riders stormed up San Juan Hill in August 1898 to liberate Cuba from Spanish tyranny and teach the Cubans how to elect good men. Nearly a century later, U.S.-led NATO troops occupied Bosnia to put an end to ethnic cleansing and teach the Bosnians how to elect good men. From 1898 to 1996 liberal America managed to launch ninety-three military interventions despite the constraints that republican institutions of governance are supposed to place on the use of force in a democracy. Indeed, only a handful of states have launched more military interventions than the United States since World War II (Tillema 1994).

The United States made a significant effort to promote democracy during thirty-three of these interventions. If liberal values guide U.S. policy, why has the United States attempted to build democracy in target states only a third of the time? If realist calculations of power and interest dominate decision-making, why has the United States pushed for democracy as often as it has?

This chapter maps out the broad patterns of the promotion of democracy during twentieth-century U.S. military interventions. It begins by defining military intervention and creating a list of experiences that qualify for inclusion in this study. It then classifies cases of the adoption or nonadoption of proliberalization policies during military interventions.

Two sets of possible explanations for the promotion of democracy during military interventions are examined. On the one hand, a realist approach suggests that presidents adopt proliberalization policies when the global and local balances of power are most permissive for the pursuit of ideological goals, and when they believe that the promotion of democracy will build a more stable allied regime in the target state. They abandon such policies when the promotion of democracy contradicts U.S. security interests. A threatening international environment, an ongoing war in the target country, and/or U.S. opposition to the government in the target state reduce the probability that U.S. presidents will experiment with liberalizing reforms.

The domestic liberal argument, on the other hand, suggests that America's liberal culture pushes it to promote democratizing reforms during interventions, but only when political actors in important institutional positions in the democratic political process use liberal appeals in support of or opposition to policy. The stronger the presence of liberal internationalists in the policy process, the greater the likelihood that the United States will promote democracy during an intervention. Democratic presidents initially choose proliberalization policies more readily than Republicans because of the strength of liberal internationalists in the Democratic Party. Even when presidents initially fail to adopt proliberalization policies, liberal ideological attacks from the Congress often compel them to shift policies. Congressional pressure can also encourage presidents to maintain a commitment to liberal reforms even in an increasingly dangerous security environment. Under these circumstances, presidents use the promotion of democracy to legitimize and build domestic political consensus for U.S. interventions.

The statistical record of twentieth-century U.S. interventions presented in this chapter supports a synthesis of the realist and domestic liberal approaches. There are two paths to the promotion of democracy during military interventions. The realist argument provides the best explanation of the initial choices of presidents. The congressional argument from the domestic liberal perspective, however, best accounts for presidents' final choices. In broad terms, the record shows how the promotion of democracy has become an important ideological tool for legitimating the exercise of American power abroad to both domestic and international audiences.

U.S. Military Intervention

This book defines military intervention as the direct or indirect use of military force focused on "changing or preserving the structure of political authority in the target society" (Rosenau 1969:161). Examining both direct and indirect uses of force brings together quantitative and qualitative literatures that concentrate on different, yet equally important, types of interventions. Quantitative studies operationalize the concept of military intervention almost exclusively as the direct use of armed forces abroad (Blechman and Kaplan 1978; Tillema 1989, 1994; Pearson, Baumann, and Pickering 1994). Qualitative studies, on the other hand, emphasize America's indirect participation in proxy wars, where the United States subsidizes local governments or insurgent movements engaged in civil wars (Barnet 1968; Klare and Kornbluh 1988; Shafer 1988; MacDonald 1992; Pastor 1992; Schraeder 1992a). Rosenau's criteria specifies which uses of force should be considered examples of military intervention: those focused on the political authority structures of target states. This definition coincides with the generally accepted meaning of the term *intervention:* the interference of one state in the internal affairs of another.

To create a comprehensive list of qualifying cases, this study relies on existing data sets to capture cases of direct military intervention and covert paramilitary intervention during the post–World War II era. It offers its own operationalization to code cases of indirect military intervention on the side of allied governments. It then applies these criteria to the 1898–1945 period to expand the data set to cover military interventions during this era.

Since cases involving the direct use of military forces during the Cold War era have been the subject of a great deal of systematic study, I use existing data sets by Tillema (1989, 1994), Pearson and Baumann (1994), and Meernik (1996) to construct this portion of the intervention inventory.[1] These data sets define military intervention in slightly different ways. Tillema defines "foreign overt military intervention" as "all combat-ready foreign military operations undertaken by regular military forces" (Tillema 1989:180). Meernik works from an updated version of Blechman and Kaplan's (1978) data set of American uses of "force without war," defining only those cases "involving ground troops of either the Army or Marine Corps in an active

---

1. I thank Herbert Tillema for sharing his data set with me. Pearson and Baumann's data set was acquired from the Inter-University Consortium for Political and Social Research (no. 6035). Meernik's data was taken from his 1996 article.

attempt to influence the behavior of other nations" as military interventions (Meernik 1996:394). Meernik's list captures most of the experiences included in Tillema's list, but also includes a variety of less intense uses of force.

Pearson and Baumann define military interventions "as the movement of regular troops or forces . . . of one country into the territory or territorial waters of another country, or forceful military action by troops already stationed by one country inside another, in the context of some political issue or dispute" (Pearson, Baumann, and Pickering 1994:209). Their operational-ization leads to the most comprehensive list of cases, including many uses of air or naval power not captured by the other data sets. They also include more than two dozen cases, most involving the evacuation of U.S. personnel from conflict zones, which did not involve efforts to shape the political authority structures of target states. These cases are excluded from the analysis.[2]

Another factor differentiating these data sets flows from Meernik's deci-sion to code only one state as the target of each intervention, while the others often code interventions as having multiple targets. Meernik, for example, codes only Kuwait as a target of U.S. intervention during the Persian Gulf War. Tillema codes Kuwait, Iraq, and Saudi Arabia. This study includes all of the multiple targets listed in any of the data sets. While the character of U.S. intervention in North Korea or North Vietnam differed from the character of U.S. intervention in South Korea and South Vietnam, it was intervention nonetheless.

Despite their differences, these three data sets complement one another in collectively capturing a large majority of the direct uses of U.S. military force abroad during the Cold War era. Thus, this book includes any case listed in any of the three that meets the definition of military intervention noted above. Cases included in more than one data set are, of course, listed only once in the intervention inventory used here.

These data sets capture only part of the universe of cases of twentieth-century U.S. military interventions because they are limited to the direct use of military force during the Cold War. The impact of the indirect military interventions emphasized by qualitative scholarship must also be evaluated, because these interventions are more likely to involve efforts to change or

2. I use Pearson and Baumann's variable measuring the "direction of intervenor supporting action," which codes whether the intervenor supports or opposes the existing government, any rebel groups within the target state, and/or any third parties that are using the territory of the target state, to determine which of their cases count as military interventions. This study excludes those cases coded as involving "non-supportive or neutral intervention." It also excludes two cases in the Tillema data set that involved the evacuation of U.S. personnel from conflict zones, Liberia and Somalia in 1991.

preserve the structure of political authority in target states than many of the limited applications of military force captured by the existing data sets. Furthermore, the subsidization by the United States of local militaries or insurgencies shares important qualities with direct military intervention. These conflicts often involve substantial U.S. direction and management of the war effort as well as a substantial commitment of U.S. money and prestige. If local forces prove unable to win the war, the conflict could escalate to involve U.S. troops. Domestic actors will react strongly to indirect interventions if they are convinced that escalation is probable and the consequences of escalation undesirable. This can generate the domestic political dynamics suggested by the domestic liberal argument.

The United States intervenes in proxy wars by bankrolling and training one side in an ongoing civil war. The most difficult task in operationalizing the concept of an indirect military intervention is determining the threshold at which U.S. financing and training of local combatants makes it a major participant in those wars. The Correlates of War data set on civil wars provides a list of potential conflicts in which the United States might have become involved (Singer and Small 1994). This study classifies wars in which U.S. military and security assistance accounted for at least half of the defense budgets of local military forces as military interventions.[3] Measuring military intervention in this way lengthens the period of time in which the United States is considered to have intervened.[4] Thus, the Pearson/Baumann, Tillema, and Meernik data sets code the U.S. intervention in South Vietnam as beginning in 1961, 1962, and 1964 respectively. It ends in early 1973, with a brief return to evacuate the embassy in April 1975. Using the criteria for indirect military intervention, the U.S. intervention began in 1950 the moment the United States paid for more than 50 percent of the French war effort. It continued until April 1975. The intervention inventory uses the most inclusive time frame in reporting the length of any intervention. It is more difficult to determine the appropriate threshold at which U.S. support

---

3. To discover whether cases fit the 50 percent aid/defense budget criteria, I obtained U.S. aid figures for military assistance and "security-supporting" economic assistance from the Department of Commerce's *Foreign Aid by the United States Government, 1940–1951* and the Agency for International Development's *U.S. Overseas Loans and Grants* congressional presentation documents. Military expenditure figures were collected from *World Military Expenditures and Arms Transfers,* produced by the Arms Control and Disarmament Agency since 1965. For pre-1965 ratios of military expenditures/U.S. aid, I used estimates provided by secondary sources.

4. Only U.S. support for the Greek government against communist insurgents in the 1940s and for the Philippine government against the New People's Army in the 1980s are not at least partially matched by other data sets.

for insurgent movements should be considered military interventions, because such support is usually covert and the military budgets of insurgent groups are harder to determine than those of governments. This study relies on Schraeder (1992b) for a list of U.S. indirect military interventions in support of such groups. Covert interventions that did not include direct support for an armed insurgency, such as Iran in 1953 and Chile in 1973, are not included in Schraeder's list of paramilitary interventions.

To complete the catalog of cases of U.S. military intervention, these criteria were then applied to the 1898–1945 period. Only direct military interventions that met any of the standards used by Tillema, Meernik, and/or Pearson and Baumann qualified for inclusion, because the United States possessed no formal military assistance program before World War II and always intervened directly when supporting insurgents.[5] Many instances of gunboat diplomacy during this era are excluded because they did not focus on the political authority structures of target states.

One could also include the American participation in both world wars as examples of military intervention. There are good theoretical reasons for excluding the world wars from a study of military interventions; however, there is no clear reason to exclude the postwar occupations of Germany, Austria, Italy, and Japan if similarly pervasive and lengthy interventions in Caribbean Basin countries and the Philippines before World War II or Korea and Vietnam after World War II are included. Indeed, Tillema, Pearson and Baumann, and Meernik exclude these interventions in large part because they fall outside of the temporal domain of their data sets.[6]

Ninety-three cases, from the Spanish-American War of 1898 to Bill Clinton's reelection in November 1996, meet these criteria. This represents about twice as many interventions as were included in a preliminary version of this analysis (Peceny 1995). This chapter analyzes numerous interventions of limited duration taken from the Tillema, Meernik, and Pearson/Baumann data sets, which were not used in the earlier study. The earlier work explicitly excluded most short-term interventions because such interventions are less

5. The most difficult case to categorize during this period was Panama. By some measures, the United States has occupied that country since its "independence" in 1903. This book classifies the 1903–36 period as an era of continual military intervention because the U.S. troops stationed in the Canal Zone regularly and routinely left that U.S.-controlled area to "maintain order" in Panama. This practice diminished somewhat after 1936, when the Roosevelt administration negotiated a new Canal Treaty in which the United States formally gave up its treaty right of intervention. After 1936 each dispatch of U.S. troops beyond the boundaries of the zone is coded as a separate case.

6. Tillema excludes these cases because they began before September 2, 1945 (personal communication).

likely to present an opportunity to promote democracy. This chapter also examines the multiple targets of U.S. intervention as separate cases, while the earlier study mirrored Meernik's practice of designating only one target per intervention. This chapter looks at an expanded group of cases to determine whether the earlier coding decisions introduced systematic bias into the analysis. Table 2.1 lists these interventions in chronological order.

What Constitutes a Proliberalization Policy?

Having constructed a list of qualifying interventions, this book considers next the policies adopted during those interventions. The term *proliberalization policies* is used rather than the broader term *promotion of democracy* because the United States has often pursued the less ambitious goal of promoting the liberalization of authoritarian regimes rather than the full-fledged democratization of target states. This book defines proliberalization policies as the combination of active support for free and fair elections with active promotion of at least one of the following: centrist political parties, reformist interest groups, reductions in human rights abuses, and/or formal subordination of the military to civilian authority.

U.S. support for elections has been selected as the most important indicator of a proliberalization policy because, since 1898, U.S. policymakers have almost universally viewed this as the central component of any "pro-democratic" policy. Therefore, despite the fact that the specific content of proliberalization policies has changed over time, focusing on the electoral connection allows for some comparison of relatively similar phenomena across time periods. Following Dahl's (1971) classic definition of polyarchy, American policymakers generally define elections as "free and fair" if all citizens are allowed to "participate" in the vote and if voters possess a choice of two or more independent "contestants." Outcomes cannot be predetermined and the actual counting of votes must be conducted in a procedurally fair manner. The definition of free and fair elections used here falls short of Dahl's standard, however, because policymakers often classify an election as free and fair even if some parties have been excluded from the electoral process and full civil liberties have not been guaranteed.[7]

---

7. The United States often supported significant restrictions on suffrage during early interventions. This is understandable given that the first interventions under consideration took place before women were allowed to vote in the United States. Southern blacks were also routinely denied the right to vote. A more relaxed standard will be applied to these early cases to reflect U.S. efforts to promote what Paul Drake (1991) has called "oligarchic republics."

Table 2.1   Twentieth-century U.S. military interventions ($N = 93$)

Cuba 1898–1902	Thailand 1962
Philippines 1898–1941	Haiti 1963
China 1900	South Korea 1963
Panama 1903–36	Saudi Arabia 1963
Cuba 1906–9	Panama 1964
Nicaragua 1909–33	Cyprus 1964
Mexico 1914	Congo/Zaire 1964
Haiti 1915–34	North Vietnam 1964–75
Dominican Republic 1916–24	Cambodia 1964–75
Mexico 1917	Dominican Republic 1965–66
Cuba 1917–22	South Korea 1965–69
Russia 1918–20	Thailand 1966–76
Honduras 1924–25	Congo/Zaire 1967
China 1927	Trinidad 1970
Italy 1943–48	Jordan 1970
Germany 1945–49	Iraq 1972–75
Austria 1945–55	Cyprus 1974
Japan 1945–52	Angola 1975–76
China 1945–49	Congo/Zaire 1978
South Korea 1945–49	Guyana 1978
Greece 1947–49	Iran 1980
Liberia 1947	Afghanistan 1980–91
Philippines 1949–52	Ecuador 1981
South Korea 1950–53	El Salvador 1981–91
North Korea 1950–53	Nicaragua 1981–90
South Vietnam 1950–75	Honduras 1982–90
Yugoslavia 1951	Egypt 1982–96
Guatemala 1954	Lebanon 1982–84
Taiwan 1954–55	Cambodia 1982–91
China 1954–55	Chad 1983
Indonesia 1956–58	Grenada 1983
China (Tibet) 1956–73	Sudan 1984
Syria 1957	Saudi Arabia 1984
Turkey 1957	Philippines 1985–88
Lebanon 1957	Angola 1985–91
Taiwan 1958	Bolivia 1986
China 1958	Libya 1986
Lebanon 1958	Guatemala 1987
Jordan 1958	Kuwait 1987–88
Cuba 1958	Panama 1988–92
Laos 1959–75	Saudi Arabia 1990–91
Panama 1959	Kuwait 1990–92
Cuba 1959–60	Iraq 1990–96
Congo/Zaire 1960–61	Somalia 1992–94
Cuba 1961	Haiti 1994–96
Dominican Republic 1961	Bosnia 1995–96
India 1962	

This study operationalizes the variable American sponsorship of "free and fair elections" in terms of the adoption of specific policies. The clearest cases involve those experiences where the United States directly supervised all aspects of the electoral process, as during the colonial era in the Philippines and the post–World War II occupations of the Axis powers. At a minimum, the United States is coded as sponsoring free and fair elections in a target country if it pursues any one of the following sets of policies: (1) active mediation with contending parties in the target state in setting the ground rules of an electoral contest, including assisting in the drafting of electoral laws and/or the creation or reformation of institutions like electoral boards, (2) the provision of financial and technical assistance for the voting process, including the payment of election workers, the management of voter registration lists, the creation of efficient procedures for the nonfraudulent counting of ballots, and/or (3) official participation in election observer missions to certify whether contests have been conducted in a free and fair manner. The elections supported by the United States need not involve the selection of the chief executive in the target country to be counted. Elections at any level qualify for inclusion.[8]

For some scholars, free and fair elections are a sufficient condition for the classification of a state as a democracy (Huntington 1991; Ray 1995; Przeworski, Alvarez et al. 1996). As Terry Lynn Karl suggests, however, democracy involves four dimensions: "(1) contestation over policy and competition for office; (2) participation of the citizenry through partisan, associational, and other forms of collective action; (3) accountability of the rulers to the ruled through mechanisms of representation and the rule of law; and (4) civilian control over the military" (Karl 1990:2). This definition of democracy suggests that proliberalization policies involve active support for the creation and maintenance of political institutions that foster greater contestation, participation, accountability, and civilian control over the military.

Certainly, elections are an important institution for enhancing these qualities in a political regime, but democracy involves more than "electoralism" (Karl 1986). American support for free and fair elections, therefore, is considered a necessary, but not sufficient, component of a proliberalization

---

8. Nearly all cases of support for free and fair elections involved some sort of national election. The most difficult case to classify because of this coding rule was the Iraqi case during the Bush administration, when the United States helped create an elected parliament in the Kurdish enclave of northern Iraq. Despite the fact that Bush made no effort to promote democracy in Baghdad, his efforts in northern Iraq led to this case being coded here as involving the adoption of proliberalization policies. I coded this as a case of nonliberalization policies in Peceny 1995.

policy. U.S. policymakers have usually combined elections with other efforts to liberalize the political system in question. Policymakers often explicitly designed these reforms to promote limited openings in the political system rather than full democratization.

U.S. support for the development of democratic associations, for example, has often taken on the character of sponsorship of or alliance with specific pro-American political parties and interest groups in opposition to other groups and parties. At the turn of the century, U.S. efforts to teach Latin Americans to "elect good men" involved U.S. support for Conservative Parties in Central America and the Caribbean in opposition to dominant Liberal Parties in the region (Munro 1964; Drake 1991). During the Alliance for Progress of the 1960s, the Kennedy administration embraced centrist, reformist parties like the Christian Democrats in an effort to marginalize leftist parties. At the same time, the AFL-CIO–associated Agency for Free Labor Development (AFIELD) worked to organize labor unions and peasant cooperatives oriented around reformist demands in a liberal democratic framework. American policymakers explicitly created these interest groups to limit the influence of radical union movements and peasant leagues (Buchanan 1991).

The American commitment to human rights has also rarely been absolute. The United States has rarely severed ties with an allied regime because of its violations of the civil rights of its citizens. It has, however, often made efforts to improve the human rights situation in allied states by reducing the number of human rights abuses (Schoultz 1981). Similarly, in supporting civilian control over the military, the United States has often settled for formal civilian control over a military that retains considerable de facto autonomy from civilian control. Nevertheless, since efforts to create "nonpartisan constabularies" in the Caribbean Basin in the 1920s or "professionalized" militaries in the post–World War II era took place in a broader context of support for other liberal reforms, they will be considered part of a proliberalization policy. They will be included despite the fact that such efforts often helped bring about personalist or military dictatorships (Millett 1977; Klare and Kornbluh 1988).

Nonliberalization policies are those which do not include active support for the combination of policies mentioned above. This has meant different things during different eras. In 1898 it meant that the United States initially imposed colonial rule in the Philippines and launched a brutal counterinsurgency war against Philippine rebels. During the 1910s and 1920s, the U.S. Marines ran Haiti as a paternalistic fiefdom. When the Haitian Parliament defied occupation authorities, armed Marines abolished the legislature

(Schmidt 1971). During the Cold War, nonliberalization policies involved support for the authoritarian dictatorships of Chiang Kai Shek, Ngo Dinh Diem, Ferdinand Marcos, and others.

For many cases the adoption of nonliberalization policies reflected the limited character of the intervention rather than an explicit decision to support an authoritarian solution. The failure to adopt proliberalization policies in Trinidad in 1970, therefore, flowed from the decision not to land the U.S. troops, which had been standing offshore during that country's Black Power riots, rather than an explicit decision to overthrow that country's democratic regime. Indeed, in cases like Wilson's occupation of Veracruz, Mexico, in 1914, even though the explicit aim of U.S. intervention might be to promote democracy, the limited character of the intervention can preclude the adoption of proliberalization policies.[9]

In this chapter, presidents' policies are coded as proliberalization or nonliberalization in the first and last two months of their administration's policies during an intervention, or in the first and last week of interventions of shorter duration. Each case, therefore, includes observations of a president's policies at both the beginning and end of that president's choices in regard to the intervention in question. An overview of the classification of proliberalization and nonliberalization policies can be seen in Table 2.2. Because many interventions, such as Vietnam, lasted through several U.S. presidential administrations, there are 156 cases of the adoption or nonadoption of proliberalization policies that emerge from the ninety-three interventions cataloged above.

The decision to break long interventions into multiple cases may lead some to question whether these observations are truly independent from one another and therefore amenable to statistical analysis. The domestic liberal argument, however, calls for distinguishing between Democratic and Republican presidents. This argument suggests that the Eisenhower and Kennedy administrations would pursue different policies in Vietnam, despite the fact that they were dealing with the same country. Considering each president's handling of an intervention, a separate case allows for a statistical evaluation of this hypothesis.

The domestic liberal argument does not expect transitions between presidents of the same party to have the same consequences for policy. Therefore, the statistical tests below will also be reanalyzed with transitions from one Republican to another or one Democrat to another consolidated into single

9. I mistakenly coded this case as involving the adoption of proliberalization policies in Peceny 1995.

Table 2.2 Adoption of proliberalization policies

Initial policy: proliberalization; final policy: proliberalization (N = 41)				
Cuba 1901–2	Panama 1903–8	Cuba 1906–8	Philippines 1909–12	Nicaragua 1909–12
Panama 1909–12	Philippines 1913–20	Nicaragua 1913–20	Cuba 1917–20	Philippines 1921–23
Nicaragua 1921–23	Dominican Rep. 1921–23	Philippines 1924–28	Nicaragua 1924–28	Dominican Rep. 1924
Honduras 1924–25	Philippines 1929–32	Nicaragua 1929–32	Haiti 1929–32	Nicaragua 1933
Italy 1945–48	Germany 1945–49	Austria 1945–52	Japan 1945–52	S. Korea 1945–49
Greece 1947–49	Philippines 1949–52	Austria 1953–55	Lebanon 1958	S. Vietnam 1961–63
Laos 1961–63	Laos 1964–68	Lebanon 1982–84*	Honduras 1982–88	Grenada 1983
Nicaragua 1989–90	Honduras 1989–90	El Salvador 1989–91	Panama 1989–92	Haiti 1994–96
Bosnia 1995–96				

Initial policy: nonliberalization; final policy: proliberalization (N = 12)				
Cuba 1898–1901	Philippines 1901–8	Panama 1913–20	Dominican Rep. 1916–20	Italy 1943–45
S. Vietnam 1964–68	Dominican Rep. 1965–66	El Salvador 1981–88	Philippines 1985–88	Cambodia 1989–91
Angola 1989–91	Iraq 1990–92			

Initial policy: proliberalization; final policy: nonliberalization (N = 4)			
Cuba 1921–22	Philippines 1933–41	China 1945–49	Iraq 1993–96

Initial policy: nonliberalization; final policy: nonliberalization (N = 99)				
Philippines 1898–1901	China 1900	Mexico 1914	Haiti 1915–20	Mexico 1917
Russia 1918–20	Panama 1921–23	Haiti 1921–23	Panama 1924–28	Haiti 1924–28
China 1927	Panama 1929–32	Haiti 1933–34	Panama 1933–36	Liberia 1947
S. Korea 1950–52	N. Korea 1950–52	S. Vietnam 1950–52	Yugoslavia 1951	S. Korea 1953
N. Korea 1953	S. Vietnam 1953–60	Taiwan 1954–55	China 1954–55	Guatemala 1954
Indonesia 1956–58	Tibet 1956–60	Syria 1957	Turkey 1957	Lebanon 1957
Jordan 1958	China 1958	Taiwan 1958	Cuba 1958	Panama 1959
Laos 1959–60	Cuba 1959–60	Zaire 1960	Zaire 1961	Tibet 1961–63

Dominican Rep. 1961	Cuba 1961	India 1962	Thailand 1962	Haiti 1963
S. Korea 1963	S. Arabia 1963	Tibet 1964–68	N. Vietnam 1964–68	Cambodia 1964–68
Zaire 1964	Panama 1964	Cyprus 1964	S. Korea 1965–68	Thailand 1966–68
Zaire 1967	S. Korea 1969	S. Vietnam 1969–73*	N. Vietnam 1969–73*	Laos 1969–73*
Cambodia 1969–73*	Thailand 1969–73*	Tibet 1969–73	Trinidad 1970	Jordan 1970
Iraq 1972–73	S. Vietnam 1973–75*	N. Vietnam 1973–75*	Laos 1973–75*	Cambodia 1973–75*
Iraq 1973–75	Thailand 1973–76*	Cyprus 1974	Angola 1975–76*	Zaire 1978
Guyana 1978	Iran 1980	Afghanistan 1980	Afghanistan 1981–88	Ecuador 1981
Nicaragua 1981–88	Egypt 1982–88	Cambodia 1982–88	Chad 1983	Sudan 1984
S. Arabia 1984	Angola 1985–88	Bolivia 1986	Libya 1986	Guatemala 1987
Kuwait 1987–88	Panama 1988	Afghanistan 1989–91	Egypt 1989–92	Kuwait 1990–92
S. Arabia 1990–91	Somalia 1992	Egypt 1993–96	Somalia 1993–94*	

*President withdraws from intervention ($n = 156$).

cases. Thus, the data will be evaluated first with Kennedy and Johnson's interventions in South Vietnam considered as separated cases and then with the 1961–68 period considered a single case.

All military interventions in which the United States used only naval and/or air forces are coded as not involving the adoption of proliberalization policies. Secondary sources were consulted for the cases involving any use of American ground forces in the intervention to determine whether the United States pursued any of the proliberalization policies noted above (Wright 1964; Drake 1991; Munro 1964, 1974; Langley 1983; Smith 1994; Huntington 1991; Barnet 1968; Tillema 1973; Herring 1986; Herz 1982; Herman and Brodhead 1984; Cumings 1981, 1990; Shafer 1988; Pastor 1992; MacDonald 1992; Arnson 1993; Schraeder 1992a; Klare and Kornbluh 1988; Muravchik 1991; Lowenthal 1991). In practice, although most cases of the adoption of proliberalization policies took place in long-term interventions, there are examples like the Grenadan and Lebanese (1958) cases that involved short-term interventions.[10]

Table 2.2 indicates that the United States has adopted proliberalization policies more than a third of the time. In forty-one cases (26 percent), presidents promoted liberal reforms at the beginning and end of their interventions. In four cases (3 percent), presidents initially adopted proliberalization policies only to abandon such policies by the end of that administration's management of the intervention. Presidents shifted from nonliberalization to proliberalization policies during the course of an intervention twelve times (8 percent). Finally, presidents failed to adopt proliberalization policies in ninety-nine cases (63 percent).

These percentages are significantly different from those reported in Peceny 1995, which found that nearly 80 percent of U.S. interventions involved the adoption of proliberalization policies. The stark differences between these studies flows from the more comprehensive set of military interventions examined in the book. As anticipated by the earlier article, virtually all of the cases that have been added here did not involve the adoption of proliberalization policies. Adding covert interventions, multiple targets, and

10. After the Iraqi case, the Lebanese cases were the most difficult ones to categorize. When not engulfed in civil war, Lebanon has exhibited a consociational form of democracy that explicitly divided the representation in parliament and most important political positions among Christians and Muslims according to a prearranged formula. During its 1958 and 1982 interventions, the United States mediated between the parties in helping the Lebanese to select their next president according to their consociational process. Despite the problems associated with classifying an electoral process with predetermined outcomes as democratic, this study classifies both of these Lebanese cases as involving the adoption of proliberalization policies.

short interventions to the data set decreases estimates of the frequency of U.S. efforts to promote liberal reforms during military interventions in comparison to the earlier study. As the statistical tests reported below demonstrate, however, adding these cases does not significantly change the results of the models evaluating the relative impact of realist and domestic liberal variables in explaining presidential choices.

Proliberalization Policies and U.S. Security Interests

Realism assumes that regime type is unimportant in shaping the international behavior of states. All states seek power and security. Idealism leads to foolish policy and can be tolerated only if a state is relatively unconstrained by the balance of power. If the United States is overwhelmingly powerful relative to all other states (Krasner 1978), or is not threatened by a powerful revisionist state (Walt 1987), it will possess greater opportunities to pursue ideological goals without placing its security in jeopardy. Conversely, the higher the level of threat faced by the United States in the international system, the less likely it is the United States will promote liberal reforms. The United States should be least likely to promote democracy when it is engaged in general war, as in 1917 and 1941, or is challenged by a powerful revisionist state, as during the Cold War.

The internal balance of power in target states also shapes the likelihood of the adoption of proliberalization policies. Internally, the central question is whether the target regime is an ally or an enemy of the United States. The United States may be eager to press enemy regimes to liberalize because this can weaken their power relative to pro-American forces in the country in question. American conquests of such regimes lead to the most opportune circumstances for the promotion of democracy. If U.S. occupation troops dominate a country in which there is no ongoing conflict, the United States possesses great opportunities to impose liberal reforms on target states. In the absence of American occupation, however, U.S. pressure to liberalize enemy regimes will rarely lead to the adoption of proliberalization policies, because the United States is not in a position to impose democracy on the target state. This is especially true in cases of covert support for insurgent movements, where the United States lacks direct leverage over the target regime.

The calculations are more complex in cases where the United States is allied with the target regime. Victory over anti-American forces in the country in question is the most crucial goal. In this context proliberalization policies carry significant risks. In general, the more intense the ongoing war, the less emphasis the United States can place on supporting liberalizing reforms. Promoting liberal reform during any war can be extremely difficult, given that governments usually place greater restrictions on political liberties during wars. Promoting liberal reforms can also pose dangerous risks of destabilizing the allied government supported by the United States. These risks have led many to argue, in the words of Richard Nixon, that America "must deal realistically with governments . . . as they are" rather than try to convert them into democracies (Ferguson 1972:326). American efforts to promote democracy often fail because most third-world societies lack the cultural or socioeconomic foundations to support democratic institutions (Huntington 1984; Kirkpatrick 1984). In this context, U.S. efforts to promote democracy are likely merely to undermine friendly tyrants in favor of anti-American insurgents (Kirkpatrick 1979).

Even when policymakers believe it possible to foster democracy, many also believe that attempts to promote a transition to democracy in the context of civil or international war entails serious risks. Long-repressed moderate sectors may not be strong enough to take the place of the existing authoritarian regime (Pastor 1987). Elections may lead to unexpected outcomes; if not the victory of anti-American forces, then perhaps for other parties at least partially antagonistic to U.S. policy in that country (Przeworski 1986). Placing human rights conditions on aid may hinder the war effort and allow anti-American insurgents to reenter the open national political arena, undermining a U.S.-allied government. Consideration of these risks often leads policymakers to support existing institutions rather than a very uncertain and possibly dangerous process of change. In the realist perspective, proliberalization policies will be adopted when they are considered necessary for winning the war. If proliberalization policies fail to build stable political regimes capable of repulsing armed insurgents, or if support for authoritarian political solutions proves effective in winning the war, proliberalization policies should be discarded in favor of some nonliberal alternative. For these reasons, realism expects the United States to be generally unlikely to adopt proliberalization policies during its military interventions.

If the domestic liberal argument is correct, however, over the long term the global spread of democracy will provide an effective guarantee of American security because democracies will not threaten the United States, their partner in the liberal peace (Smith 1994). Other liberal great powers are unlikely to band together to oppose the United States if they see it as the "leader of the free world" rather than as a domineering hegemon. The adoption of proliberalization policies could simply be a step toward building the liberal pacific union to guarantee American security.

In the short and medium term, however, realists believe the United States intervenes to defeat anti-American actors in the country in question. Proliberalization policies will be adopted when they are considered essential for winning the war or keeping the peace during a U.S. occupation. Many U.S. presidents have supported liberal reforms in third-world states because they perceived democracy to be the antidote to the tyranny and poverty that cause instability within those states. By promoting liberal reforms to address the sources of instability, U.S. policymakers hope to keep anti-American actors from capitalizing on legitimate domestic grievances to seize power (Wright 1964; Ferguson 1972; Pastor 1987; Schoultz 1987; Shafer 1988; MacDonald 1992; Smith 1994; Steinmetz 1994). Democracies are more stable, it is argued, because they confine political conflict to nonviolent, mutually agreed upon channels that circumscribe both radical changes in policy and radical means of accomplishing policy goals. The 1984 Kissinger Commission Report, chartered by the Reagan Administration to review U.S. policy toward Central America, provides a cogent example of the realist logic behind the promotion of democracy during U.S. interventions:

> Experience has destroyed the argument of the old dictators that a strong hand is essential to avoid anarchy and communism, and that order and progress can be achieved only through authoritarianism. Those nations in Latin America which have been moving to open their political, social and economic structures and which have employed honest and open elections have been marked by a stability astonishing in the light of the misery which still afflicts the hemisphere. The modern experience of Latin America suggests that order is more often threatened when people have no voice in their destinies. Social peace is more likely in societies where political justice is founded in self-determination and protected by formal guarantees. (Kissinger 1984:14)

This logic has been most clearly articulated and put into practice in the Kennedy administration's Alliance for Progress for Latin America (Schlesinger 1965; Levinson and de Onis 1970).

This chapter quantitatively tests the realist hypotheses that a threatening international environment, opposition to the target regime, and war in the target state dissuade the United States from promoting democracy. It is more difficult to test quantitatively the proposition that presidents adopt proliberalization policies because they "perceive" them to be the best way to achieve U.S. security interests. These concerns, however, will be a central focus of the case studies.

Domestic Liberalism, American Culture, and the Adoption of Proliberalization Policies

One of the central goals of this book is to connect the literature analyzing the "democratic peace" to the voluminous literature examining the impact of American liberalism on U.S. foreign policy. These two literatures should be closely related, yet few scholars have taken advantage of the potential synergy between them. On the one hand, thinking of U.S. policy in comparative terms, as the foreign policy of a liberal state not unlike other liberal states, can generate new insights about American foreign policy. On the other hand, while scholars of the democratic peace agree that liberal values and liberal institutional constraints shape the foreign policies of liberal states in profound ways, they tend to operationalize these concepts in very broad terms. If this literature is going to deepen our understanding of the conflict behavior of liberal states, it is going to have to develop more complex understandings of these concepts. The literature on American foreign policy provides some useful insights on how to accomplish this goal. This section examines how America's liberal culture shapes its military interventions, while the next examines the impact of liberal institutions.

Liberal values of respect for self-determination and a norm of nonviolent conflict resolution generate peaceful relations among like-minded states. This is the central insight of the domestic liberal argument about the impact of liberal values on foreign policy. Scholars of U.S. foreign policy have long argued that America's liberal values fundamentally shape its foreign policy, but they suggest that these values often work in ways that do not adhere to the expectations of advocates of the democratic peace.

The American "liberal ideal" argument suggests that America has been "an unusually altruistic and generous nation on the world scene" because its people are driven by a missionary commitment to promote liberal democracy in the world (Quester 1982:56; Packenham 1973; Huntington 1981). America's liberal culture is so pervasive, according to this argument, that central decision makers are as committed as any American to this moral crusade.[11]

---

11. Doyle (1983b) goes farther than other scholars of the liberal peace in suggesting that missionary impulses to spread democracy abroad might be a natural component of all liberal cultures rather than a specifically American preoccupation.

As Hartz (1955) suggests, however, America's peculiarly "totalitarian" liberalism exhibits three different tendencies: crusading liberal internationalism, isolationism, and excessive anticommunism. Each has different implications for the democracy question. Cycles of international interventionism and isolationism in the history of American foreign policy both flow from the same cultural pathologies. "An absolute national morality is inspired either to withdraw from 'alien' things or to transform them: it cannot live in comfort constantly by their side" (Hartz 1955:286). Thus, America either attempts to remake the world in its own image or to separate itself as completely as possible from that world.

The messianic character of American liberal internationalism may explain why the United States has so often attempted to promote democracy when it seemed to contradict America's narrowly conceived security interests, as well as why it has so often overcome institutional constraints that should have placed greater limits on U.S. military intervention abroad. American "liberal internationalists" have, therefore, often strongly supported interventions that successfully promoted democracy and human rights. Of equal importance for this study, they have also launched principled challenges to U.S. military interventions when they believed these interventions undermined democracy, both at home and abroad. At home, the expansion of a powerful and secretive "national security state" has often stifled democratic debate on U.S. foreign policy, according to these liberals. In third-world countries, they argue, U.S. interventions have often involved support for dictatorship and the brutal repression of civil liberties (Huntington 1981:221–65). Thus, the aggressive liberal internationalist strain in American culture can support U.S. intervention abroad, but only if that intervention serves liberal goals.

In contrast, the other two elements of America's liberal culture can support the adoption of nonliberalization policies. Isolationists reject any efforts to remake a decadent world. Hartz also traces the roots of the extreme anticommunism of McCarthyism to America's liberal culture. "When the nation rises to an irrational anticommunist frenzy, it replies to the same instinct which tends to alienate it from Western democratic governments that are 'socialist.' When it closes down on dissent, it answers the same impulse which inspires it to define dubious regimes elsewhere as democratic" (1955:285). Anticommunism is consistent with American liberal culture because communism represents the antithesis of liberalism, but it has often led to support for a variety of anticommunist allies who also happened to be antidemocratic. Anything done to oppose communism, however, is justified as serving liberal values abroad. Thus, aspects of America's liberal culture can help explain why the United States has chosen to adopt nonliberalization policies in two-thirds of its military interventions.

America's liberal values clearly do not compel presidents to embark on missionary crusades to promote democracy abroad. These values, however, shape policy in two important ways. First, some actors in the policy process are motivated primarily by their commitment to liberal ideals. Second, various actors in the policy process can use liberal themes to manipulate public opinion to serve interests having no relationship to the promotion of liberal values abroad. Some actors use liberal appeals to attack presidential policy while others use these appeals to build support for intervention. Because of the variety of liberal appeals available to political actors, a variety of outcomes are possible. It is the power of liberal internationalists and liberal internationalist appeals in the policy process that leads to the promotion of democracy during U.S. military interventions.

Domestic Liberalism, Institutional Constraints, and the Adoption of Proliberalization Policies

If the people who pay the costs of war in lives and treasure have a say in the decision, states are less likely to go to war. This is the basic insight of the institutional argument from the domestic liberal perspective. Scholars have paid less attention to the question of precisely what kinds of institutional constraints are most crucial in shaping democratic foreign policy. Are elections the key institutions constraining the war-making capability of liberal states (Gaubatz 1991; Bueno de Mesquita and Siverson 1995)? Are checks and balances between the legislature and the chief executive more important (Morgan and Campbell 1991)? What are the roles of political parties, interest groups, a free press, or public opinion in constraining presidential power? Do America's specific republican institutions place a unique set of constraints on foreign policy decision-making?

The case studies will pay attention to the full range of potential institutional constraints imposed on presidents by American democracy. The central foci of the quantitative analysis as well as the case studies are the constraints imposed by the presidential election process and the U.S. Congress. The impact of parties, interest groups, the press, and public opinion will be evaluated, for the most part, by their impact on presidential elections and congressional pressure. I argue that the presidential selection process places limited constraints on presidents when it comes to the adoption of proliberalization policies during military interventions. It is Congress that plays the crucial role in compelling presidents to adopt proliberalization policies in circumstances in which they would prefer not to do so.

Presidents, Political Parties, and the Promotion of Democracy

Although the U.S. Constitution gives the president and the Congress shared power over foreign policy, only the president is institutionally suited to seizing the initiative in the foreign policy realm (Koh 1990:118–23; Fisher 1995). Therefore, the rise of America to superpower status during the twentieth century has given presidents ample opportunities to build an "imperial presidency" (Schlesinger 1973). The president's direct control over the enormous capabilities of the U.S. defense establishment, exercised through the National Security Council, has made the president the most important actor in the American foreign policy process, especially since World War II. Congressional delegation of authority to the president and judicial affirmation of presidential prerogatives has reinforced this pattern (Koh 1990:123–49).

The president's role in the world as the principal military and diplomatic representative of the United States means that he, more than any other elected official, must learn to operate in an anarchic external environment that has traditionally operated largely on realist principles. The president is, therefore, compelled by this external environment to pay attention to realist considerations in a way that members of Congress are not. This provides part of the explanation for why presidents are more likely to adopt proliberalization policies in response to realist calculations than in response to direct political pressure through the electoral process.

This tendency is reinforced by the nature and limitations of the domestic political constraints that can be placed on presidential policy through the electoral process. The commitment of candidates to the promotion of democracy can reflect their efforts to win over the crucial centrist swing voters who provide the margin of victory in any general election with two major candidates (Downs 1957; Aldrich, Sullivan and Borgida 1989). Indeed, presidential candidates usually do announce that they favor the promotion of democracy, at least in the abstract. In most presidential elections, however, domestic economic issues have overshadowed U.S. interventions, especially in cases where U.S. troops have not been placed in combat. In these instances there is little pressure from the general electorate on the issue of U.S. interventions.

In those cases where U.S. interventions have become a central issue in presidential campaigns, general elections have usually provided too blunt an instrument for forcing presidents to adopt proliberalization policies. Larger considerations than the specific characteristics of interventionist policies are likely to stand out. Presidents will be judged on whether they are winning or losing the war. If the war is still in its initial stages, the public is likely to "rally around the flag." If the United States wins the war, it will add to the incumbent's electoral support. The longer the war continues and the higher the cost in lives and money, however, the more the war effort will be considered a failure and the more likely the incumbent will be unseated (Mueller 1973).[12] In this context, opposition candidates have an incentive merely to promise vaguely to end the war without giving specific details on how that will be accomplished, as was true of Eisenhower's promise to "go to Korea" in the 1952 election and Nixon's "secret plan" to end the Vietnam War in 1968 (Divine 1974:69–86; Karnow 1983:582–83). Given these political dynamics, general election campaigns rarely serve as the mechanism for bringing about a pro-democratic compromise.

Presidential elections involve a two-step process, however. Candidates must first win the nomination of their party before they can compete in the general election (Fenno 1978). This distinction between the nomination of candidates and the general election is crucial because the strength of liberal internationalists within the Democratic Party makes it likely that Democratic presidents will commit to the promotion of democracy during the nomination process (MacDonald 1992:29–43).

Both parties include people who adhere to each of the tendencies present in America's liberal tradition. In fact, the earliest liberal internationalist opponents to U.S. intervention were Civil War–era Republicans who opposed McKinley's interventions in Cuba and the Philippines. The Republican Party has subsequently counted many prominent liberal internationalists among its ranks, as represented for many years by the eastern establishment wing of the party. Historically, however, the liberal presence has been much weaker in the Republican Party than in the Democratic. Between the world wars, isolationist rather than liberal internationalist sentiment dominated Republican ranks. After the war, advocates of the anticommunist position in the cultural debate, such as Ronald Reagan, were strongly represented in the party. This has led to a different set of intra-party coalition-building dynamics within the Republican Party than has been true of the Democrats.

The Democratic Party has attracted liberal internationalists, in part, because of its general commitment to activist government at home and abroad

---

12. Bueno de Mesquita and Siverson (1995) make a similar argument about democracies more generally. Victory or defeat in war matters most for the electoral prospects of democratic leaders.

that emerged during the New Deal. Part of this connection is also explained by historical chance. Democrats were the opposition party during two crucial eras when liberal internationalists launched some of their most heated attacks against the morality of U.S. military interventions. The relationship between liberal internationalism and the Democratic Party has its roots in the anti-imperialist coalition forged in the critical realigning election of 1896 by William Jennings Bryan (Burnham 1970; Brady 1973). Bryan reinforced the anti-imperialist character of the Democratic Party in 1900 in his second run against the Republican architect of the Spanish-American War and colonial rule in the Philippines, William McKinley. If the Spanish-American War and the War of the Philippine Insurrection had been fought under Democrat Grover Cleveland, these liberals may have remained in the Republican Party (Tompkins 1970). Liberal attacks against U.S. intervention in Vietnam reached their apex during the Republican presidency of Richard Nixon. If Lyndon Johnson had run for and won reelection in 1968, the connections between liberal internationalism and the Democratic Party might not have been nearly as strong.

More important, Democrats held the presidency during each of the world wars. Woodrow Wilson's entry into World War I "to make the world safe for democracy" and Franklin Roosevelt's entry into World War II under the principles of the Atlantic Charter solidified the Democrats' position as the party of liberal internationalism. If Republicans had been in office during these crucial periods, they might have used liberal internationalist rhetoric to mobilize Americans for war and could have built the same kind of connection between liberal internationalists and the Republican Party that now exists with the Democrats.

The presence of significant concentrations of liberal internationalists at the negotiating table or in the primary electorate have made them an important part of nominating coalitions within the Democratic Party. At times, liberal internationalists have possessed the strength to nominate openly anti-interventionist liberal candidates like George McGovern in 1972. In most cases liberals have had an important, though limited, influence. They have usually been able to gain the commitment of the nominee to include some pro-democratic emphasis in his policies and to assign liberal internationalists to important foreign policy posts, as when John F. Kennedy defeated more conservative opponents like Lyndon Johnson for the 1960 Democratic nomination, in part, by appealing to the liberal foreign policy wing of the party (Halberstam 1969).

There are important limitations to this argument. Two of the most active Democratic presidents, Harry Truman and Lyndon Johnson, assumed office without having initially to win their party's nomination for the presidency. Other liberal presidents, such as Franklin Roosevelt and Jimmy Carter, justified their failure to adopt proliberalization policies as a principled commitment to nonintervention (Bemis 1943; Commission on U.S.-Latin American Relations 1975, 1976). Because the Democratic Party has represented an extremely broad coalition, at least since Roosevelt's presidency, liberal internationalists are rarely able to push a completely like-minded candidate to the nomination. Successful candidates must appeal to a wide range of constituencies within the party. In addition, as noted above, the candidates must move to the center of the larger national political spectrum after winning their party's nomination if they are going to appeal to swing voters in the general election. This further limits the influence of liberal internationalists. Finally, once the party has chosen a nominee, it has almost no ongoing institutional mechanisms for controlling his behavior after he is elected president.

Yet, early coalition-building during the nomination process gives liberals some lasting power and influence within Democratic administrations. In addition, although there may be few institutional mechanisms compelling a Democratic president to follow through on this original position, he may do so simply because he genuinely believes proliberalization policies to be the most appropriate. Because of the identification of the Democratic Party with liberal internationalist ideals, and the strength of liberal internationalists within the party, Democrats are simply more likely to attract and select candidates committed to the promotion of democracy as a matter of principle. Democratic presidents generally attempt to reconcile their liberal predisposition with realist imperatives by emphasizing the security benefits associated with the promotion of democracy. For these reasons, I expect the relationship between a president's party and his support for proliberalization policies to be identifiable but weak. Furthermore, the presidential path to the promotion of democracy inherently blurs the lines between the realist and domestic liberal arguments because of the strategies presidents use to reconcile these potentially contradictory elements. The following section argues that the congressional argument from the domestic liberal approach provides a more persuasive explanation for changes in policy over time.

The Congressional Path to the Adoption of Proliberalization Policies

In the American context, the U.S. Congress places the most significant institutional constraints on presidential power. Strong liberal attacks emanating from the Congress can compel presidents to shift to proliberalization policies. Through its constitutionally granted rights to declare war, give advice and consent on treaties, and control the appropriations process, Congress has always possessed a substantial number of instruments for influencing a president's foreign policy. Of these, control of the appropriations process has provided the most important constraint because military interventions are costly ventures and the president must convince Congress to appropriate the substantial funds necessary to win the war.[13]

The institutional reforms of the 1970s gave Congress expanded powers over foreign policy (Franck and Weisband 1979; Crabb and Holt 1989; Pastor 1992; Lindsay 1994). The War Powers Act was crafted to limit the president's ability to send U.S. troops without congressional approval (Auerswald and Cowhey 1997). The foreign policy bureaucracies were compelled to report regularly to Congress on a wide variety of subjects that had previously escaped congressional review, thus expanding Congress' ability to monitor executive branch compliance with its wishes through the use of "fire alarm" oversight rather than more intrusive "police patrol" methods (McCubbins and Schwartz 1987; Lindsay 1994). Human rights legislation called for the State Department to report on the human rights records of countries receiving U.S. aid (Schoultz 1981; Forsythe 1988). The CIA was required to inform the newly created intelligence oversight committees of any planned covert actions (Treverton 1990). Congress created new bureaucratic institutions, like the human rights bureau of the State Department, to ensure that congressional priorities were represented in the executive branch (Schoultz 1981; Forsythe 1988:120–29). The placement of conditions on the disbursement of aid, often accompanied by provisions for a legislative veto, became a common practice in the post-1974 period. Members of Congress increasingly depend on liberal allies in the interest group community to augment their resources by providing alternative sources of information, helping to monitor executive branch policy, and acting as informal whips in support of liberal legislation (Schoultz 1981). The use of any of these instruments to attack a president's interventions as illiberal can lead them to respond by changing policy.

Members of Congress may use these institutional mechanisms to serve their reelection goals. Foreign policy generally presents a set of issues where members use "position-taking" or "credit claiming" strategies to respond to constituent and interest group pressure (Mayhew 1974). While vocal

13. The powers to declare war and ratify treaties have become less important in the post–World War II era as presidents increasingly circumvented congressional restrictions by using force without asking for a declaration of war and by signing executive agreements rather than treaties.

liberal internationalists almost never form a majority in any congressional district, their active support or opposition can have a marginal effect on congressional campaigns. Because of the deep roots of the democratic ideal in American culture, adopting a pro-democratic position, either in support of or opposition to the president entails virtually no cost to legislators and can appeal to or diminish the opposition of liberal constituents. Because most of their constituents will generally hold the president responsible for the success or failure of U.S. foreign policy (Nincic 1992), symbolic votes against a president's policy also entail little risk of inflicting electoral damage to members of Congress.

Much of the literature discussing congressional action on foreign policy and defense issues suggests that members are motivated, for the most part, by ideological and partisan considerations (Lindsay 1990; McCormick and Wittkopf 1990; Bernstein and Anthony 1991; Nincic 1992). From this perspective, accusations that a president is violating fundamental American democratic values in the conduct of his intervention may reflect either the principled opposition of ideologically committed liberals or the use of liberal rhetoric to serve partisan ends.

Some members of Congress are clearly motivated by an ideological commitment to liberal internationalist ideas. These representatives often serve on the House Foreign Affairs and Senate Foreign Relations Committees. Most members view participation on these committees as detrimental to their reelection chances, given the unpopularity of the Foreign Aid Bill. Only members wishing to pursue "good public policy," therefore, have clear incentives for joining these committees (Fenno 1973:9–12; 141–42).[14] This suggests that members actively involved in foreign policy debates are more likely to be driven by an ideological commitment to a preferred set of policies than by other considerations.

If Congress is controlled by one party while the presidency is in the hands of the opposition, however, interventionist policies can also become a

14. The importance of ideological motivations is not as strong for the armed services or full appropriations committees, which provide a variety of important resources to members of Congress besides opportunities to pursue good public policy. This is part of the explanation for why the Foreign Affairs and Foreign Relations Committees have been consistently more liberal than the Armed Services Committees in both houses. While the importance of ideology in shaping the character of the foreign policy committees has often meant that members of both parties have been internationalists, ideological splits between liberal internationalists and conservatives on these committees have increased in recent years. In a Republican-dominated Congress, the ideological motivations of members of the Foreign Relations and International Affairs Committees may lead to different political dynamics.

congressional vehicle for partisan attacks on the executive. Sharp ideological attacks against a president's policy as antidemocratic and un-American can be used to undermine public support for the president. In this situation party leaders may force members who do not agree with the arguments of the liberals to go along for partisan purposes. Conversely, if the same party controls both Congress and the executive, liberal internationalist ideologues may be forced to support policies with which they disagree.

The historical concentration of liberal internationalists in the Democratic Party often leads to the combination of these ideological and partisan motivations. Liberal internationalist control of important congressional committees combined with partisan battles between a Democratic Congress and a Republican president will virtually guarantee the adoption of proliberalization policies. In the congressional path to the adoption of proliberalization policies, therefore, the usual pattern is for Republican presidents to adopt proliberalization policies to blunt partisan ideological attacks by liberal Democrats in Congress. At times, liberal Democrats in Congress might be willing to give Democratic presidents the benefit of the doubt, not only out of partisan loyalty but because they trust their fellow liberal internationalist in the White House to adopt proliberalization policies eventually. Under certain circumstances, liberal control of important congressional committees alone may be sufficient to force a change in policy, even against a Democratic administration. The relative importance of partisanship and ideology depends, in part, on the institutional structures of the Congress.

Political parties and committees are the principal institutions through which the Congress is organized. Parties dominated Congress during the first years of the twentieth century (Brady 1973). For the majority of the period under study, however, committees dominated the decision-making processes of both houses (Fenno 1973). This distinction is important because a small group of ideologically committed members could have an important impact over presidential policy in a decentralized, committee-based system. In a centralized system based on strong party institutions, however, partisan divisions between Congress and the president may be a necessary condition for the adoption of proliberalization policies.

Thus, when the Republican McKinley administration imposed colonial rule on the Philippines in 1899, he could ignore, to some extent, the liberal attacks of congressional Democrats. In the House of Representatives, Reed Rules, named after Speaker Thomas Reed (R-Maine), granted the Speaker of the House extraordinary power, while party discipline was enforced by effective party caucuses. Most issues were decided by straight party-line votes (Brady 1973). Not only did the Republican House leadership not allow votes on McKinley's policy toward the Philippines, they rarely allowed the opposition Democrats to speak on the issue on the floor of the House. Partisan rule was also most pronounced in the Senate during the first decade of the twentieth century, though this was due more to the homogeneity of the parties than to the institutions of the Senate (Brady, Brody, and Epstein 1991). A strong and disciplined party caucus in the Republican-dominated Senate minimized congressional attacks on the Republican president.

When committees dominate congressional decision-making, ideologically committed members can overcome partisan politics. The Senate Foreign Relations Committee has played an especially important role in constraining presidential policy. Under the leadership of Senator William Fulbright (D-Ark.), for example, that committee was able to compel the Johnson administration to shift toward proliberalization policies in the Dominican Republic and South Vietnam despite the fact that the committee and the Senate as a whole was controlled by the president's own party.

Regardless of whether liberal attacks from the Congress flow from ideological, partisan, or reelection motivations, and whether they emerge from the full Congress or certain important committees, such attacks usually compel presidents to respond by promoting democracy in the country in question. In the congressional path, proliberalization policies serve to build domestic policy legitimacy and domestic support for interventionist policies (George 1980; Herman and Brodhead 1984). Genuine efforts to promote democracy can convince some ideological liberals to support the intervention. More generally, the adoption of proliberalization policies provides ideological cover for those involved in the interventionist policy consensus. Supporters of the intervention can avoid being attacked as in league with brutal dictators and repression while associating themselves with core American values. Substantial pressure from liberal internationalists will, in most cases, lead to a compromise involving the adoption of proliberalization policies in the context of military interventions. If liberal internationalist pressure is sufficiently intense, however, it may force a president to withdraw from a military intervention.

American liberal ideals do shape U.S. policy, as suggested by the domestic liberal argument, but only when used by people in positions of institutional strength in the policy process. They are often used by members of Congress to strengthen the institutional constraints on the executive branch. At other times they are used by presidents to neutralize those institutional constraints. The promotion of democracy, therefore, has become a central way that the U.S. government tries to overcome the public's reluctance to pay the costs of war in lives and treasure.

Analyzing the Adoption of Proliberalization Policies

I now test the realist and domestic liberal approaches through an examination of the 156 cases of the adoption or nonadoption of proliberalization policies during military interventions listed in Table 2.2. I first review the hypotheses and discuss how each of the independent variables is operationalized. Then a series of logit models are presented that use these variables to explain presidents' initial and final choices. These results confirm that the realist arguments do an excellent job of explaining initial choices, while the domestic liberal argument about congressional pressure provides a better explanation of presidents' final choices.

The Realist Hypotheses

The first hypothesis of the realist argument is that the international balance of power shapes presidential policies.

Hypothesis 2.1: The presence of a significant threat to the United States in the global balance of power makes presidents less likely to adopt proliberalization policies during military interventions.

The logic of this argument applies equally to the initial and final choices of presidents. To measure the international threat hypothesis, three periods are classified as times when the United States faced significant threats in the global balance of power: World War I (1914–18), World War II (1939–1945), and the Cold War (1947–89). The years 1898–1914, 1918–38, 1945–47, and 1989–96 are classified as periods of low international threat.

Classifying the entire Cold War era as a period of high threat, of course, oversimplifies a complex reality. The United States was clearly more powerful than the Soviet Union at the beginning of this era. The détente era of the 1970s was less conflictual than the norm for the rest of the era. Finally, there was a relaxation of tensions in the late 1980s before the definitive end of the Cold War. To take account of these differences, I experimented with a variety of alternative time periods for this variable. Of these alternatives, classifying the end of the Reagan administration as occurring at a time of low international threat generated the strongest coefficient for the impact of the level of threat on the final choices of presidents. I therefore report results with this coding decision in Table 2.4.

There are three hypotheses related to the second realist insight, that the internal balance of power in the target country shapes U.S. decisions. The second hypothesis suggests that America's relationship to the target regime shapes its opportunities to promote liberal reforms.

Hypothesis 2.2: U.S. opposition to the government in the target state makes presidents less likely to adopt proliberalization policies during military interventions.

Cases are coded as involving U.S. opposition to the target government if the United States either supported insurgents fighting that government or had taken some kind of offensive military action against the target government. In either instance, the United States usually lacks the kind of control over the government in the target state that would be necessary to work actively for elections and other liberal reforms. Cases that did not involve such actions were coded as involving support for the target government. Support for the government need not imply a formal alliance relationship.

Another element of the internal balance of power, the existence of a state of war, should have a negative impact on support for liberal reforms, as suggested by the third hypothesis:

Hypothesis 2.3: The existence of an ongoing war in the target country makes presidents less likely to adopt proliberalization policies during military interventions.

The logic of this hypothesis also applies equally to the initial and final choices of presidents. This variable is measured using the Correlates of War data on civil and international wars, which sets a threshold of 1,000 total battle deaths for international wars and 1,000 annual deaths in civil wars (Singer and Small 1994).

The fourth realist hypothesis to be examined in this book also relates to the internal balance of power:

Hypothesis 2.4: Presidents will adopt proliberalization policies when they believe such policies are most likely to build a stable pro-American government in the target state.

As noted above, I was unable to devise a systematic way to measure the perceptions of presidents across all twentieth-century interventions as to the utility of proliberalization policies in building stable pro-American governments. This hypothesis, therefore, will not be examined in the statistical tests below but will be evaluated in the case studies.

The Domestic Liberal Hypotheses

The domestic liberal argument offers two hypotheses that are examined here. First, it suggests that the concentration of liberal internationalists in the Democratic Party generates significant partisan differences in the choices of presidents. This leads to the fifth hypothesis to be studied.

Hypothesis 2.5: Presidents from the Democratic Party are more likely than Republicans to adopt proliberalization policies during military interventions.

This argument should apply to both the initial and final choices of presidents. As noted above, however, I expect the relationship between a president's party and the adoption of proliberalization policies to be identifiable but weak.

The congressional argument from the domestic liberal approach applies only to the final choices of presidents, viewing final presidential choices as a response to congressional pressure.

Hypothesis 2.6: A strong liberal internationalist response from the Congress makes presidents more likely to adopt proliberalization policies during military interventions.

A liberal internationalist response from Congress is considered strong if (a) at least one congressional committee with important jurisdiction over foreign policy held oversight hearings and/or voted on policy initiatives, and (b) if liberal themes were prominent in the hearing deliberations. Evidence of liberal internationalist themes in the congressional debate could include either attacks against administration policies as supporting dictators or repression, or positive statements calling for the adoption of free and fair elections, reductions in human rights abuses, and other liberalizing reforms. A weak liberal internationalist reaction is defined as one in which Congress took no action or in which liberal internationalist themes were not prominent in the debate.

If Congress passes significant legislation demanding liberal reforms during an intervention, this is certain to have some impact on a president's policies. However, I deliberately chose a low threshold for my measure of the strength of the liberal internationalist response from the Congress. I did this in order to examine whether even congressional actions that place no immediate constraint on a president's policy can nevertheless lead to a change in policy.

One additional consideration is essential for assessing the impact of Congress on U.S. military intervention. The logic of the congressional argument suggests that two types of outcomes can be considered evidence of the success of liberal pressure from Congress. Liberal pressure can force presidents to adopt proliberalization policies during an ongoing intervention. If that pressure is sufficiently intense, however, it can also compel presidents to withdraw from an intervention rather than try to legitimate the intervention by promoting liberal reforms. When examining the final choices of presidents, therefore, the results will be evaluated first with cases of presidential withdrawal (marked by an asterisk [*] in Table 2.2) coded as the adoption of nonliberalization policies. The model will then be analyzed with the withdrawal cases coded as the functional equivalent of the adoption of proliberalization policies.

Explaining the Initial Choices of Presidents

Because presidents are coded as either adopting or not adopting proliberalization policies during military interventions, it is appropriate to examine presidential choices using logit, a statistical test that analyzes models with dichotomous dependent variables. Table 2.3 presents two logit analyses examining presidents' initial choices of whether to adopt proliberalization policies. The results for the test, which looks at "all cases" listed in Table 2.2, demonstrate that, with the exception of the war variable, the realist argument provides the best explanation of the initial choices of presidents.

There is a strongly significant, negative relationship between a threatening international environment and the initial adoption of proliberalization policies. Presidents initially failed to adopt proliberalization polices 84 percent of the time (87 of 104) when faced by a hostile global balance of power. Thus, presidents generally adopted nonliberalization policies at the outset of America's Cold War interventions. In contrast, they adopted proliberalization policies 54 percent of the time (28 of 52) when faced with a nonthreatening international environment.

There is also a significant and negative relationship between American opposition to a target regime and the initial adoption of proliberalization policies. Presidents initially adopted proliberalization policies only 12 percent of the time (6 of 48) when they opposed the target government. In contrast, they adopted proliberalization policies 36 percent of the time (39 of 108) when supporting local governments.

This model also shows the anticipated positive, though weak, relationship between a president's party and the initial adoption of proliberalization policies. This variable just misses statistical significance at the .05 level. Democratic presidents actually chose not to adopt proliberalization policies a majority of the time. Republican presidents, however, were even less likely to choose proliberalization policies. Democrats chose such policies 32 percent of the time (19 of 59) while Republicans did so 27 percent of the time (26 of 98). The weakness of this relationship indicates that the domestic liberal argument fails to provide as powerful an explanation of the initial choices of presidents as does realism.

Table 2.3   Initial presidential choices

Variable	All Cases: Coefficient (standard error)	Same Party: Coefficient (standard error)
Threat	−2.063*** (.442)	−1.775*** (.492)
Oppose government	−1.228** (.514)	−1.076* (.589)
War	.246 (.420)	.413 (.477)
President's party	.683 (.431)	.711 (.468)
Constant	.220 (.361)	−.247 (.495)
−2 log likelihood	154.494	118.179
Model chi-square	32.946*** (4 df)	19.591*** (4 df)
Correctly predicted	75%	73.6%
Number of cases	156	125

* $p < .05$; ** $p < .01$; *** $p < .001$; one-tailed tests.

The second test in Table 2.3, labeled "same party," evaluates whether considering each president's policies toward a single country as separate cases introduces a substantial bias into the analysis. For this test, any time a Republican president replaced another Republican or a Democrat followed a Democrat during a long-term intervention, these cases were consolidated into a single observation. The results for these 125 cases indicate a moderate reduction in the strength of the findings, with the "oppose government" variable becoming significant at the .05 rather than the .01 level. The fact that these results generally confirm those found in the more inclusive sample suggests that separating cases by each president's policies during long-term interventions does not significantly bias the results.

Explaining the Final Choices of Presidents

Table 2.4 examines the final choices of presidents using logit. As in Table 2.3, the analysis here examines all cases listed in Table 2.2 and the sample that consolidates consecutive administrations from the same party into single

Table 2.4   Final presidential choices

Variable	All Cases: Coefficient (standard error)	Same Party: Coefficient (standard error)	Threat 88: Coefficient (standard error)	Withdrawal: Coefficient (standard error)
Threat	−1.440* (.648)	−1.602** (.643)	−1.870** (.693)	−.639 (.659)
Oppose government	−.222 (.866)	−.208 (.887)	−.411 (.912)	−.120 (.736)
War	−.441 (.694)	−.556 (.683)	−.341 (.716)	−.031 (.677)
President's party	.505 (.438)	−.201 (.664)	.937 (.700)	−.466 (.623)
Liberal congress	2.506*** (.737)	2.779*** (.719)	2.446*** (.765)	3.754*** (.710)
Initial proliberal	4.563*** (.776)	3.864*** (.823)	4.913*** (.852)	4.461*** (.796)
Constant	−2.157*** (.682)	−1.579* (.717)	−2.243*** (.688)	−2.338*** (.702)
−2 log likelihood	80.381	69.400	73.591	86.499
Model chi-square	119.569*** (6 df)	87.318*** (6 df)	126.446*** (6 df)	124.709*** (6 df)
Correctly predicted	89.10%	88.00%	89.68%	89.10%
N	156	125	156	156

* p. < .05; ** p. < .01; *** p. < .001; one-tailed tests.

cases. Table 2.4 also adds two tests that address potential biases noted above. The third test, labeled "Threat 88," reports results that code the Reagan administration as ending in 1988, during an era of low rather than high international threat. The fourth test, labeled "withdrawal," codes cases in which presidents withdrew from unpopular interventions as the equivalent of the adoption of proliberalization policies.

The realist hypotheses receive more limited support in the analysis of final presidential choices. Whether presidents adopt proliberalization policies at the end of their interventions appears to be unrelated to the existence of war or U.S. opposition to the target government at that time. Only the existence of a high level of international threat at the end of a president's intervention continues to have a significant impact on presidential choices. The highest level of significance for the threat variable occurs when 1988 (at the end of the Reagan administration) is coded as a period of low international threat, as recorded in the "Threat 88" test in Table 2.4. The threat variable just misses the .001 level of significance in that test. Thus, according to the realist argument, the shift to the promotion of democracy that gathered steam during Reagan's second term could be explained by the opportunities provided for the pursuit of ideological goals in a less hostile world.

The results in the "withdrawal" test of Table 2.4, however, suggest that the strength of the realist variable is contingent on the classification of cases of presidential withdrawal from unpopular interventions. When those thirteen cases are coded as the adoption of proliberalization policies, the statistical relationship between international threat and the adoption of nonliberalization policies fades to insignificance. These withdrawal cases should be considered challenges to the realist argument. The failure to promote liberal reforms in these cases did not flow from calculations of how best to win the wars in question. Rather, domestic opposition compelled presidents to abandon these countries to adversaries of the United States in the context of a hostile international environment.

A president's partisan affiliation also has no significant impact on final presidential choices in any of the tests reported in Table 2.4. Indeed, the "same party" and "withdrawal" tests indicate that Republican presidents were more likely to adopt proliberalization policies at the end of an intervention than were Democrats. For the "same party" test, this reflects the elimination of numerous cases of the adoption of nonliberalization policies when consecutive Republican presidents are consolidated and the elimination of cases of proliberalization policies when Democratic administrations are combined. The change in sign in the "withdrawal" test reflects the fact that the painful withdrawals from Southeast Asia occurred during Republican administrations.

Only two variables were strongly significant in each of the tests reported in Table 2.4. Not surprisingly, the most powerful variable for explaining final presidential decisions of whether to promote democracy during military interventions was whether they initially adopted proliberalization policies. While one president's policies during an ongoing intervention can be considered independent of the choices of his predecessors, it is not clear that a single president's policies at time $t + 1$ can be considered fully independent from his policies at time t. Table 2.4, therefore, includes each president's initial policies as an independent variable to help account for his final policies. The strong positive relationship between these variables indicates that there was usually substantial inertia and continuity from the beginning to the end of most president's policies during interventions.[15]

Beyond this, only the liberal reaction of Congress had a significant impact on final presidential choices. This variable is significant at the .001 level in each of the four tests in Table 2.4. Three times as many cases of change in policy recorded in Table 2.2 involved a change from nonliberalization to proliberalization policies rather than from proliberalization to nonliberalization policies. Nearly all of these positive changes occurred in the context of a strong liberal reaction from Congress. Table 2.4 suggests that liberal pressure from Congress has a significant impact on presidential policy even when using a conservative measurement of that impact. Sixty percent of the cases (30 of 50) of a strong liberal response from the Congress ended in the adoption of proliberalization policies. Only 22 percent (23 of 106) of the cases lacking a strong congressional response ended in proliberalization policies. The reduced statistical significance of the realist variables can be accounted for in part by the fact that many cases in which the adoption of proliberalization policies is associated with a strong liberal response from Congress—such as South Vietnam, 1964–68; the Dominican Republic, 1965–66; El Salvador, 1981–88; and the Philippines, 1985–88—involved change in policy in a security environment not conducive to the adoption of proliberalization policies.

As noted above, the adoption of proliberalization policies during military interventions is only one possible presidential response to congressional pressure. Presidents can also capitulate to congressional pressure and withdraw from the intervention. Thus, while the Nixon and Ford administrations did not pursue proliberalization policies in Vietnam, Cambodia, and Laos, they did respond to domestic political pressure by systematically withdrawing U.S. troops from these countries. First, Nixon withdrew U.S. troops, but maintained U.S. indirect intervention in these conflicts. Then Congress denied the Ford administration the resources necessary to continue funding the Thieu regime in South Vietnam and the counterpart regimes in Laos and Cambodia. These congressional actions prompted Richard Nixon to complain in his memoirs that "the war and the peace in Indochina that had

15. The decision to control for initial proliberalization policies explains part of the reason for the reduced statistical significance of the realist variables in the examination of final presidential choices. The international threat variable was stronger in logit models that excluded the "initial proliberal" variable from the analysis. It is difficult to know whether final presidential choices reflect a continual process of the evaluation of the level of threat in the international environment or simple inertia. This issue will be evaluated more thoroughly in the case studies presented in subsequent chapters.

been won at such cost over twelve years of sacrifice and fighting were lost within a matter of months once Congress refused to fulfill our obligations. And it is Congress that must bear the responsibility for the tragic results" (Nincic 1992:60). These cases illustrate the general argument that presidents cannot sustain antidemocratic interventions in the face of strong liberal internationalist pressure from the Congress. When cases where presidents withdrew from interventions in the face of liberal attacks from Congress are added to those in which presidents adopted proliberalization policies, as in the "withdrawal" test in Table 2.4, congressional pressure has an even more profound impact on presidential policy. The percentage of cases in which a strong liberal reaction from the Congress led to a change in policy increased from 60 to 82 percent (41 of 50).

Case Selection

An examination of America's twentieth-century efforts to promote democracy during military interventions provides substantial evidence that there are indeed two paths to the promotion of democracy during U.S. military interventions. Realism provides the best explanation for the initial choices of presidents, while the congressional argument from the domestic liberal approach best explains their final choices. Subsequent chapters supplement these statistical findings with the in-depth analysis of several cases to determine whether a detailed "process tracing" of events reveals the expected causal patterns in U.S. decision-making (George 1979).

I have chosen the following six cases for intensive study: Cuba, 1898–1901; the Philippines, 1898–1901; Vietnam, 1961–63; El Salvador, 1981–84; Haiti, 1994–96; and Bosnia, 1995–96. These cases were chosen to illuminate elements of the theoretical arguments noted above. They were also chosen because they represent important turning points in the forging of America's identity as a liberal great power. Although they don't match the importance of the American experiences during the world wars and the origins of the Cold War (Ruggie 1997), these cases involved significant efforts by American presidents to legitimize the exercise of U.S. power to the American people and the world as essential for the cause of democracy and the liberal peace.

The Spanish-American War, discussed in Chapter 3, inaugurated America's entrance into the global balance of power as a great power. The contrasting American experiences in Cuba and the Philippines after the war led Americans to promote democracy in its subordinate states rather than impose European-style colonial rule. These cases confirm elements of both the realist and domestic liberal arguments. The McKinley administration initially adopted nonliberalization policies toward Cuba, yet shifted toward the promotion of democracy by the end of the intervention. This case provides an excellent example of the power of congressional pressure in changing presidential policy. It also supports certain elements of the realist argument, in that the lack of a significant threat to the United States in the global balance of power and the end of the insurgent war on the island presented a permissive security environment for the adoption of proliberalization policies.

Because Filipino insurgents decided to fight the American occupation of their country, the McKinley administration possessed less flexibility to adopt liberal reforms there, despite the strong liberal attacks on McKinley's policy from the Congress. The Filipino case is important because it provides one of the few cases in which congressional pressure did not lead either to the adoption of proliberalization policies or to American withdrawal. This case reveals the importance of congressional institutions, because the strong partisan institutions governing Congress at the turn of the century kept a Republican Congress from launching a full-fledged attack against a Republican administration.

Chapter 4 examines Kennedy's policies toward South Vietnam because the American experience in Vietnam epitomized the extension of American power under the bipartisan Cold War consensus. America's failure in Vietnam, of course, shattered that consensus. This case provides a good test of the presidential argument to determine whether Kennedy's partisan identity or realist concerns were most crucial in shaping his decisions. Despite the fact that the broad security environment was not conducive to the adoption of proliberalization policies, a close examination of this case suggests that Kennedy policy was shaped most by security concerns.

Analyzing a case from the Reagan administration can help resolve one of the uncertainties brought to light by the statistical analysis. The relative strength of the realist and domestic liberal arguments hinges in part on how one classifies the security environment faced by the Reagan administration. Therefore, Chapter 5 looks at Reagan policy toward El Salvador. Reagan used his interventions in Central America to convince Americans to move beyond the constraints of the Vietnam syndrome and reassert American power in the world. El Salvador became his first laboratory for using the promotion of democracy to build a new foreign policy consensus in favor of the assertion of American power abroad. This case provides the clearest distinction between the realist and domestic liberal approaches. Reagan initially adopted nonliberalization policies because he viewed the promotion of democracy to be completely inappropriate, given the security situation in that country. Despite this, he shifted to the adoption of proliberalization policies when faced with strong liberal opposition to his policies in the Congress.

Finally, as the case studies in Chapter 6 indicate, the Clinton administration's policies of democratic enlargement involve an effort to use the promotion of democracy to legitimate a continuation of American leadership in the international system in the post–Cold War era. Both the Haitian and Bosnian cases illustrate the possibilities for democracy promotion when the political dynamics of both the realist and domestic liberal perspectives push in the same direction. The global and local balances of power allowed the United States to pursue ambitious efforts to build democracy that might not have been possible a decade before. From the domestic liberal perspective, as a Democrat, Clinton was predisposed to adopt proliberalization policies, while liberal internationalist attacks from Congress, coming from liberal Democrats in the Haitian case and conservative Republicans in the Bosnian case, reinforced this liberal predisposition. The extreme vacillation and limited responses of the Clinton administration in both cases suggests, however, that the strengthening of institutional constraints and isolationist sentiment might also lead presidents to abandon proliberalization policies in favor of withdrawing from the intervention in question.

3

The Spanish-American War and the Foundations of the Pro-Democratic Compromise

The Spanish-American War heralded America's emergence as a great power in the international system. The United States had already become the world's most prosperous state by 1898, but its army numbered only 25,000 and its isolationist tendencies led to its exclusion from European great power politics during most of the nineteenth century. Then the United States delivered a crushing blow to decadent Spain, acquired the remnants of its colonial empire, and was finally recognized by Europe as an important force in the global balance of power. What kind of great power would the United States be? How would it use its newfound power and influence in the world? How would it exercise its authority over its new possessions?

President William McKinley pursued similar nonliberalization policies in Cuba and the Philippines in the immediate aftermath of the Spanish-American War of 1898. He initiated long-term U.S. military occupations to pacify each nation to prevent political instability or the emergence to power of revolutionary forces antagonistic to U.S. interests. Thus, realist concerns about the potential negative consequences of the promotion of democracy led McKinley to ignore the opportunities for the pursuit of liberal goals afforded by an unthreatening global balance of power.

By mid-1899, however, the McKinley administration was pursuing very different policies in the two countries. On the one hand, the United States adopted proliberalization policies in Cuba, leading to a grant of formal independence to an elected Cuban government in 1902. In the Philippines, on the other hand, the United States engaged in a brutal counterinsurgency war against Filipino nationalists and erected the framework for long-term colonial rule. Why did the McKinley administration switch to proliberalization policies in Cuba? Why was there no similar shift in policy toward the Philippines?

I argue that McKinley shifted policy in Cuba in response to congressional pressure, as expected by the domestic liberal argument. The president was pushed toward an electoral solution by liberal arguments that the Spanish-American war had been fought to liberate Cuba from Spanish tyranny and that the United States should fulfill its promise to hand over power to the elected representatives of the Cuban people. Because this intervention occurred during a time of strong party institutions in Congress, however, partisanship was more important in determining this outcome than were the activities of ideologically committed liberal internationalists. Republicans lacked a working majority in the Senate during the Fifty-fifth Congress. Opposition parties in the Senate, therefore, successfully used liberal rhetoric to attack the Republican McKinley administration for its "antidemocratic" policies toward Cuba. This dynamic was reinforced by the search for a pro-democratic compromise by many congressional Republicans who had been hemmed in by their own rhetorical attacks against the previous Democratic administration of Grover Cleveland. The adoption of proliberalization policies was also facilitated by the end of insurgent war in Cuba, as expected by the realist argument.

The nature of congressional institutions also explains why the McKinley administration did not shift policies in the Philippines when the domestic liberal argument would have expected such a shift. By 1899, McKinley's colonial policies in the Philippines faced a strong ideological attack from the liberal anti-imperialist movement. The efforts of the anti-imperialists came to naught, however, because Republicans firmly dominated the Fifty-sixth Congress. The Republican leadership in both chambers used their institutional powers to thwart anti-administration legislation. This allowed McKinley to maintain his illiberal policies in the Philippines, at least in the short term. The emergence of armed opposition to the United States in the Philippines placed an additional obstacle in the path of the adoption of proliberalization policies there.

Despite McKinley's apparent success in maintaining nonliberalization policies in the Philippines, America's imposition of colonial rule in the Philippines generated substantial opposition at home and an insurgent movement in the Philippines. U.S. support for free and fair elections in Cuba to choose a nominally independent government, however, proved popular in the United States and was accepted by most Cubans. Through these contrasting experiences, American leaders discovered that the promotion of democracy and the liberal idea of the democratic peace proved an effective way of building domestic support for and international acceptance of an expansionist foreign policy. America's experiences in the Spanish-American War helped it forge a unique liberal identity as a great power.

Military Occupation for Cuba and Colonial Rule for the Philippines

Rather than embrace the insurgent movements who shared America's goal of defeating Spain in Cuba and the Philippines, the McKinley administration refused to recognize them as representatives of their nations. In his war message of April 11, 1898, McKinley suggested that the United States would intervene as a neutral "to place hostile constraints on both parties in Cuba." He came out against both a recognition of the insurgent Cuban Republic as the government of an independent Cuba and a recognition of the belligerency rights of the rebel Cuban Liberating Army, because "to commit this country now to the recognition of any particular government in Cuba might subject us to embarrassing conditions of international obligation toward the organization so recognized." Instead, McKinley sought to establish "a stable government capable of maintaining order and observing its international obligations insuring peace and tranquillity and the security of its citizens as well as our own" (State 1901:755–59). Similarly, when Emilio Aguinaldo announced the independence of the new Philippine Republic in June 1898, Commodore George Dewey, commander of the U.S. fleet that had annihilated Spain's Pacific fleet in Manila Harbor on May 1, 1898, refused to send a U.S. representative to the ceremonies.

The United States then excluded both insurgent groups from the military operations that led to Spain's final defeat, despite the years of struggle between these insurgents and Spain that had preceded American intervention. General William Rufus Shafter, the commander of the U.S. expeditionary force in Cuba, began this process by relegating his erstwhile Cuban allies to subservient noncombat roles during the July 1898 battle for Santiago in order to minimize the Cuban role in the expected victory over Spain

(Pérez 1983:196–210). Cuban forces were not allowed to participate in the acceptance of the surrender of Spanish forces and were informed by General Henry Lawton that "interference from any quarter would not be permitted. The Cuban insurgents . . . must recognize the military occupation and authority of the United States and the cessation of hostilities proclaimed by this Government" (State 1902:230).

Within days of Dewey's victory at Manila Bay, McKinley sent 5,000 troops to the Philippines to occupy Manila. These troops were sent "for the twofold purpose of completing the reduction of the Spanish power in that quarter and of giving order and security to the islands while in the possession of the United States" (State 1904:676–78). Giving order and security to the islands would mean the pacification of Aguinaldo's insurgent forces. Commodore Dewey had brought the exiled Aguinaldo back to the Philippines in hopes that he could help in the war effort, but by August 1898, McKinley had ordered General Merritt's troops to exclude the insurgents from the surrender of Spanish forces in Manila (State 1904:743, 754).

After the Spanish army had been dispatched, the Americans began to lay the foundations for long-term military occupations of both nations. "As I view it," General Shafter acknowledged in late 1898, "we have taken Spain's war upon ourselves" (Pérez 1983:215). Consequently, by March 1899, long after the defeat of Spain, the United States had posted more than 45,000 troops on Cuba, a force which dwarfed the one that had engaged the Spanish at Santiago (Department 1904:16–17). General John Brooke was appointed military governor on January 1, 1899, as U.S. forces officially took control of the island from Spain. The McKinley administration had announced no timetable for the termination of the military governorship or the withdrawal of U.S. forces and seemed ready to settle down for a long-term occupation. General William Ludlow, who at first took command of the occupation of Santiago and later served as military governor of Havana, suggested that a long period of U.S. rule would be necessary to civilize the Cubans—perhaps a "generation" (Healy 1963:115). General Leonard Wood, who served as military governor in Santiago in 1899 and as governor of the entire island from late 1899 through 1902, suggested in April 1899 that "the sentiment for our remaining here forever is becoming very strong in this part of Cuba, and I think we shall have hard work to get away" (Healy 1963:90). Many of McKinley's principal advisers agreed with the sentiments of U.S. Ambassador to Spain Stewart Woodford when he told the president: "I have at last come to believe that the only certainty of peace is under our flag. . . . I am thus, reluctantly, slowly, but entirely a convert to the early American ownership and occupation of the Island. If we recognize independence, we may turn the Island over to a part of its inhabitants against the judgment of many of its most educated and wealthy residents" (State 1901:687–88).

U.S. policy in the Philippines differed from Cuba in the McKinley administration's decision to annex the islands. McKinley may have decided in favor of annexation as early as May 1898, before the cessation of hostilities with Spain, but he was noncommittal in public (Morgan 1965:82; Gould 1980:117). When Spain surrendered to the United States in August, McKinley postponed discussion of the Philippine question to the Paris Peace Conference. When he chose his negotiating team, however, three of the five members of the commission clearly favored retention of the Philippines. A fourth, Secretary of State William Day, would follow the president's wishes. In his September instructions to the negotiating team, McKinley demanded only the retention of the island of Luzon, but by the end of October, McKinley had instructed his commissioners to demand the retention of all the islands, which Spain accepted in the December 1898 Treaty of Paris that terminated the Spanish-American War. On December 21, 1898, McKinley wrote a proclamation to the people of the Philippines explaining that the United States intended to assert its sovereignty over the entire archipelago and to institute a temporary military government of the Philippines. McKinley promised to protect the Filipinos "in their personal and religious rights," but made no promise of future self-government. This proclamation solidified his policy to create a colonial government for the Philippines (Welch 1979:18).

McKinley's decision to forego the adoption of proliberalization policies in these two nations can be partially explained by the lack of constraints imposed during the presidential selection process. Although the platform under which McKinley ran for president in 1896 did call for a pro-Cuban policy, McKinley did not have to adopt liberal foreign policy positions to attain the Republican nomination.[1] In part, this was because liberal internationalists were not a strong constituency in the party. More important, McKinley did not face any serious opposition for his party's nomination. During the general election campaign, McKinley emphasized his support

---

1. The Republican platform stated: "From the hour of achieving their own independence the people of the United States have regarded with sympathy the struggles of other American peoples to free themselves from European domination. We watch with deep and abiding interest the heroic battle of the Cuban patriots against cruelty and oppression and our best hopes go out for the full success of the determined contest for liberty. The government of Spain, having lost control of Cuba, and being unable to protect the property or lives of resident American citizens, or to comply with its treaty obligations, we believe that the government of the United States should actively use its influence and good offices to restore peace and give independence to the island" (Congress 1897:955).

for sound money and protectionist trade policies in opposition to the free silver and free trade platform of his Democratic opponent, William Jennings Bryan (Gould 1980:1–20). While the domestic liberal argument may explain why McKinley was relatively unconstrained by domestic forces in making his initial choices, it does not provide a powerful explanation of those choices.

Security Interests and McKinley's Decision to Subject Cuba and the Philippines to Military Occupation

Realist considerations dominated the McKinley administration's initial decisions about Cuba and the Philippines. In terms of the hypotheses examined in Chapter 2, however, Cuba should have been a case most likely to involve the initial adoption of proliberalization policies. The global balance of power presented only limited threats to the United States. Spain had tried very hard to enlist the support of the European great powers against American intervention in Cuba, but those powers showed little interest in opposing the United States in the Caribbean Basin. The strongest response of the great powers involved a diplomatic démarche days before the American declaration of war urging the United States to pursue a peaceful settlement of the dispute. Even this limited démarche was made only after it had been welcomed by the McKinley administration in an effort to dampen public enthusiasm for war with Spain (Offner 1992:29–30, 89–90, 162–68). The state possessing the greatest capabilities to threaten the United States, Great Britain, was the most supportive of the American position (Offner 1992:199–200). Internally, the quick surrender of Spanish forces, the decision by the Liberating Army not to oppose U.S. troops and the presence of a 45,000 strong occupation force should have facilitated the initial adoption of proliberalization policies in Cuba.

The security situation in the Philippines was less congenial to the promotion of democracy. While the European powers were reluctant to challenge U.S. authority ninety miles from the American coast, they were less likely to accede to U.S. wishes in the Pacific. Within two months of Dewey's victory, his squadron faced a group of "neutral" naval vessels from several great powers, including Germany, which threatened to claim the Philippines if the United States withdrew (Gould 1980:114–15; Trask 1981:377–88). When fighting broke out between American occupation forces and the army of the newly proclaimed Philippine Republic on February 4, 1899, this further constrained America's opportunities to promote democracy.

Despite the imperfect relationship between the realist factors emphasized in Chapter 2 and the initial policies of the McKinley administration, realist considerations did indeed cause McKinley to adopt nonliberalization policies in Cuba and the Philippines. The United States possessed significant strategic and economic interests in both nations. Ninety miles from the U.S. coast, Cuba was of obvious strategic importance and was already substantially integrated with the U.S. economy. The Philippines would serve as America's principal base in its expansion into the Pacific to penetrate the huge China market. America's material interests, therefore, demanded that friendly and stable governments ruled in Cuba and the Philippines. The McKinley administration decided to exercise direct political control over both possessions because it believed that neither nation could produce such a government.

McKinley hesitated to support an independent Cuba because he agreed with Ambassador Woodford, who stated: "I do not believe that the population is today fit for self government . . . acceptance of a practical protectorate over Cuba seems to me very likely the assumption of the responsible care of a madhouse" (State 1901:687). When asked his opinion about self-government for the Cubans, General Shafter replied, "Self-government! Why these people are no more fit for self-government than gun-powder is for hell!" (Healy 1963:36). This pessimism was reinforced by racist attitudes about the dark-skinned population of Cuba (Hunt 1987). Policymakers pointed to the example of the violent and constantly unstable politics of the black republic of Haiti for a model of what they expected in Cuba should the Liberating Army achieve power (Healy 1963:91). Thus, McKinley feared that the adoption of proliberalization policies in Cuba would lead to a complete breakdown of stable government.

McKinley feared a stable anti-American government almost as much as he feared chronic instability. The rebels of the Liberating Army fought for a radical notion of independence, which the spiritual leader of the revolution, José Martí, proclaimed would involve independence from the United States as much as from Spain (Foner 1972:13). Furthermore, the insurgent strategy against Spain had been to destroy the sugar economy of Cuba (Foner 1972:14–34). The substantial U.S. economic interests in the island were inevitably affected. McKinley did not want to make any "embarrassing commitments" to a movement that combined a commitment to real independence from the United States with direct attacks on American economic interests (State 1898:558–61). Indeed, Grover Cleveland's secretary of state, Richard Olney, had dismissed the Liberating Army as a gang of arsonists (Atkins 1926:213–14). Free and fair elections, whether in an independent Cuba or in the context of U.S. military occupation, would probably lead to a victory by the popular revolutionary forces, an outcome McKinley was determined to avoid.

McKinley's analysis of the capabilities of the Filipinos to govern their own affairs was equally pessimistic. As with Cuba, racism influenced U.S. assessments of the possibility for the Filipinos to govern themselves, thus rendering policymakers less than fully rational in their realist calculations (State 1904:840–52). In addition, there was a sense that the Philippines were so riven with ethnic divisions that it would be impossible to gain the consensus necessary for republican rule. McKinley viewed Aguinaldo as little more than a "petty Tagalog chieftain" trying to impose his tyranny over dozens of other tribes (Welch 1979:15). Therefore, McKinley could not leave the Filipinos to themselves, as he explained to a group of ministers, "for anarchy and bloodshed would follow in the wake of native ignorance and inability to govern; so there was nothing left for us to do but to take them all, and to educate the Filipinos, and uplift and civilize and Christianize them, and by God's grace do the very best we could by them, as our fellow-men for whom Christ died" (Morgan 1965:96).

McKinley was able to maintain nonliberalization policies in the Philippines throughout the remainder of his administration. By mid-1899, however, he had shifted to proliberalization policies in Cuba by sponsoring a series of electoral contests that culminated in the grant of formal independence to an elected Cuban government in 1902. The congressional argument from the domestic liberal approach offers the best explanation for this shift in policy.

Congressional Pressure and the Move to Proliberalization Policies in Cuba

On December 1, 1899, after a year in which the United States prepared for an indefinite military occupation of Cuba, Secretary of War Elihu Root announced a clear timetable for Cuban elections and promised a relatively quick pace for the withdrawal of U.S. forces and the advent of Cuban independence (War Department 1904:41–44). Municipal elections were scheduled for mid-1900 after the completion of a census. Elections for a constitutional convention were scheduled to follow soon after. As part of this process, occupation authorities began to create the institutional infrastructure of democracy virtually from scratch.

I argue that the McKinley administration shifted to a more pro-democratic policy in Cuba because Congress proclaimed the Spanish-American War to be a war to liberate Cuba. The Teller Amendment to the congressional war resolution stated: "The U.S. hereby disclaims any disposition or intention to exercise sovereignty, jurisdiction or control over said island except for the pacification thereof, and asserts its determination when that is accomplished to leave the government and control of the island to its people" (Congress 1898:3993). This "self-denying ordinance" provided the crucial initial congressional constraint on McKinley's policy in Cuba. Continued liberal pressure from Congress against McKinley's policies in both Cuba and the Philippines compelled him to adopt proliberalization policies in Cuba. Partisan dynamics within the Republican caucus in Congress, however, played a more crucial role in turning these liberal attacks into an effective constraint on the chief executive. As expected by the domestic liberal argument, liberal ideals did push the United States to promote democracy in Cuba, but only because people in positions of institutional strength in Congress used those ideals to partisan advantage.

Liberal Ideals and Congressional Support for Cuban Democracy

Congress agitated on the Cuban question almost from the beginning of the insurrection in Cuba in 1895. In early 1896, both houses of Congress almost unanimously passed a concurrent resolution that recognized Cuban belligerency rights and resolved that the president should use his "friendly offices" to obtain the "recognition of the independence of Cuba."[2] Belligerency resolutions passed the Senate Foreign Relations Committee in December 1896 and the full Senate in June 1897. Throughout these congressional debates, members of Congress almost universally identified with the Cuban cause and attacked Spanish colonial policy on that island.

The American indictment of Spain was twofold. First, Americans viewed Spain as a decadent Old World monarchy (Owen 1994). The central theme of three years of congressional debates and resolutions was that the United

---

2. The belligerency resolution resolved that "in the opinion of Congress, a condition of public war exists between the Government of Spain and the government proclaimed and for sometime maintained by the force of arms by the people of Cuba; and that the United States should maintain a strict neutrality between the contending powers, according to each the rights of belligerents in the ports and territories of the United States." Belligerency rights would allow the Cubans to purchase and transport weapons from the United States with impunity (Congress 1896: 1065–68). The resolutions passed the Senate 64 to 6 on February 28 and the House 247 to 27 on April 6, 1896.

States should support the Cuban cause because they were fighting for democracy and freedom against Spanish monarchical tyranny. Representative William Sulzer (D-N.Y.) summed up the character of the debate when he said in 1896:

> Mr. Speaker, these brave, noble, heroic Cuban patriots are fighting a battle of republicanism against monarchy; of democracy against plutocracy; home rule against the bayonet; the sovereignty of the individual against the sanctity of the king; the ballot against the throne; American liberty against foreign tyranny, and above all and beyond all they are fighting a battle for the rights of man. (Congress 1896:2349)

The Cubans were portrayed as the moral equivalent of the founding fathers of the United States. Cuba was fighting for "the same principles that we contended for at Bunker Hill, Bennington, Princeton and Yorktown—the principles of local self-government and the doctrine that taxation without representation is tyranny," according to Senator Gallinger (Congress 1896:2248).

This message was skillfully reinforced by the "Cuban junta" in New York, which gave voice to tens of thousands of Cubans who had emigrated to the United States in the wake of the Ten Years' War. This group focused its energy on lobbying Congress to recognize the belligerency rights and independence of the Cuban insurgents. Most participants in the propaganda campaign, including the leader of the junta, Tomás Estrada Palma, were white, English-speaking, middle-class, naturalized U.S. citizens. These expatriates consciously emulated the U.S. model and frequently drew comparisons between their struggle for freedom and the American Revolution against British colonial rule (Rubens 1932:326–29). Some even favored annexation or the establishment of a U.S. protectorate over the island (Pérez 1983:110–37). They were successful in building support for their cause because they projected a peculiarly North American message.

A wide variety of groups became champions of the Cuban cause. The American Federation of Labor, spurred on by the Cuban-American members of the cigar makers' union, voted to ask the U.S. government to recognize Cuban belligerency rights (Foner 1972:xxv). Patriotic groups like the Grand Army of the Republic held rallies in support of the Cuban cause while Protestant ministers welcomed the opportunity to expel Catholic Spain from the island (May 1961:69–82). Both northern blacks and southern white jingoes voiced their support. All of these groups equated the Cuban struggle with the American Revolution.[3]

Second, Americans attacked Spain for the practice of its colonial rule in Cuba. Spain had sent more than 200,000 troops to Cuba, commanded by General Valeriano Weyler, a man who been labeled "Butcher" Weyler for his conduct in an earlier civil war in Cuba, the Ten Years' War, 1868–78. During his two years as captain-general (1896–1897), Weyler pursued a brutal and expensive counterinsurgency strategy. At least 100,000 Cubans died of disease and starvation in *reconcentración* camps. Thousands more were killed by Spanish troops.

Senator William Allen's denunciation of Spanish rule spoke for many in Congress:

> Your treatment of the Cubans for the last 50 years has been brutal and inhuman; you have shocked the moral sense of the civilized world; . . . you have stifled the cries of the Cubans for liberty and have drenched every acre of their soil with the blood of innocent men, women and children and now in the spirit of our free institutions, the people of the United States, being the chief guardians and advocates of popular liberty upon this hemisphere, will require you to relax your hold upon these people and give them that freedom and right of self-government that is inalienable to all people. (Congress 1896:2252)

John Sherman (R-Ohio), chair of the Senate Foreign Relations Committee, warned that "if this line of conduct is pursued by Spain in Cuba . . . there is no earthly power that will prevent the people of the United States from going over to that island, running over its length and breadth, and driving out from the little island of Cuba these barbarous robbers and imitators of the worst men who ever lived" (Congress 1896:2247).[4]

The brutality of the war effort was a central theme of the press coverage of the war. The Cuban junta provided a constant flow of news stories on the conflict to the sensationalist New York papers at a regular 4 p.m.

---

3. It is difficult to determine the precise impact of this constituent pressure on members of Congress. The chairs of the congressional committees dealing with the Cuban issue both claimed that they took action on the Cuban issue in response to intense constituent pressure (Congress 1896:2347). As is true today, Florida's representatives were swayed by pressure from Cuban expatriates (Congress 1896:486–89).

4. Sherman was clearly more concerned with Weyler's atrocities than with Cuban independence. After attacking Weyler's policies, he also suggested that Cuba should be attached to Mexico (Congress 1896:2246).

"peanut club" at the offices of the junta (Rubens 1932:204–5; Wisan 1934). Their reports, which emphasized the rape and murder of Cuban civilians by Butcher Weyler's soldiers, were then sent out over the news wires to papers all over the country and became the principal source of news on Cuba for much of the country. The constant bombardment of the public with stories of Spanish atrocities convinced most readers that Spanish rule in Cuba was inherently brutal, repressive, and illiberal (Wisan 1934:88–98, 187–237).

Some Americans focused on the broader and more devastating impact of disease and starvation in the reconcentration camps. In an important speech that helped push the country to war, Senator Redfield Proctor declared at the end of his fact-finding trip to Cuba that Spain's reconcentration policies had led to a state of affairs that

> is not peace nor is it war. It is desolation and distress, misery and starvation. . . . Torn from their homes, with foul earth, foul air, foul water and foul food or none, what wonder that one-half [of the *reconcentrados*] have died and that one-quarter of the living are so diseased that they cannot be saved. . . . To me the strongest appeal is the spectacle of a million and a half people . . . struggling for freedom and deliverance from the worst misgovernment of which I have ever had knowledge. (Congress 1898:2916–19; Linderman 1974:37–59)

Some of the members who made these liberal arguments in favor of the Cuban cause, probably including Senators Gallinger and Allen, did so because they were ideologically committed to spreading liberal democracy to Cuba. There were not enough ideologically committed liberals in the Congress to build a majority in favor of proliberalization policies for Cuba, however. The crucial role played by liberal internationalists was that they set the terms of the debate over Cuba. Even though members of Congress were motivated by a wide range of concerns, they all publicly cited the issue of freedom and democracy for Cuba as the central issue of the congressional debate.

Partisanship and Congressional Action on Cuba

A set of partisan dynamics that originated in the debates over Cuban policy in early 1896 turned these liberal attacks into effective congressional constraints on the president. Congressional Republicans used the 1896 concurrent resolutions in favor of Cuban independence and belligerency rights to attack the Democratic president. Because these initiatives were offered as concurrent resolutions, they only expressed the wishes of Congress, thus allowing Cleveland to ignore them. While these resolutions did not provide an effective instrument for changing policy, they did provide an excellent vehicle for launching partisan attacks against a Democratic president.

A majority of congressional Democrats also voted in opposition to their party's president. By 1896, Cleveland's eastern establishment wing of the Democratic Party had been overwhelmed by the southern and western agrarian populist portions of the party. These factions coalesced around William Jennings Bryan, the party's nominee for president in the 1896 elections. Therefore, both major parties repudiated Cleveland's reluctance to challenge Spanish policy in Cuba in their party platforms and congressional resolutions (May 1961). The Republicans were the most pro-Cuban of the parties.

Thus, when the Republican candidate, William McKinley, won the presidential election of 1896, congressional Democrats were already on record in support of *Cuba Libre*. Democrats (and Populists) in the Congress, therefore, used increasingly expansive liberal rhetoric to launch partisan attacks on McKinley's policies. More important, the president's own party in Congress was strongly committed to a pro-independence and pro-democratic policy for Cuba. As noted above, however, McKinley was not committed to these policies. Throughout the next two years, McKinley had to fight not only Democrats but also members of his own party.

The problem of maintaining control over congressional Republicans manifested itself most openly in the Senate, where the traditional lack of institutional mechanisms for forcing party loyalty and central control made it difficult for anyone to compel members to support the administration. The Senate Foreign Relations Committee voted unanimously in support of a joint resolution recognizing Cuban independence and belligerency status in December 1896 during the final days of the Cleveland administration. The committee agreed to postpone consideration of the measure in the full Senate only after McKinley named the chair of the Committee, Senator Sherman, as his nominee for secretary of state (Dennison 1943:97). During the special first session of the Fifty-fifth Congress, the Senate passed a belligerency proclamation 41–14, with significant Republican support (Congress 1897:1186).

The April 1898 votes on the congressional war resolution demonstrated an even more critical problem for the president. A split in the ranks of the Republican Party had robbed the regular Republicans of a working majority in that chamber. Republicans possessed fifty out of the ninety seats in the Senate of the Fifty-fifth Congress, but seven of these were Silver Republicans from western states who had supported the free-silver platform of Bryan and the Democrats in the 1896 elections. Silver Republicans like Senator Teller often allied themselves with the Democrats, making it difficult for the Republicans to turn their numerical majority into a legislative majority.

Therefore, when Senators Joseph Foraker (R-Ohio) and David Turpie (D-Ind.) offered an amendment to the war resolution recognizing the independence of the Cuban Republic, Republicans provided the margin of victory in a 51 to 37 vote.[5] Eleven regular Republicans and all seven Silver Republicans voted with a majority of the Democrats for an amendment that the president had vowed to veto (Gould 1980:87; Offner 1992:189). For many regular Republicans, this represented a vote for principle against partisanship. For others, it represented an effort to avoid being labeled a hypocrite in the next elections. The Senate then voted by voice vote in favor of the Teller Amendment. There was no serious debate on this measure because at the time of its passage it appeared superfluous, given the Senate's approval of the Turpie-Foraker independence resolution.

Throughout this period, the Republican-controlled House of Representatives never voted against the president. Indeed, the House rarely debated the Cuban issue.[6] This was because the House of the 1890s operated under "Reed Rules," named after the Speaker of the House, Thomas Brackett Reed (R-Maine) (Brady 1973:143–79). Under Reed Rules, the Speaker made all committee appointments, controlled what legislation the House would consider, when it would be considered, and how long it would be debated. The Speaker ruthlessly exercised this extraordinary authority to enforce party discipline and exclude the minority party from any influence on legislation. There was, however, an important tension between the institutional power of the Speaker and the principles of responsible party governance that legitimated the institutional structures of the House. House Republicans ran on a pro-Cuba platform in 1896. Thus, while Speaker Reed was able to use his institutional power to restrain House action on Cuba for almost two years, many Republicans chafed under the violation of the implicit rule that

5. This initiative, approved on April 16, 1898, was the minority position of the Foreign Relations Committee. As a compromise measure, the committee had adopted the language that the people of Cuba "are, and of right ought to be, free and independent," a clause that was an indirect recognition of Cuban independence. When Senator Frye of Maine offered an amendment to strike the words "are, and" from the resolution, the Senate voted 55 to 33 against it (Congress 1898:3988). The Senate's vote for the minority rather than majority resolution of the committee provides evidence for the weakness of committees in the institutional structures of the Senate at this time.

6. Democratic leaders were able to comment on Cuba only while making "parliamentary inquiries" or "points of personal privilege," at which point the Speaker would usually silence them for being "out of order." See, for example, Congress, 1898, pp. 3810–21.

the Speaker was supposed to use his power to represent the majority position of the party.

On March 29, 1898, the day after McKinley submitted his report on the sinking of the battleship *Maine* in Havana harbor, nearly fifty discontented Republicans met to discuss means of forcing the Cuban issue. The next day, they threatened to vote with the Democrats in favor of Cuban independence unless the House Foreign Affairs Committee promised immediate action. That evening, more than one hundred Republicans met once again to demand Cuban independence. The president and the House leadership capitulated to this revolt and McKinley asked Congress for a declaration of war (Offner 1992:150–54).

This incident marked one of the only times in nearly two decades of strong speakership in the House, beginning with Reed's reign and ending with the revolt against Speaker Joseph Cannon in 1910, that House Republicans had revolted against their party's leadership. Reed resigned at the end of the session as a direct result of this incident (Beisner 1968:209–10). The extraordinary nature of this revolt illuminates the more general point that the institutional structures of the House made it extremely difficult for the Congress to place an effective constraint on the president if both the presidency and the House were controlled by the same party.

House Republicans supported the president on every subsequent foreign policy initiative. On April 13, 1898, the House overwhelmingly approved an open-ended war resolution approved by the president.[7] House Republicans unanimously voted down a Democratic alternative calling for the recognition of the Cuban Republic, despite the fact that a majority of the party had expressed their support for such a measure. After several days of contentious debate, a House-Senate conference committee agreed to a compromise that maintained the Teller Amendment while striking out the Turpie-Foraker Amendment from the final declaration of war.[8]

7. The House voted 325 to 19 in favor of a resolution stating: "The President is hereby authorized and directed to intervene at once to stop the war in Cuba, to the end and with the purpose of securing permanent peace and order there and establishing by the free action of the people thereof, a stable and independent government of their own on the island of Cuba. The President is hereby authorized and empowered to use the land and naval forces of the United States to execute the purpose of this resolution" (Congress 1898:3819–21).

8. The final resolution approved by both houses of Congress had four parts: "First, the people of the island of Cuba are, and of right ought to be free and independent; Second, that it is the duty of the United States to demand, and the government of the United States does hereby demand that the government of Spain at once relinquish its authority and government in the island of Cuba and withdraw its land and naval forces from Cuba and Cuban waters; Third, that the President of the United States be, and hereby is directed and empowered to use the entire

House Republicans and the eleven regular Republican senators who had originally voted for the Turpie-Foraker Amendment gladly accepted the Teller Amendment compromise. This suggests how members reconciled the potentially conflicting values of ideology and partisanship. Regular Republicans forged a pro-democratic compromise where supporters of *Cuba Libre* and the administration could meet.[9]

They had also saved themselves from a possible electoral disaster in the 1898 elections if their president had not gone to war to free Cuba. Democrats had threatened to make Cuba their critical campaign issue in the 1898 congressional elections if the president did not act. Representative Sulzer (D-N.Y.) warned:

> Before the election when you were looking for votes, you pretended to be great friends of the Cuban patriots; but now that you have the opportunity to demonstrate that friendship you are absolutely silent. The people are watching you and you will hear from them in the fall. . . . The Democrats in the House are in favor of passing the joint resolution granting belligerent rights to the Cubans. The Republicans have persistently refused to permit a vote on the question. The people of this country will hold the Republican Party responsible for that action at the coming election. We will tell of your recreancy on this important question and the people will condemn you. (Congress 1898:763)

One Senator voiced a similar threat to Assistant Secretary of State William Day: "Don't your president know where the war-declaring power is lodged? Well, tell him . . . that if he doesn't do something, Congress will exercise the power and declare war in spite of him! He'll get run over and the party with him!" (Pérez 1983:173)

House Republicans were especially afraid that the label of "Reed's caucus of *reconcentrados,*" as House Democratic Leader Representative Joe Bailey

---

land and naval forces of the United States, and to call into the actual service of the United States the militias of the several states to such extent as may be necessary to carry these resolutions into effect; Fourth, that the United States hereby disclaims any disposition or intention to exercise sovereignty, jurisdiction or control over said island except for the pacification thereof, and asserts its determination when that is accomplished to leave the government and control of the island to its people" (Congress 1898:4062).

9. Senate conferees sacrificed the Turpie-Foraker amendment when it became clear that regular Republicans would no longer support the resolution. The Senate conferees did hold out for a statement that the Cubans "are, and of right ought to be independent." The final compromise was approved 43 to 25 on April 18 (Congress 1898:4031).

of Texas had taken to calling them, would stick (Congress 1898:3433–45). In the Senate, Republican stalwart Henry Cabot Lodge (R-Mass.) warned: "If the war in Cuba drags on through the summer with nothing done, we shall go down in the greatest defeat ever known . . . it will be deadly. I know that it is easily and properly said that to bring on or even threaten war for political reasons is a crime and I quite agree. But to sacrifice a great party and bring free silver upon the country for a wrong policy is hardly less odious" (Pérez 1983:174). According to Senator Knute Nelson (R-Minn.), "A popular war might do more than anything else to relieve the country from the nightmare of the free silver question. The success of Bryanism, Populism and free silver would inflict infinitely more damage on this country than a short, sharp war with Spain" (Offner 1992:153). "In the final analysis," according to historian John Offner, "Republicans made war on Spain in order to keep control of Washington" (Offner 1992:ix).

In sum, partisan politics caused Congress to push McKinley to go to war under conditions he did not support. In the compromise that had brought America into the war, McKinley made a commitment to Cuban independence without recognizing the Cuban rebels as the government of that island. While the Teller Amendment gave the administration substantial room to maneuver in crafting a Cuban government to its liking, it also closed off the options of immediate annexation or colonial rule. McKinley was constrained even by his own rhetoric. In December 1897 he had stated unequivocally: "I speak not of forcible annexation, for that cannot be thought of. That, by our code of morality, would be criminal aggression" (State 1898:xx). Therefore, when Spain urged the United States to assume sovereignty over Cuba in the treaty negotiations that followed the American victory over Spain, McKinley replied simply that "we must carry out the spirit and the letter of the resolution of Congress" (State 1901:927). McKinley did not want to derail an established compromise by openly breaking with the will of the Congress as expressed in the Teller Amendment. The Teller Amendment forced the McKinley administration to set aside the option of colonial rule for Cuba. Subsequent congressional pressure pushed McKinley to promote democracy there.

McKinley's behavior in the latter half of 1898 indicates that he operated under a congressional constraint in regard to his policy in Cuba that he did not appear to face in his policy toward the Philippines, where Congress failed to keep McKinley from pursuing a colonial policy. The next section examines this anomaly and offers an explanation for the failure of the anti-imperialist movement to compel McKinley to adopt pro-democratic policies toward the Philippines.

U.S. Annexation of the Philippines
and the Treaty Ratification Debate

On December 10, 1898, U.S. representatives signed the Treaty of Paris, which terminated the war with Spain and ceded the Philippines to American control. On February 6, 1899, the Senate voted 57 to 27 to ratify the treaty, a one-vote margin of victory. They did so despite the vocal complaints of liberals that the treaty would legitimate the imposition of undemocratic colonial rule in the Philippines. These liberal attacks should have been sufficient to force McKinley to adopt proliberalization policies toward the Philippines.

The fighting that broke out between Americans and Aguinaldo's Filipino forces just before the Senate vote explains in part both McKinley's decision not to adopt proliberalization policies and the Senate's decision to ratify the treaty. Indeed, McKinley indicated as much in a February 16, 1899, speech in Boston defending his Philippine policy. McKinley disclaimed imperial designs, declared his intention of aiding the Filipinos toward self-government, and affirmed that Americans were not the masters but the emancipators of these people. At the same time, however, he caustically remarked: "It was not a good time for the liberator to submit important questions concerning liberty and government to the liberated while they are engaged in shooting down their rescuers" (Leech 1959:361–62). Any movement toward independence and democracy would be postponed until after the Filipinos had laid down their arms and proclaimed allegiance to the United States.

As noted above, however, the McKinley administration decided not to promote democracy and independence in the Philippines months before Aguinaldo's troops fired on American soldiers. Aguinaldo's attack, therefore, can be seen as a consequence of McKinley's decision not to promote democracy in the Philippines as much as a cause of that policy. The congressional argument from the domestic liberal perspective offers an explanation for McKinley's failure to shift to proliberalization policies that focuses on the importance of partisanship in determining outcomes in an era when parties dominated the decision-making structures of Congress.

The Anti-Imperialist League and Liberal Internationalism

The coalition that rallied around the anti-imperialist cause differed from that which supported the liberation of Cuba. There was no comparable expatriate community of Filipinos in the United States to rally support for their cause. While the Cuban cause had met with support at all levels of society, the anti-imperialist movement possessed a strikingly elitist character, with former presidents like Grover Cleveland and Benjamin Harrison, retired cabinet officers like John Sherman, senators and governors listed among the prominent opponents of imperialism. Finally, while liberal rhetoric may have masked ulterior motives in the Cuban case, the most prominent anti-imperialists were clearly motivated by a principled commitment to American liberal ideals.

The anti-imperialists argued that imperialism undermined democracy at home and abroad and violated the fundamental principles upon which America had been founded. Moorfield Storey expressed these central themes in a June 15, 1898, public meeting at Boston's Faneuil Hall:

> [We insist that] an attempt to win for the Cubans the right to govern themselves shall not be made an excuse for extending our sway over alien peoples without their consent . . . to seize any colony of Spain and hold it as our own, without the free consent of its people is a violation of the principles upon which this government rests. . . . [If we pursue an imperialist policy,] we will become a military power burdened with a standing army and an enormous navy, . . . our domestic difficulties will be neglected, . . . our taxation will increase, our currency become more disordered, and worst of all the corruption which threatens us cannot fail to spread. . . . When Rome began her career of conquest, the Roman Republic began to decay. . . . Let us once govern any considerable body of men without their consent, and it is a question of time how soon this republic shares the fate of Rome. (Tompkins 1970:124–25)

This public meeting led to the creation of the Anti-Imperialist League, the group which provided the most spirited and consistent organized opposition to McKinley's policies in the Philippines. The financial support of industrialist Andrew Carnegie guaranteed that the message of the league would be disseminated nationwide from the league's central office in Chicago.

The most active members of the league were descendants of the first puritan settlers of New England (Tompkins 1970:144–46). For these Boston elites, opposition to imperialism reflected a lifetime of efforts to recapture the ideals of their forefathers. Many had begun their public life in the abolitionist cause before the Civil War. They later became the "mugwumps" who formed the Massachusetts Reform Club during the 1870s to agitate for civil service reform and similar causes. Imperialism reflected yet another example of America's movement away from the hallowed principles of its past, yet another corruption of the Republic (Beisner 1968:5–138; Welch 1979:43–57).

That this was primarily an ideologically based movement is attested to by the partisan composition of the organization. Although the league counted some conservative Democrats among its membership, many of its principal leaders were Republicans who had participated in the founding of the party in the 1850s as principled opponents of slavery. The first president of the league, George Boutwell, and John Sherman had been staunch Republicans during their entire political lives. Others, like Carl Schurz, Samuel Bowles, Erving Winslow, and Moorfield Storey (league president in the early 1900s) had been founding members of the party. The presence of so many Republicans willing to oppose their party's president suggests that ideological considerations outweighed partisan considerations for these members of the Anti-Imperialist League.

While many of the members of the league were old guard Republicans who could trace their political careers to the origins of the party, most of them were old men who had retired from the Congress. They represented the party's past (Beisner 1968:186–211). Two Republicans who shared the sentiments of the league still served as important leaders in the Senate, George Hoar of Massachusetts and Eugene Hale of Maine. Hoar, who became the most famous of the anti-imperialists in the Senate, opposed the annexation of the Philippines because it violated basic American liberal ideals (Congress 1899:544). In 1902 Hoar summed up his opposition to McKinley's policy in the Philippines:

> We changed the Monroe Doctrine from a doctrine of eternal righteousness and justice, resting on the consent of the governed, to a doctrine of brutal selfishness looking only to our own advantage. We crushed the only republic in Asia. We made war on the only Christian people in the East. We converted a war of glory into a war of shame. We vulgarized the American flag. We introduced perfidy into the practice of war. We inflicted torture on unarmed men to extort confession. We put children to death. We established *reconcentrado* camps. We devastated provinces. We baffled the aspirations of a people for liberty. (Beisner 1968:162)

Hoar and Hale provided the only regular Republican votes against ratification of the Treaty of Paris. The fact that only two Republicans voted against the treaty indicates the importance of partisan considerations in accounting for the president's ability to maintain a nonliberalization policy in the Philippines.

Partisanship and Senate Ratification of the Treaty of Paris

In contrast to the Cuban issue, McKinley managed to call upon nearly complete party unity in support of his policies in the Philippines. He did this first by rallying public opinion to support his policies during a national speaking tour. Although McKinley had probably decided to annex the Philippines in May 1898, he waited until the end of October to announce his decision and made it appear that he had only reluctantly accepted the "duty" of governing the country. When the Republicans did much better than expected in the off-year elections a week later, many credited McKinley and his expansionist policies (Gould 1980:135–37). This helped him to weld Senate Republicans into a unified block behind his policies. The administration and the Republican leadership in the Senate also placed enormous partisan pressure on wavering Republicans. These Republicans were promised patronage and good committee assignments by Republican leader Nelson Aldrich (R-R.I.) if they sided with the president. They were threatened with punishment if they failed to support the party line (Morgan 1965:107–8).

A vote against the treaty at this point would not have merely been a vote advising against a decision to take the Philippines. It would have been a vote to repudiate the president's policies of the previous six months. As Senator Lodge, who led the fight for ratification, argued: "The president cannot be sent across the Atlantic, in the person of his commissioners, hat in hand, to say to Spain with baited breath: 'I am here in obedience to the mandate of a minority of one-third of the Senate to tell you that we have been too victorious, and that you have yielded too much, and that I am very sorry that I took the Philippines from you'" (Congress 1898:5790–92). It was very difficult for Republicans to embarrass their president in this way. Several Republicans who originally indicated their opposition to the treaty on ideological grounds voted for the treaty in the end (Congress 1899:528–30; Winslow 1976:31).

In the case of these wavering Republicans, promises to promote democracy during military intervention helped members reconcile ideological and partisan considerations. McKinley privately assured doubtful Republican senators like Wellington (Md.) and Mason (Ill.) that the administration intended to give some form of self-government to the Philippines after a not too lengthy period of U.S. tutelage. These Republicans' concerns were further assuaged in January 1899 by McKinley's appointment of two members who had expressed opposition to colonial rule to a Commission that would make recommendations about the future of the Philippines.[10]

Votes from regular Republicans were insufficient to gain the two-thirds majority necessary for ratification, however. McKinley needed the support of some Silver Republicans, Populists, and/or Democrats in order to guarantee passage. Most Senate Democrats, led by Arthur Pue Gorman of Maryland, opposed the treaty. Although many were principally motivated by partisanship, they expressed their opposition in liberal terms. They denounced colonialism as unconstitutional, antidemocratic, and un-American.[11] Two-thirds of the Democrats in the Senate voted against ratification, providing 22 of the 27 negative votes (Tompkins 1970:192–93).

William Jennings Bryan, national leader of the Democratic and Populist Parties, feared that the opposition parties would suffer electorally by opposing the treaty, however. He advised Democrats and Populists to approve the treaty and then offer a resolution proclaiming that the United States pledged to give the Philippines its independence at the earliest possible moment. By voting for ratification, the Democrats would allow a Republican administration to fight a brutal imperialist war against a people fighting for their freedom. By forcing Senate Republicans to vote against independence for the Philippines, the Democrats would place the Republicans on record as opponents of basic American ideals. When Senator Augustus Bacon (D-Ga.) offered this independence resolution, Vice President Hobart was forced to cast the deciding vote in a 29–29 tie. Dozens of Republican senators conveniently found themselves absent from the floor when they were called upon to vote against self-determination for the people of the Philippines. In sum, instead of opposing imperialism by stopping ratification of the treaty, Bryan hoped to make imperialism an important campaign issue in 1900 (Tompkins 1970:188–91). Although it is not clear how many Democratic votes Bryan changed, two Populist Party senators, including Senator Allen of Nebraska, apparently did shift their vote based on this advice (Winslow 1976:31).

10. The First Philippine Commission was led by Cornell University President Jacob Gould Schurman, and included University of Michigan Professor Dean Worcester, former U.S. Minister to China Charles Denby, and the U.S. military commanders in the Philippines, General Elwell Otis and Admiral George Dewey. Both Schurman and Worcester had been on record as opposing long-term colonial rule for the Philippines.

11. See, for example, the words of the Vest Amendment, offered to provide an open forum for a discussion of the Philippines while the actual treaty debates took place in executive session: "Under the constitution of the United States, no power is given to the Federal Government to acquire territory to be held and governed permanently as colonies. . . . All territory acquired by the Government . . . must be acquired and governed with the purpose of ultimately organizing such territories into States suitable for admission into the Union" (Congress 1899:20).

Finally, McKinley was able to win the vote because the members of the lame-duck Senate knew that the incoming Senate would probably ratify the treaty if they failed to do so. The Republicans gained six seats in the Senate and could count on a solid Republican majority there when the Fifty-sixth Congress convened in December 1899. Many Democrats realized that their opposition efforts were likely to be futile. Several important swing voters, therefore, decided to trade their votes for patronage while their votes were still valuable to the administration.[12]

The failure of the Anti-Imperialist League and Senate Democrats to over-turn the Paris Treaty on the issue of colonial rule in the Philippines suggests that liberal members of Congress and vocal interest groups will find it difficult to triumph over a determined president with partisan majorities in the Congress, especially at a time when Congress is dominated by strong parties. Warfare in the target country, as the realists anticipate, also kept the McKinley administration from adopting proliberalization policies in the Philippines. At the same time, however, McKinley won this battle with only one vote to spare. His difficulty in selling a colonial policy for the Philippines made it even more imperative to avoid a similar dispute over his Cuba policies.

Elections for Cuba and War for the Philippines

During the final years of the McKinley administration, the domestic political links between the Cuban and Philippine cases both reinforced the pressure to maintain proliberalization policies in Cuba and allowed the continuation of colonial policies in the Philippines. On the one hand, the strong domestic political pressure over the Philippines helped convince the McKinley ad-ministration to stick to proliberalization policies in Cuba even when it had serious misgivings about the security consequences of those policies. On the other hand, McKinley's policies in Cuba helped convince many wavering supporters of the president within the Republican Party that the president eventually intended to pursue similar policies in the Philippines.

---

12. Eleven Democrats voted in favor of ratification, four of whom had previously announced their opposition to imperialism. Senator Kenny (Del.) received assistance in extricating himself from legal problems. Senator McLaurin (S.C.) was promised control over the distribution of postmaster positions in his state. Senator McEnery (La.) was allowed to choose several recipients of federal judgeships in Louisiana. Senator Gray (Del.) was named to a federal judgeship, although his vote probably reflected his service on the treaty negotiating team (Gould 1980:144).

The McKinley administration also discovered, somewhat unexpectedly, that the promotion of democracy could serve as an effective means of serving U.S. power and security interests in subordinate states. The McKinley administration asserted naked domination over Filipinos and was met with armed rebellion in the Philippines and substantial domestic opposition. It pursued a more liberal policy in Cuba, at least partially in tune with the rhetoric that had legitimated the war. This policy was more successful in dampening opposition to U.S. domination in Cuba and in crafting a domestic consensus in support of American policy.

Congress, Cuban Elections, and the Platt Amendment

Throughout the intense debate about the future of the Philippines during the ratification process in early 1899, Republicans pointed to the administration's presumed commitment to leave Cuba as soon as a stable democratic government could be established on the island as evidence of the administration's good faith. Republican leaders who had loyally stood by the president in all legislative battles, like Senator John Spooner of Wisconsin, made a point of arguing that:

> Of course we cannot take Cuba. I hope, for the honor of America, no man would think of such a thing. We promised the world to make Cuba free and to enforce law and order in that Island until the people there could form a government. When that is done our pledge will have been splendidly redeemed. . . . I hope it will not be long before our flag is taken down in Cuba and the island is left to govern itself. (Congress 1899:1385)

This sentiment was reinforced by a vote on March 3, 1899, the last day of the lame-duck session, on an amendment to the Army Appropriation Bill offered by Senator Foraker. The proposed amendment forbade the granting of franchises or concessions of any kind in Cuba by U.S. authorities for the duration of the occupation. In his speech before the Senate, Foraker clearly laid out the purpose of the amendment. A program of granting franchises would begin a rapid expansion of U.S. economic penetration of Cuba which would mean "that the U.S. will not get out of Cuba in a hundred years." A vote for the Foraker Amendment was a vote for a quick end to the American occupation and early self-government for the Cubans. Republicans and Democrats voted enthusiastically for this proposal (Congress 1899:2807–12). Thus, as the McKinley administration and occupation authorities were becoming increasingly convinced that a long-term military occupation government was necessary in Cuba, Congress proclaimed its opposition to such a course of action in favor of adhering to the spirit of the Teller Amendment.

Fortuitously, the Teller Amendment and support for free and fair elections in Cuba proved to be a useful tool for achieving American control over the island at a minimal cost. The Cuban Liberating Army initially refused to demobilize in the face of the U.S. military occupation. The commanding general of the Liberating Army, Máximo Gómez, maintained the integrity of his army as a guarantee of Cuban independence. In February 1899, soon after Aguinaldo's troops had fired on U.S. troops in the Philippines, McKinley sent a special representative to General Gómez in Cuba to assure him that the U.S. occupation would not last longer than required to "pacify" the island in line with the terms of the Teller Amendment (Pérez 1983:262–63). Convinced by this pledge, Gómez agreed to disband the Liberating Army by the summer of 1899. "We should aid by every pacific means in completing the work of the Americans," Gómez argued. "We must forget past antipathies and disagreements and unite all elements completely.... We must make the presence of foreigners on our soil unnecessary by our behavior ... to demonstrate to them the legitimate desires and sufficient capacity to govern ourselves" (Pérez 1983:294).

Without a credible pledge that it would fulfill the terms of the Teller Amendment, the United States could have found itself at war with the Liberating Army. Instead, the Cubans disbanded their army to convince the Americans that they were worthy of self-government. The Cuban experience, therefore, suggests a reversal of the causal argument suggested by hypothesis 2.3 in Chapter 2. It wasn't the absence of war in the target country that made the U.S. more likely to promote democracy. It was the promise to promote democracy that made war with the Liberating Army less likely. American officials still wanted to annex Cuba, but they realized that forcible annexation could lead to war with remobilized veterans of that army.

General Wood, who became Military Governor of Cuba in December 1899, embodied the solution to this dilemma. "Forcible annexation he had refused to consider; annexation by guile he had effectively opposed; but annexation by acclamation had been his dream from the beginning" (Hagedorn 1931:371). Wood wanted to prepare the Cubans for independence in such a manner that they would want to join the union of their own free will. As Secretary of War Elihu Root explained, "It is better to have the favors of a lady with her consent, after judicious courtship, than to ravish her" (Pérez 1983:279).

Wood and Root believed, however, that "annexation by acclamation" would require perhaps decades of direct American tutelage. Congressional pressure forced them instead to move rapidly to create an American protectorate over a friendly Cuban government, in hopes that Cubans would apply for admission into the Union after a generation of independence. Among occupation officials, only General James Wilson, commander of Matanzas and Santa Clara provinces, had argued for this course of action (Healy 1963:94–96).

Wood, therefore, attempted to create a coalition of local elites who would see annexation to the United States as the appropriate destiny for Cuba. The most crucial element of this coalition was the Cuban expatriate community. A majority of the Cubans chosen to serve in the occupation government were the English-speaking, naturalized U.S. citizens associated with the Cuban junta (Pérez 1983:284–301). These Cubans possessed strong separatist credentials acquired during the war with Spain, but, like President Estrada Palma, warmly embraced the idea of a close relationship with the United States.

Root and Wood sought to legitimize this path by ensuring that the "better elements" of Cuban society, including the Spanish residents who had bitterly opposed a free Cuba, were selected by the Cuban people in "free and fair" elections.[13] They constructed an electoral law that allowed only male property owners, literates, and Liberating Army veterans to vote because they believed that universal adult male suffrage would lead to victories by revolutionary elements of the Liberating Army. Wood took the extra step of encouraging the formation of a pro-American political party and campaigning for its candidates. Senator Ben "Pitchfork" Tillman (D-S.C.) denounced the elections as the equivalent of the post–Civil War reconstruction elections in the American South:

> [T]he President has proclaimed that he is not a friend of free Cuba. He does not believe in the Republic and he has not wanted a republic. . . . [U]nder his reconstruction policy . . . he will have the right to determine who are the "people of Cuba" . . . and yet you propose to have those gallant soldiers told "You are not the free people of Cuba, but the Spaniards who are in Havana and in the other cities, who have ruined your homes who have burned your houses and destroyed your

---

13. The December 1899 announcement of the electoral initiative was timed both to distract attention from an intensification of the war in the Philippines and to start the new congressional term on a positive note.

industries, in truth, they are to be brought in and recognized as the people of Cuba." We expel the Spaniards. We will pacify the Island. We will go there ignoring the present Cuban government. We will order an election; we will say it will be an honest election; that there shall be no cheating; no counting in or counting out; no military interference, except to see a free vote and a fair count. And when the representatives of that government meet, who can recognize it as a stable government? Can this Congress do it? Will this Congress act? (Congress 1898:3889–90)

Wood supervised two sets of elections in 1900. First, municipal elections were held on June 16, 1900. Then elections for a constitutional convention took place on September 3, 1900. Rather than elect the "best men" to represent them, the Cubans sent representatives of "the extreme and revolutionary element" connected to the Liberating Army to the Constitutional Convention in September 1900. "I should say that we have about ten absolutely first class men and about fifteen men of doubtful qualifications and character and about six of the worst rascals and fakirs in Cuba," Wood reported to Washington (Healy 1963:148).

The McKinley administration feared precisely such an outcome when it had initially decided not to adopt proliberalization policies. The 1900 elections brought to office men that McKinley's principal advisers believed both incapable of sustaining stable government in Cuba and quite capable of writing a constitution damaging to American interests. Despite the realization of its fears, the McKinley administration remained committed to the promotion of democracy through the remainder of the intervention. Indeed, Wood pushed up the date of the constitutional convention elections despite his expectation of a negative outcome for U.S. interests, given the results of the municipal elections. Despite his deep concern about the document that such a convention might produce, Wood took great pains to cooperate with the Constitutional Convention.

The McKinley administration continued its proliberalization policies in the face of the threat to its security interests posed by the Cuban elections because of two types of domestic political pressures emphasized by the domestic liberal argument. First, while the solidly Republican Fifty-sixth Congress generally supported the Republican president, it proved more difficult to handle than expected because members were preparing for the 1900 elections. Congressional pressure on the Cuban issue built to such an extent that Senator Platt confessed that "the whole Congress is nervous, liable to take the bit in its teeth and say we ought to get out of Cuba, and it requires a sort of steady hand to keep things straight now in the last days of the session." Platt added that he had intended to suggest a modification of the Foraker Amendment, but "to tell the truth I do not dare to do it now," because it would encourage the Democrats to reopen the Cuba debate (Healy 1963:141–42).

Second, William Jennings Bryan, the Democratic and Populist nominee in the 1900 presidential race, promised to make opposition to imperialism in the Philippines the "paramount issue" of his campaign. Bryan spoke almost exclusively about imperialism in his acceptance speech at the Democratic convention in Indianapolis in August (Bryan 1976:43–47). Later in the campaign, Bryan downplayed the issue in favor of his preferred issues of free silver and economic populism. McKinley was still sufficiently concerned about the impact of Bryan's campaign attacks that he continued proliberalization policies in Cuba to blunt those attacks.

Wood explicitly pushed up the timing of the Constitutional Convention elections so that they would occur before the American elections. Wood wrote to Root in June, "I want to go ahead with the Constitutional Convention as fast as possible, and follow it by the legislative assembly; . . . I believe the adoption of a constitution here and the legislative assembly to be a fine thing for the Cubans and for the administration at home" (Healy 1963:145). Before the Cuban elections, Wood had warned: "If they send a lot of political jumping jacks as delegates they must not expect that their work will be received very seriously" (Healy 1963:148). Wood accepted the "jumping jacks" selected by the Cuban people in order to "keep things as quiet as possible in Cuba" before the American elections (Rubens 1932:400).

The electoral victories of the most radical elements of the Cuban revolutionary coalition signaled a defeat for the purest expression of the American effort to dominate Cuba by promoting "annexation by acclamation." These elections, however, effectively demobilized the most dangerous opponents of U.S. domination over Cuba. Their victories caused the strongest advocates of Cuban independence in the U.S. Congress to support a protectorate relationship with the United States.

This protectorate relationship was codified in the Platt Amendment, passed by the Senate on February 25, 1901. This amendment gave the United States substantial authority to control Cuban affairs. The United States demanded that Cuba include limitations on treaty-making powers, public debt, and public sanitation programs in their constitution as conditions for granting independence to Cuba. All edicts of the military government would be respected by the Cuban government. In addition, Cuba would cede naval bases to the United States, and America would retain the right to intervene at its discretion to protect stable and republican government in Cuba (Congress 1901:2954).

Congressional opposition to the Platt Amendment was limited because it reflected a reasonable compromise for members of Congress who wanted either to fulfill the promise of the Teller Amendment or to continue U.S. domination over the island. The acceptance of the Platt Amendment by Cuba allowed the United States to fulfill the pro-democratic compromise by turning over Cuba to an elected government led by President Tomás Estrada Palma in early 1902. While many Cubans grumbled about the limitations imposed on Cuban sovereignty by the Americans, the relative peace with which Cubans accepted American domination stood in stark contrast to the American experience in the Philippines.

Benevolent Assimilation and Counterinsurgency War in the Philippines

When McKinley announced his intention to exercise absolute sovereignty over the Philippines in December 1898, he promised that it was "the earnest and paramount aim of the military administration to win the confidence, respect and affection of the inhabitants of the Philippines by assuring them in every possible way that full measure of individual rights and liberties which is the heritage of free peoples, and by proving to them that the mission of the United States is one of benevolent assimilation, substituting the mild sway of justice and right for arbitrary rule" (State 1904:719). This soothing rhetoric did not promise the liberation from colonial rule that Aguinaldo's followers desired. There was no Teller Amendment for the Philippines that could assuage the fears of Filipino nationalists that the United States intended to replace Spain as colonial master. Because of this, Americans soon found themselves fighting a brutal counterinsurgency war there.

U.S. forces commanded by General Arthur MacArthur launched a major military offensive in October 1899 against the Filipino insurgents. When the Filipinos responded to this offensive by adopting guerrilla tactics, MacArthur pursued policies not unlike the ones "Butcher" Weyler had adopted in Cuba. He began herding Filipinos into concentration camps in order to "protect" them from the insurgents and empty the countryside of potential supporters of the republic. By disrupting existing patterns of subsistence agriculture, MacArthur denied the rebels crucial food supplies. By turning the countryside into a "howling wilderness" he created free-fire zones in which anyone discovered would be shot (Welch 1979:24–42). Meanwhile, the Schurmann Commission's recommendations for "home rule" were shelved because the administration believed in the necessity of achieving military victory before allowing greater participation by Filipinos (State 1900–1901:82–91). "Benevolent assimilation" would begin after the war. These results are precisely what one would expect according to the realist argument that war limits the opportunities to promote liberal reforms.

The cooperative Fifty-sixth Congress allowed McKinley to pursue these illiberal policies during 1899–1900, despite the fact that the Anti-Imperialist League had reached the zenith of its activism at this time, with a national office opened in Chicago in October 1899 in preparation for the 1900 elections. Senator Lodge used his chairmanship of the special Senate committee on the Philippines to minimize congressional attacks on McKinley administration policy. Republican leaders in both houses were able to keep Congress from adopting anti-administration legislation regarding the Philippines. As noted above, however, as the 1900 elections approached, it became increasingly difficult to control congressional action on McKinley's colonial policies. The administration-sponsored Spooner Act for the governance of the Philippines had to be shelved until the next session in order to avoid the possibility that party leaders might lose control of the Congress on this contentious issue.

McKinley responded to the domestic attacks against his Philippine policies in part by asking MacArthur to postpone the full implementation of his counterinsurgency policies until after the American elections (Welch 1979:36). McKinley did not wish to announce an even harsher and more repressive policy for the Philippines at a time in which it might cost him votes in the coming election. Rather than repression, McKinley publicly emphasized benevolent assimilation. McKinley appointed William Howard Taft as the head of a second Philippine Commission that argued for uplifting the natives by building schools and roads and providing other social services. Limited self-government was promised although independence was not discussed. McKinley had not wanted to begin these policies until after the insurgents had been crushed, but decided to move toward a civil government in mid-1900, with Taft appointed the first civil-governor of the Philippines, in order to answer domestic critics and to assist in the pacification process. McKinley even briefly considered announcing his support for Philippine independence in response to a suggestion by Senator Hoar (Leech 1959:552). Finally, as noted above, McKinley responded to attacks against his Philippine policies by deepening his commitment to the promotion of democracy in Cuba and timing his liberal Cuban initiatives to coincide with less popular initiatives in the Philippines. He then implicitly pointed to the move toward democracy and independence in Cuba as an example of what might be expected in the Philippines.

Meanwhile, General MacArthur's counterinsurgency policies had proved quite successful in gaining the American initiative in the war. In March 1901 his forces captured Aguinaldo and broke the resistance in the central island of Luzon. By mid-1902 the insurgency was pronounced completely defeated and Americans settled in for a long period of colonial rule that would not officially end until 1946. The United States had won the war, but at a great cost. The Philippine war generated substantial opposition within the United States. More Americans died fighting the Philippine Republic than had died fighting Spain. Tens of thousands of Filipinos died fighting for their independence. The United States had suppressed the rebellion but it had not won the allegiance of its new subjects, who clearly did not consent to colonial domination.

Conclusion

The American occupation of Cuba in the wake of the Spanish-American War presents an apparent anomaly from the realist perspective. Cuba was a likely case for the initial adoption of proliberalization policies. There was no ongoing war in Cuba, and the United States operated in an international system that presented no serious threats. Nevertheless, the details of this case indicate that realist considerations did guide McKinley's initial decision not to promote democracy in Cuba. He simply did not believe the Cubans would elect a stable pro-American government without a long-term American military occupation of the island. Indeed, U.S. troops were ordered back to Cuba several times over the next few decades as hostilities broke out with each new round of fraudulent elections, just as McKinley had anticipated.

The domestic liberal argument provides the best explanation for McKinley's shift in policy, however. Liberal pressure from Congress compelled him to adopt proliberalization policies. Liberal internationalists in the Congress, assisted by interest groups, focused the domestic political debate on the question of democracy and independence for Cuban freedom fighters. The lack of a solid Republican majority in the Senate in 1898 gave congressional opponents of the McKinley administration the leverage they needed to force McKinley to fulfill Congress' promise to liberate rather than subjugate Cuba.

Republican supporters of *Cuba Libre* played a central role in forging a pro-democratic compromise as a method for reconciling partisan and ideological goals.

Realism provides a good explanation for the failure to adopt proliberalization policies in the Philippines, especially during the War of the Philippine Insurrection. The Philippine case, however, presents an apparent anomaly for the domestic liberal argument, because significant liberal attacks from the Congress and the anti-imperialist movement did not lead McKinley to abandon his support for counterinsurgency warfare and colonial rule for the Philippines. A closer examination of this case, however, demonstrates that the internal dynamics of Congress can account for the failure of liberal attacks to force a change in policy. The extraordinary power of party institutions in the Congress during this era, and the Republicans' firm control of both houses of Congress after the 1898 elections, allowed them to turn back serious congressional efforts to challenge administration policy. Even then, it took the positive example of U.S. policy toward Cuba to convince many Republicans to continue supporting McKinley's policies in the Philippines.

A crucial legacy of the Spanish-American War was that American leaders learned how to use the promotion of democracy to achieve America's material interests. Promoting the war as necessary for the liberation of Cuba from Spanish tyranny helped build a powerful domestic consensus in the United States in favor of the war. By granting independence to a freely elected government in Cuba, the United States convinced many Cubans that it was in their interest to pursue policies that served the interest of the United States. Although the United States failed in its most ambitious efforts to achieve annexation by acclamation, Cubans accepted American leadership much more readily than did Filipinos, who fought a bitter guerrilla war against their American occupiers. Thus, the promotion of democracy served to legitimate American expansionism at home and abroad.

The success of the American occupation of Cuba, in comparison to the Philippine experience, led American policymakers to emulate the Cuban rather than the Philippine model in subsequent interventions. After the debacle in the Philippines, the United States would never again try to impose colonial government on a subordinate people. By the presidency of Woodrow Wilson, the United States had taken definitive steps toward eventually granting the Philippines its independence. Teaching Central Americans and the inhabitants of Caribbean isles to "elect good men" became the centerpiece of U.S. interventions in the Caribbean Basin between 1898 and 1934. Nicaragua, the Dominican Republic, Haiti, and Honduras all became targets of American proliberalization policies during this era. In by far the most successful application of this policy in the history of U.S. foreign policy, U.S. occupation governments transformed Nazi Germany and Imperial Japan into liberal democratic allies in the wake of World War II. With the advent of the Cold War, however, policymakers began again to question the utility of the promotion of democracy during U.S. military interventions. In Vietnam the Truman and Eisenhower administrations first supported the reimposition of French colonial rule and then the personalist dictatorship of Ngo Dinh Diem in the newly minted country of South Vietnam. Only in 1961 did the United States make any significant effort to promote liberal reforms in that country. This book now turns to the Kennedy administration's tortured efforts to promote democracy in Vietnam.

4

Kennedy and Diem

The Presidential Path to the Promotion of Democracy

America's experience in Vietnam poses puzzles for both the domestic liberal and realist approaches. America fielded a half million soldiers in combat and spent tens of billions of dollars on the war in Vietnam before the institutional constraints emphasized by the domestic liberal argument began to place significant limits on U.S. intervention there. The United States also engaged in a variety of behaviors that violated liberal values. While the realist argument can account for some of these illiberal actions, it cannot explain why the United States would waste so many financial and human resources in a war that had only a peripheral impact on American national security.

This chapter examines the adoption of proliberalization policies in Kennedy administration policy toward South Vietnam to discover what role the promotion of democracy played in America's early involvement in that war. The Vietnamese case provides an excellent example of the presidential path to the adoption of proliberalization policies. Twice in 1961 the Kennedy administration made significant attempts to pressure the authoritarian regime of Ngo Dinh Diem to adopt a series of political, economic, and military reforms. In 1963 the Kennedy administration supported Diem's overthrow in a November 1963 military coup.

Kennedy pursued liberalizing reforms in Vietnam in January 1961 in part because he had needed to adopt a pro-democratic stance to win the support of liberal internationalists to gain the nomination of the Democratic Party in 1960. There were, however, few ongoing institutional mechanisms by which these liberals could force Kennedy to continue his support for proliberalization policies. This weakness of the domestic constraint in the presidential path allowed him to base subsequent policy choices for the most part on security calculations. As has often been the case, however, the Democrats had chosen a candidate who was genuinely committed to liberal internationalism. Kennedy, therefore, kept returning to proliberalization policies in an effort to reconcile realist imperatives with liberal ideals by emphasizing the security benefits of the promotion of democracy.

With the exception of this predisposition toward liberal security policies, the realist approach provides the most persuasive explanation for the pattern of U.S. policy throughout Kennedy's term. While the Vietnamese case appears anomalous from the realist perspective, in that Kennedy made efforts to promote democracy at the height of the Cold War in a country at war, Kennedy's policies showed great sensitivity to international constraints. His efforts to promote democracy reflected his judgment that a democratic South Vietnam would be more likely to prevail against the Viet Cong in the long term. Kennedy shifted to nonliberalization policies in mid-1961 and again in 1962 because he feared the short-term instability that might arise from the risky strategy of pushing for liberal reforms.

Only liberal pressure from the Congress could have forced Kennedy to stick with proliberalization policies. That pressure was nonexistent in 1961 and only barely visible in 1963. As was true of the Philippine case, congressional liberals were reluctant to challenge their party's president. Despite this, Kennedy was deeply concerned with the reaction of Congress. What worried him, however, was the potential pressure from hard-line anticommunists, not the potential pressure from liberal internationalists. This concern reinforced the need to find the best possible realist solution to defeat the communist insurgency in South Vietnam.

Kennedy's Initial Proliberalization Policies

Kennedy's first decision on Vietnam was to approve a comprehensive counterinsurgency plan that called for the United States to fund a 20,000-man increase in the Army of the Republic of Vietnam (ARVN) and a 30,000-man increase in the Vietnamese Civil Guard. In return for this increased funding, the Kennedy administration asked the Diem regime to adopt a series of military, economic, and political reforms. In contrast to the Eisenhower administration, Kennedy allowed U.S. ambassador to South Vietnam, Eldbridge Durbrow, to hold off on giving the "green light" for the expanded aid until Diem adopted a series of liberalizing political reforms (State 1988:1–12).

Kennedy's proposed political reforms called for a significant liberalization of the Diem regime. The Kennedy administration suggested that Diem enlarge the powers and autonomy of the Vietnamese National Assembly, allowing it powers of legislative oversight over executive bureaucracies. It asked Diem to relax censorship so that the press could investigate charges of corruption as well as provide an avenue for a broader range of free speech than had existed previously. It also pushed Diem to include one or two opposition members in his cabinet in order to broaden the base of his government. The Kennedy administration criticized Diem's repression of noncommunist dissent and asked that the head of the secret intelligence service, Tran Kim Tuyen, be transferred to a diplomatic post abroad because of his "growing identification in the public mind with alleged secret police methods of repression and control" (State 1986:577). It challenged Diem to disband the Can Lao Party, an underground party that served as an instrument of political repression and a conduit for managing corruption, and to ship his brother Ngo Dinh Nhu, the leader of the party, to a diplomatic post abroad (State 1986:579).

Support for free and fair elections played an ambiguous role in Kennedy's initial proliberalization policies because Diem was in the process of engineering his reelection to the presidency. All previous electoral contests in South Vietnam had led to overwhelming victories for Diem obtained through blatant fraud.[1] As the April 1961 Vietnamese elections approached, the Kennedy administration made no attempt to push Diem to have a free and fair electoral

---

1. The United States had acquiesced in extraordinary levels of fraud in each of these contests. In October 1955, Diem won 98 percent of the vote in a referendum asking voters to choose whether to depose the emperor, Bao Dai. His American advisers had recommended a more modest 60 to 70 percent margin. In 1956 Diem abolished local village elections and replaced local officials with appointed ones. When a single opposition candidate was elected to the National Assembly in 1959, Diem had him arrested. Most important, the United States backed Diem in his determination to refuse to participate in the 1956 reunification elections called for in the Geneva Accords because "almost any type of election that could conceivably be held in Vietnam in 1956 would, on the basis of present trends, give the Communists a very significant, if not decisive advantage" (Kahin 1986:89, 95–98).

process at the presidential level. Instead, they encouraged Diem to make the other liberalizing reforms in connection with the election campaign in hopes that these would contribute to the liberalization of the electoral process, if not to a completely free and fair election. Some pointed to the fact that Diem won only 64 percent of the vote in Saigon while winning 90 percent of the vote nationwide as evidence that the elections were not rigged in the capital city (State 1988:70–71).[2] Since many of the liberalization measures were aimed at opening up the political process within the capital, some officials interpreted this as evidence of the impact of U.S.-inspired liberalization.

The Kennedy administration also pushed for the opening up of the electoral processes at lower levels of the political system, emphasizing the reinstatement of village-level elections. Diem agreed to take a small step in this direction by calling for free and fair elections for youth representatives for village councils. Although this was an extremely limited measure, Diem assured the American ambassador that "he had given strict orders youth elections be fully democratic since this first step in electoral process to be implemented later on broader scale and therefore public must be assured these honest elections" (State 1988:50).

The 1960 Nomination Battle and the Initial Adoption of Proliberalization Policies

As anticipated by the domestic liberal argument, Kennedy's battle for the Democratic nomination in 1960 helped lead to his initial support for proliberalization policies in Vietnam. As a northerner and a Catholic, he had little hope of winning southern votes for his candidacy, which were likely to go to Senate Majority Leader Lyndon Johnson (D-Tex.) (White 1961:56–60). Kennedy, therefore, relied on support from the more liberal northern and Pacific Coast party delegations. He adopted a pro-democratic stance as part of his strategy to win liberal support for his nomination.

Democratic Party organizations in the northern and western states in 1960 reflected one of two patterns. Some state parties were run by traditional political machines. To win the support of the machine bosses, Kennedy had to prove that he could overcome the electoral handicaps imposed by his youth

---

2. General Lionel McGarr, chief of the Military Assistance Advisory Group in Vietnam (MAAG) and General Lyman Lemnitzer, chairman of the Joint Chiefs, agreed (State 1988:82, 90–91). On the other hand, CIA chief Allen Dulles suggested that "the outcome of the election did not truly represent the popularity of President Diem and that, in essence, the elections were rigged" (State 1988:82).

and Catholicism by winning contested primaries outside of his New England base (White 1961:63–73; Sorenson 1965:108–13, 126–28; O'Donnell, Powers, and McCarthy 1972:158–81). Other states were dominated by reformist, liberal, citizen-based movements that had grown in opposition to corrupt party machines. To win in states controlled by liberal activists, he had to demonstrate his commitment to liberal domestic and foreign policies. To win the nomination, Kennedy had to gain the support of both political bosses and liberal activists.

Kennedy faced two main competitors in the battle for the support of party liberals. Senator Hubert Humphrey (D-Minn.) was the only candidate to challenge Kennedy in the primaries. The populist Humphrey, "by temperament, record and rhetoric, better fitted liberal specifications than Kennedy" (Schlesinger 1965:14). Humphrey represented a Minnesota Democratic Party that was "a model of clean and practical politics . . . led by intellectuals, untainted by scandal, solidly backed by the money and troops of the great labor unions, [and] loved by the farmers of Minnesota" (White 1961:43). Humphrey personified the beliefs and experiences of liberal activists throughout the country. In contrast, many liberals found Kennedy too cool, too moderate, and too weak in opposing McCarthyism to warrant their support (Schlesinger 1965:14).

This was an important problem for Kennedy in the state of Wisconsin, where he went head to head with Humphrey in the Minnesotan's own back yard. The Democratic Party in Wisconsin was a reformist citizen-based party inspired by the Minnesota experience (White 1961:97–100). The state was divided between the Protestant farming communities of the west, which supported Humphrey, and the Catholic industrial cities of the east, which voted for Kennedy. The state capital, Madison, which held a crucial balancing position in this electoral equation, was a bastion of liberalism (White 1961:99). Although Kennedy narrowly won the Wisconsin primary, his failure to take Madison symbolized the difficulty Kennedy would have in winning the confidence of liberal activists in the party when there were more liberal candidates in the race. Kennedy's narrow victory in Wisconsin forced a second primary fight in West Virginia, one of only thirteen primary states in 1960. Kennedy's victory there pushed Humphrey out of the race.

The greatest liberal threat to Kennedy's nomination, however, was the "sleeping candidacy" of Adlai Stevenson, the party's standard-bearer in the two previous elections against Eisenhower (Schlesinger 1965:17). Stevenson did not openly declare his candidacy for the 1960 nomination, but would have accepted a draft at the party convention in Los Angeles. Kennedy would have had a difficult time defeating an active Stevenson campaign, because the liberal reformers of the postwar era looked to Stevenson as their leader. Stevenson was also clearly the most prestigious exponent of liberal internationalist foreign policy ideas in the party and the country as a whole. The more foreign policy appeared to be at the top of the national agenda, the more party liberals looked to Stevenson for guidance. Thus, the downing of a U-2 plane by the U.S.S.R. and the subsequent breakdown of a superpower summit in mid-1960 brought a surge in support for Stevenson (White 1961:136–44; Divine 1974:205–11).

Kennedy emphasized the liberal parts of his foreign policy in order to overcome liberal rivals for the nomination. He convinced many liberals of the sincerity of his pro-democratic rhetoric by wooing the party's top liberal foreign policy experts to his banner. He first appealed to the foreign policy experts on the Harvard and MIT faculties who had worked with him during his tenure as a congressman from Massachusetts (Schlesinger 1965:14–16; Sorenson 1965:117–18). The most critical move in this direction was his decision to name Connecticut Democrat Chester Bowles, whose father had been a leading anti-imperialist in 1898, as his chief foreign policy adviser early in the campaign. With the exception of Stevenson, Bowles was the principal icon of the liberal foreign policy wing of the party. Kennedy chose him because it would ease the doubts of liberals about his candidacy. "Through countless liberal psyches would flash the idea, precisely as Kennedy had intended it to: Bowles as Secretary of State. Or better still, Bowles as a holding action for a couple of months and Adlai as Secretary of State" (Halberstam 1969:21; Bowles 1971:288). Early in the campaign, Kennedy nearly offered Stevenson the secretaryship in return for his endorsement (Schlesinger 1965:25–26).

By the end of the primary season, Kennedy needed to gain approximately 150 votes to secure the nomination. Many of the delegates most likely to shift to Kennedy were liberals holding out for a Stevenson candidacy (Schlesinger 1965:24; Sorensen 1965:150). A "draft Stevenson" movement designed to deny Kennedy a first-round victory in hopes that a deadlocked convention would turn to Stevenson nearly swayed enough delegates to deny Kennedy that first-round victory (White 1961:144–48, 183–93; Schlesinger 1965:33–40). Kennedy won a close contest on the first ballot with 45 votes to spare, however, because he managed to maintain just enough liberal support to put him over the top (White 1961:195). While Humphrey supported Stevenson, Humphrey's protégé, Minnesota Gov. Orville Freeman nominated Kennedy. The Michigan delegation, dominated by a liberal activist/UAW coalition led by Gov. G. Mennon "Soapy" Williams and UAW President Walter Reuther, threw its support to Kennedy, in part because he had passed their test of ideological purity on the issues (White 1961:161–63; Sorensen 1965:148–49).

Williams was later named assistant secretary of state for African affairs. While Kennedy was not always successful in swaying liberal voters, he gained enough liberal support to win the nomination. If he had not moved in a more liberal direction during the nomination process, he might not have attained the necessary majority.

Once he was nominated, however, Kennedy moved back toward the center of the general electorate in his campaign against Nixon. Where liberal themes had dominated his primary campaign speeches, his fall campaign focused on the "missile gap" and the loss of Cuba as his principal foreign policy themes (Divine 1974:235–87). He emphasized that proliberalization policies were a more effective means of waging the Cold War in the Third World.

Once Kennedy was elected, the principal foreign policy positions in his administration went to establishment figures, not to liberals. CIA Chief Allen Dulles was held over from the Eisenhower administration. NSC Adviser McGeorge Bundy was a Republican. Robert McNamara at Defense was a technocratic executive from the Ford Motor Company. Secretary of State Dean Rusk had served both Republican and Democratic administrations.[3]

Some important liberals did get second-level positions in the new administration. Adlai Stevenson was named U.S. ambassador to the United Nations. Chester Bowles was named undersecretary of state for political affairs, the number-two spot in the State Department. George Ball, who had led the effort to draft Stevenson at the Los Angeles convention, was named undersecretary of state for economic affairs. Cambridge liberal intellectuals like Arthur Schlesinger also received posts. These liberals in the administration were the sole ongoing institutional constraint on Kennedy policy that survived the nomination process. This was a limited constraint, however, given that Stevenson was ignored by Kennedy and Bowles was fired by the end of 1961 (Bowles 1971:352–68). Ball was kept around only to provide "domesticated dissent" in administration counsels (Thomson 1968:49).[4] The liberals had little influence.

Thus, Kennedy's initial commitment to proliberalization policies reflected a compromise position that helped him win his party's nomination and later the general election. During the nomination battle, he emphasized

---

3. Halberstam (1969:9–17) illuminates this point by beginning *The Best and the Brightest* with the visit of the ultimate establishment figure, Robert Lovett, to Kennedy. Most of Lovett's candidates were appointed to the cabinet.

4. George Ball reports: "I was on the periphery; I was a Stevenson protégé; I had not been for Kennedy before Los Angeles; I had not taught or studied on the Charles River" (Ball 1982:164). When Ball warned Kennedy that his policy was likely to lead to the introduction of 300,000 U.S. troops in a war that could not be won, Kennedy replied: "George, you're just crazier than hell. That just isn't going to happen" (Ball 1982:366).

support for liberal institutions to establish his commitment to the liberal ideal. During the general election campaign, he emphasized support for democracy as a more effective means for pursuing U.S. security interests. This initial commitment to liberal internationalism did not solely reflect strategic behavior by candidate Kennedy, however. Party liberals might not have thrown their support to Kennedy if they had not sensed that he possessed a genuine belief in the tenets of liberal internationalism. As president, Kennedy hoped to harness his liberal vision to a security policy that would provide an effective response to the security threats faced by the United States in the international system.

This emphasis on democracy shaped Kennedy's initial policies throughout the Third World. In his inaugural address, Kennedy proclaimed that his administration would "pay any price, bear any burden, meet any hardship, support any friend, oppose any foe to assure the survival and the success of liberty" (Sorensen 1965:246). Soon after, he announced an ambitious program to promote democracy in Latin America, the Alliance for Progress. In Vietnam, Kennedy's campaign for democracy led to the less ambitious set of proliberalization policies described above.

Realism and Shifts in Kennedy Policy from Mid-1961 to Mid-1963

While Kennedy was pushed to adopt proliberalization policies initially by the domestic liberal constraints of the presidential nomination process, there were few ongoing institutional mechanisms that could force him to maintain his commitment to these policies. Kennedy's ability to shift from proliberalization to nonliberalization policies several times during his administration testifies to the weakness of the liberal domestic constraints upon his Vietnam policy. Realist considerations explain the Kennedy administration's policy shifts between mid-1961 and mid-1963. Kennedy believed that Diem would have to broaden and democratize his regime in order to defeat the Viet Cong over the long term. In the short term, however, pressure on Diem to adopt liberal reforms might hinder the war effort or lead to a complete collapse of the Vietnamese government. These conflicting realist imperatives led to considerable vacillation in U.S. policy. Kennedy pushed for reforms on several occasions only to back off when it appeared that further pressure might hurt the war effort or lead to short-term instability. While Kennedy's long-term security vision can be at least partially explained by the domestic liberal argument, only the realist approach can provide an adequate explanation for the relative ease with which he abandoned proliberalization policies when the security situation within Vietnam seemed to warrant it.

Democracy, Economic Growth, and Counterinsurgency: Kennedy's Program for the Long Term

Soviet Premier Nikita Kruschev's January 1961 speech proclaiming expanded support for wars of national liberation in the Third World convinced Kennedy that the United States needed to concentrate its efforts on countering Soviet threats there (Hilsman 1967:414). To do so, the new administration replaced Eisenhower's reliance on nuclear strategy with a strategy of "flexible response" that would emphasize building up U.S. capabilities to fight in a wide range of conflicts with reciprocal force (Gaddis 1982:198–236). Kennedy was especially concerned with the question of countering guerrilla war, as he explained to the West Point graduating class of 1962:

> This is another type of war, new in its intensity, ancient in its origins— war by guerrillas, subversives, insurgents, assassins; war by ambush instead of by combat; by infiltration instead of aggression, seeking victory by eroding and exhausting the enemy instead of engaging him. . . . It requires in those situations where we must counter it . . . a whole new kind of strategy, a wholly different kind of force, and therefore a new and wholly different kind of military training. (Hilsman 1967:415)

Kennedy took several steps to make sure that this new concern with fighting counterinsurgency wars would be institutionalized in the foreign policy process (Blaufarb 1977:52–138; Cable 1986:183–286). He set up a special interagency group to address problems of counterinsurgency on a global basis. All foreign service officers and military advisers being sent to Third World countries were required to attend courses on counterinsurgency war. Green Berets and other Special Forces units were created to serve as specialists in this new kind of warfare.

Kennedy believed that U.S. support for economic development and political reform in the Third World were crucial components of a winning strategy against communist insurgency. If the United States did not support political, social, and economic change, disfranchised workers and peasants might be attracted to communist insurgencies that claimed to represent their interests. "Those who make peaceful revolution impossible make violent revolution inevitable," argued Kennedy. This combination of proliberalization reforms, socioeconomic development projects, and counterinsurgency was most clearly codified in the Alliance for Progress, but it reflected the general logic Kennedy applied to all Third World conflicts (Levinson and de Onis 1970).

The Latin American experience also clearly demonstrated that the commitment to democracy was contingent on security considerations. "There are three possibilities in the Dominican Republic," Kennedy suggested, "a decent democratic government, a Trujillist authoritarian government, or a Castroite regime. We should shoot for the first, but we shouldn't rule out the second until we are sure we can avoid the third" (Schlesinger 1965:769). This attitude reflected the general approach to Third World democracy of the Kennedy administration. Kennedy was convinced that democratic regimes were necessary over the long term to guarantee the kind of stable friendly regimes that could successfully stave off communist revolution. During the short term, however, the pursuit of more democratic outcomes might lead to dangerous instability and "Castroite" revolution. Therefore, the vacillation of Kennedy policy toward South Vietnam represented the common Kennedy pattern. Kennedy pushed for democracy throughout the world, yet usually backed off when it appeared that pressure could lead to short-term instability and the undermining of allied regimes facing insurgencies.

The May 1961 Task Force Report on Vietnam

The Kennedy administration first retreated from a strong emphasis on the promotion of democracy in Vietnam in May 1961, with the completion of the report of a presidential task force on Vietnam. This report acknowledged that it was necessary "to develop political and economic conditions which will create a solid and widespread support among the key political groups and the general population for a Vietnam which has the will to resist Communist encroachment and which in turn stems from a stake in a freer and more democratic society" (State 1988:96–97). As Theodore Sorensen, George Ball, and McGeorge Bundy argued in support of this position:

> To the extent that [success in Vietnam] depends on wider popular support among the Vietnamese, tax and foreign exchange reforms from Diem and his agreement to the military and governmental reorganizations required, the outcome is speculative at best. . . . There is no clearer example of a country that cannot be saved unless it saves itself—through increased popular support; governmental, economic and military reforms and reorganizations; and the encouragement of new political leaders. We do not want Vietnam to fall—we do not

want to add to Diem's burdens—and the chief purpose of insisting upon such conditions should not be saving of American dollars but the saving of Vietnam. (State 1988:84)

The recommendations of the final report, however, backed away from the earlier insistence that Diem adopt significant political reforms before his regime received expanded U.S. aid. The report indicated that "to accomplish the following [reformist goals] it will be necessary to work through and support the present Vietnamese government despite its weaknesses. No other feasible alternative exists at this point in time which does not involve an unacceptable degree of risk" (State 1988:97). Kennedy appointed a new ambassador, Frederick Nolting, charged with rebuilding strained relations with Diem (Nolting 1988). He sent Vice President Johnson to Vietnam, who lauded Diem as the "Winston Churchill of Southeast Asia" as a sign of American commitment to the Diem regime (State 1988:135–57; Newman 1992:67–80).

Army Chief of Staff General Lyman Lemnitzer summed up the argument for supporting Diem and dropping the insistence on prior reforms:

The problem of Vietnam, from the U.S. point of view, is very simple and very clear. I believe that it can be stated in these words: Does the U.S. want Vietnam to follow the path of Laos (with all the effect that would have on the rest of Southeast Asia) or does the U.S. really want to maintain Vietnam as an independent noncommunist state closely aligned with the West? Stated another way, does the U.S. intend to take the necessary military action now to defeat the Viet Cong threat or do we intend to quibble for weeks and months over details of general policy, finances, Vietnamese government organization, etc., while Vietnam slowly but surely goes down the drain of Communism as North Vietnam and a large portion of Laos have gone to date. (State 1988:126–27)

At first glance, the outcome of this policy debate appears to reflect bureaucratic political dynamics rather than realist calculations. State Department representatives on the task force argued for reforms, while Defense Department personnel pushed for immediate military aid. The original draft of the task force report, drafted by the staff of Undersecretary of Defense Roswell Gilpatric, unambiguously reflected the Defense Department's view. Afterward, the State Department succeeded in getting approval for an alternative draft, which Gilpatric thought "watered down too much the emphasis on antisubversion activity and linked too tightly antisubversive measures to the political social reforms which we have been trying to achieve" (State 1988:87–88).

These two positions, however, represented both sides of the realist dilemma of short-term versus long-term strategy which Kennedy had to take into account in making his decision. Two realist considerations helped tip the balance in favor of the Pentagon view at this time. First, Ambassador Durbrow failed in his effort to use the threat of aid suspension to bring about reforms. It wasn't clear that a pressure strategy would work regardless of the desirability of the proposed reforms. American setbacks in Laos, where Kennedy was forced to accept a neutralist government and Cuba, after the Bay of Pigs fiasco, reinforced these concerns (Defense 1971:1–5). Kennedy backed Diem because he did not see reasonable alternatives at a time when the United States faced important challenges in other parts of the world.

Deputy National Security Adviser Walt Rostow's comments on the final draft of the task force report, however, suggest the tenuous and contingent nature of Kennedy's support for Diem. The Kennedy administration's long-term strategy had not changed and policymakers had only temporarily set aside the strategy of using aid conditionality to get reforms from Diem:

> Although we have no alternative except to support Diem now, he may be overthrown. . . . If so, we should be prepared to move fast with the younger army types who may then emerge. Such a crisis is not to be sought, among other reasons because its outcome cannot be predicted; but should it happen, we may be able to get more nearly the kind of military organization and perhaps even the domestic political program we want in Vietnam but have been unable to get from Diem. . . . The paper urges a series of domestic political and economic moves in Vietnam. It should be understood clearly that these are measures which we have pressed for a long time on Diem, without notable success; and that we have still to find the technique for bringing our great bargaining power to bear on leaders of client states to do things they ought to do but don't want to do. (State 1988:131)

The Taylor-Rostow Mission, October 1961

Kennedy made another attempt to condition an expansion of U.S. aid to political and economic reforms when he sent his military adviser, General Maxwell Taylor, and Walt Rostow of the NSC on a special mission to Vietnam in late 1961. The Viet Cong had sharply stepped up its attacks on the Diem government in late 1961. Kennedy sent Taylor and Rostow to Saigon to make recommendations as to whether the United States should introduce combat troops to counter this threat and whether the United States should insist that Diem adopt political, economic, and military reforms in return for increased U.S. aid (Rostow 1972:270–79; Taylor 1972:227–45).

The familiar division between representatives of the Defense and State Departments reemerged in Taylor's report when the participants on the trip were asked to comment on the wisdom of pressuring Diem to make reforms. Taylor argued that the most significant problem with Diem was that his divide-and-conquer political tactics, designed to thwart coup attempts, made it impossible for the ARVN to take effective coordinated action (State 1988:486–88). Taylor rejected the option of pursuing a coup because of the dangers of creating a destabilizing process that would be beyond U.S. control (State 1988:493). He opted, instead, for a strategy of "limited partnership." American advisers would be inserted at every level of the ARVN to ensure that the proposed vast increase in U.S. military aid and equipment would be used more effectively. The only reforms he proposed were for the military and intelligence bureaucracies of Vietnam.

In their addenda to the main report, however, the State Department representatives on the mission, Sterling Cottrell and William Jordan, made a strong case for pushing for liberalizing reforms (State 1988:505–9). Jordan, for example, argued that this was an "opportunity for the U.S. to stand once again for change in this part of the world, to press for measures that are both efficient and more democratic. We must identify ourselves with the people of Vietnam and their aspirations, not with a particular man or administration" (State 1988:512). He argued that the Vietnamese people had lost confidence in the Diem regime because:

> Many men of intelligence and ability have been kept out of government or have been forced to resign, if their complete loyalty to the president came into doubt. The National Assembly has become a rubber stamp for presidential measures. Elections are a meaningless exercise that can only produce contempt for the democratic process. A chance remark in a cafe can produce a jail sentence. Those who express political opposition are harassed. Men are held indefinitely without indictment or even the placing of charges. One member of the National Assembly has been in jail for a year. (State 1988:513)

The list of reforms suggested by State Department personnel in Vietnam were quite modest. To build support among elites, Diem should (1) appoint independent cabinet members; (2) remove Diem's sister-in-law Madame Nhu from the public scene; (3) release noncommunist political prisoners and place some of these in high government positions; (4) grant permission to all noncommunist political parties to organize and participate in the 1962 National Assembly elections; (5) liberalize press censorship laws; (6) set up a public tribune's office; (7) establish an independent judiciary; (8) grant greater freedom to the National Assembly to debate and criticize government policy; and (9) ensure that deputies lived in the districts they represented (State 1988:659). To build mass support, Diem should (1) include Cao Dai or Hoa Hao members in the government; (2) make frequent informal visits to the countryside; (3) give frequent radio "fireside chats"; (4) tell people what they want to hear, that "things are getting better and soon they will feel safe in their homes," rather than emphasizing "sacrifice" and "discipline"; (5) publicize public works programs that employ many refugees in the cities; (6) increase welfare programs; and (7) set up provincial councils (State 1988:660).

On November 15, 1961, Kennedy sided with the State Department against the recommendations of General Taylor. Despite the fact that Taylor had led Diem to believe that he would get 8,000 U.S. troops without pressure for reforms, Kennedy decided not to send U.S. combat troops. Furthermore, National Security Action Memorandum No. 111 argued that Vietnam should undertake "prompt and appropriate legislative and administrative action to put the nation on a war footing (this would include decentralization and broadening of the government so as to realize the full potential of all non-communist elements in the country willing to contribute to the common struggle)" (State 1988:657). As suggested by the wording of the memorandum, security considerations prompted the insistence on reforms. Kennedy believed the Diem regime to be too narrowly based and dictatorial to win. Liberalization of the regime would broaden the political base of the government and make it a stronger opponent to the Viet Cong. The significant gains the Viet Cong had made in 1961 reinforced Kennedy's perception that reforms were necessary to win the war.

Within three weeks, however, the Kennedy administration once again backed off from its reformist program. Kennedy retreated because of Diem's steadfast refusal to pursue any liberalizing reforms. Diem's brother Nhu began an anti-American press campaign and Diem complained to Ambassador Nolting that he would not let his country become a "protectorate" of the United States (State 1988:649–52). The Kennedy administration was faced with the choice of acquiescing to Diem's dictatorial practices or supporting a military coup. In late 1961 the Kennedy administration still judged that the instability that could arise from a coup attempt would be more damaging to the war effort than a continuation of Diem's autocracy. They, therefore, accepted Diem's offer of a "limited partnership" on military matters without political changes.

Improved Security Conditions and Reduced Pressure, 1962

Kennedy rapidly expanded the amount of military aid and advisers going to Vietnam between January 1962 and May 1963. Advisers numbered 20,000 by the end of 1963. During this time, the United States made no demands that the Diem regime adopt any further liberalizing reforms, because the advances made by Vietnamese forces in 1962 meant that there was no realist imperative to change an apparently successful policy (McNamara 1995:45). Improvement in two areas convinced U.S. policymakers that no changes were necessary during 1962. First, U.S.-supplied helicopters gave ARVN forces a significant short-term military advantage against the Viet Cong.[5] Second, American advisers were pleased that the Vietnamese government had enthusiastically embraced the "strategic hamlet" program, which was considered the most essential component of the overall plan for the defeat of the Viet Cong (Hilsman 1967:424–67; Defense 1971:128–59).

According to the American conception of the strategic hamlet program, the Vietnamese military would first provide basic security for peasants by concentrating them in fortified villages and setting up local police and self defense forces to provide basic protection. Then, civic action teams would be sent into the hamlets to provide basic government services, agricultural credit, and public works projects in order to win the hearts and minds of the peasants. Finally, elections would be held to select councils for the governance of the hamlet (Tregaskis 1963:353–63).

This program represented an excellent example of how proliberalization policies were fundamentally tied to counterinsurgency programs that were often deeply repressive. "Relocating" peasants in secure hamlets involved the forcible eviction of hundreds of thousands of people from their homes. These same "beneficiaries" of increased security were often compelled to build the

---

5. Before the introduction of U.S. helicopters, Viet Cong insurgents had ample time to escape the clumsy ground sweeps of ARVN forces. With helicopters, ARVN troops could now rapidly arrive in force to surprise Viet Cong units. American military advisers exercised their limited partnership by taking control of ARVN operations from behind the scenes to attempt to make sure that the new mobility capacity was being used properly. Within a year, Viet Cong forces had adapted to the new technology and tactics, but during 1962, their forces were caught off guard by these new weapons and tactics and suffered several important defeats (Sheehan 1988:37–125).

hamlets without compensation. Police "protection" for the residents of the hamlets involved repression and intimidation of those they were ostensibly there to serve. Only after the hamlet was "secure" would controlled elections be held and aid distributed.

In any event, American officials were so pleased with the progress in the war effort that McNamara ordered contingency plans to be drawn up for the eventual withdrawal of American advisers from Vietnam. An initial 1,000-man reduction in the American presence was scheduled for late 1963 (Defense 1971:160–200). They could make these optimistic plans and soft peddle political reforms precisely because there did not appear to be a realist imperative to make radical changes during 1962. Things seemed to be getting better.[6] Thus, the pattern of Kennedy administration responses from mid-1961 through 1962 reflected realist concerns. It must be kept in mind, however, that this could only happen because of the weakness of the liberal domestic political constraint involved in the presidential path to the adoption of proliberalization policies.

Congressional Pressure and Kennedy Policy in 1961–1962

It would have taken liberal pressure from Congress to have forced the president to maintain proliberalization policies throughout this period. That liberal pressure was almost totally lacking in 1961 and 1962. This was reinforced by the almost total lack of criticism from liberal interest groups. There were liberals in positions of institutional strength within the Congress who had serious misgivings about continued support for the Diem regime in South Vietnam. As leaders of a relatively small Democratic majority in Congress dealing with a Democratic president, however, they felt compelled to give their party's president the benefit of the doubt. Because they believed that his commitment to liberal internationalism was sincere, they accepted Kennedy's departures from this ideal as necessary short-term expedients that would be soon rectified. Congressional liberals, therefore, cooperated as much as possible with the Kennedy administration. Whatever concerns they had about Kennedy's policies were presented in private.[7]

---

6. According to Newman, military officials in the MAAG, in cooperation with their superiors at the Pentagon, systematically misrepresented the intelligence sent to Washington in an effort to mislead the president and Secretary McNamara into thinking the war was being won (Newman 1992:173–327). Even if the improvement in Vietnam was illusory, the impression that the situation was improving had the same impact on policy that an actual improvement would have had.

7. Senator William Fulbright (D-Ark.), chair of the Senate Foreign Relations Committee, for example, publicly declared his support of Kennedy's policies toward Vietnam. He reiterated

Most prominent among those liberals who expressed private concerns was Sen. Mike Mansfield (D-Mont.), who replaced Lyndon Johnson as Senate majority leader in 1961. Mansfield almost always publicly supported the president in 1961 and 1962 (Gibbons 1986:31, 109). This support reflected, in part, Mansfield's early support for Diem in 1954 as the United States began its attempt to build a noncommunist South Vietnam. By 1961, however, Mansfield had begun to have serious reservations about the Diem regime. In a letter written to Kennedy during the deliberations surrounding the 1961 Taylor report, Mansfield argued strongly against sending U.S. troops to Vietnam. Instead, he wrote, the United States should support:

> (1) A Vietnamese foreign policy and propaganda program which hold out some hope of a unification of Vietnam by means other than the sword; (2) A vast coordinated effort in the field of economic development which bears a Vietnamese hallmark and our name in small print no matter how much we contribute to it; (3) A rapid introduction of democratic practices at the village and provincial levels; (4) A dramatic and sincere effort to enlist Vietnamese intellectuals in all aspects of the government's activities, primarily by the lifting of the shroud of fear which hangs over political life in Saigon and by acceptance of a genuine opposition in the National Assembly; (5) A campaign by Diem and his officials to develop close personal ties with the people by a continuous Johnson-like shirt-sleeve campaign from one end of the country to the other. (State 1988:469)

Mansfield's proposals reflected probably the most liberal position being advocated by a member of Congress at this time, and even this was not being presented in the Congress.

This public silence by the most prominent liberals in Congress led to a lack of public debate about whether or not Kennedy policy in Vietnam lived up to American ideals. This allowed Kennedy to push for or move away from liberalizing reforms depending on what he thought was best for U.S. security interests. Congressional liberal Democrats went along with this in part because they didn't want to embarrass a Democratic administration. They also gave Kennedy the benefit of the doubt because they realized that he too was searching for a more pro-democratic policy. They accepted his judgment on whether that was possible.

---

this support privately, but also probed the administration in executive hearings of his committee about whether it was exploring more democratic alternatives to the Diem regime (Gibbons 1986:22, 29–30, 47–50, 109–10).

This explains part of why Congress took almost no action contrary to administration policy on Vietnam during 1961 or 1962. Special hearings to discuss Vietnam were held by no congressional committee. That country rarely came up in hearings where administration officials were called to answer a general range of questions about U.S. foreign policy. There was some increased debate during the regular foreign aid hearings than there had been in previous years, but Congress passed all of Kennedy's increased aid requests with little argument.

This does not mean that Kennedy felt no congressional constraint, however. On the contrary, Kennedy's margin of support was seriously limited by the power of the conservative coalition of southern Democrats and Republicans in the Congress. These members were more concerned with whether Kennedy was being vigorous enough in his efforts to fight communism in Vietnam and other areas of the world than in whether the United States was promoting democracy. Therefore, when Lyndon Johnson addressed fifty-seven senators after his May 1961 trip to Saigon, some Republicans responded that the Kennedy administration wasn't doing enough to support the Diem regime and that the United States should send combat troops as soon as possible (Gibbons 1986:47).

This pressure from anticommunists in the Congress was felt most profoundly not on the issue of Vietnam but on the issues of Cuba and Laos, where the United States appeared to be retreating before communism—in one instance because of the failure of the Bay of Pigs invasion and in the other because the Kennedy administration was negotiating for the neutralization of Laos. Senator Barry Goldwater (R-Ariz.), for example, stridently condemned administration policy for its "continued drifting in the wrong direction; for inaction on all major Cold War fronts; for further costly implementation of an outmoded, weak kneed foreign policy which accomplishes nothing but more and greater losses of freedom's territory to the forces of international communism" (Dietz 1986:42). Republican leaders continually hammered on Kennedy to take a harder line against Soviet-inspired communism. In addition, Kennedy could not be sure of the support of conservative southern Democrats if he were to abandon South Vietnam.

In sum, Kennedy was constrained by domestic politics but not by liberal internationalists. He was concerned that the loss of South Vietnam could "stimulate bitter domestic controversies in the United States and would be seized upon by extreme elements to divide the country and harass the administration," as was suggested by Rusk and McNamara in their memorandum reflecting the president's response to the Taylor report (Defense 1971:111). Kennedy feared a repeat of McCarthyism and the debate over "who lost China" that had ravaged the Democratic Truman administration (Rostow 1972:270). He was determined to avoid a repeat of that debate over Vietnam (Ellsberg 1971). While this congressional pressure reflected America's peculiar brand of liberal culture, it also reinforced the realist need to avoid losing Vietnam to communism.

The Buddhist Crisis and the Overthrow of Diem

The Kennedy administration had not placed significant pressure on Diem to adopt proliberalization reforms between January 1962 and mid-1963. Then, on May 8, 1963, Vietnamese government troops fired into a peaceful demonstration in the old imperial capital of Hue, killing at least seven. The protesters had been demonstrating against the Diem government's refusal to allow them to fly special flags to commemorate Buddha's birthday. This event triggered a political crisis in South Vietnam that caused Kennedy to renew his efforts to push Diem to adopt liberal reforms and later to push for Diem's ouster in a military coup.

Buddhist political leaders, led by the charismatic Thich Tri Quang, responded to the May 8 attack by mobilizing a demonstration of 10,000 protesters the next day. They demanded that the Diem regime (1) cancel the ban on religious flags; (2) give Buddhists the same legal rights as Catholics; (3) stop government persecution of Buddhists; (4) allow Buddhists freedom to preach their faith; and (5) compensate the families of the Hue victims and punish those responsible for the event (Rust 1985:95). The Buddhist crisis soon blossomed into a full-scale political crisis for the Diem government. A movement that had begun in Hue rapidly spread to the pagodas of Saigon. Buddhist leaders sponsored further political demonstrations and antigovernment propaganda, even as they opened up negotiations with the government. Many of the leading monks went on hunger strikes to protest government policy. On June 11, an elderly monk named Quang Duc burned himself to death on a busy street corner as a protest measure. This was only the first in a series of self immolations that were to galvanize the attention of both the Vietnamese and American publics to this protest movement. The crisis intensified as students demonstrated in Saigon and Hue in support of the Buddhist protesters and army officers prepared for a coup.

Madame Nhu showed her contempt for the Buddhists by saying that she would be happy to provide the fuel for future "barbecues" of Buddhist monks. Diem approached the Buddhist crisis with more tact, but was wary about giving in to political pressure for fear that this would lead to similar pressure from a wide range of groups. When Diem's halting and limited steps toward conciliation during the first month of the crisis failed to quell the protest, he resorted to repression. On August 21, 1963, Special Forces units attacked Buddhist pagodas across the nation. Some 1,400 nuns and monks were arrested, including nearly all the major leaders of the protest movement.

Throughout the Buddhist crisis, the Kennedy administration responded by pushing the Diem regime on numerous occasions to reach some form of compromise with Buddhist leaders that would include a complete acceptance of all the five demands presented by the Buddhists in early May (State 1991a:335, 339, 348, 350, 364, 366, 376, 383). Deputy Chief of Mission William Trueheart, who was in charge of the mission during Ambassador Nolting's absence, told Vietnamese Secretary to the Presidency Nguyen Dinh Thuan that "U.S. support for the government of Vietnam could not be maintained in the face of the bloody repressive action at Hue" (State 1991a:350). After the self-immolation of Quang Duc, Trueheart warned Thuan that if Diem did not take more drastic action to reconcile themselves with Buddhist demands, "he might be faced with public U.S. government disassociation and disapproval of its handling of the Buddhist crisis" (State 1991a:376). In addition, the Americans encouraged Diem to create some form of government commission led by Buddhist Vice President Nguyen Ngoc Tho to resolve the crisis and serve over the longer term for the guarantee of religious freedom in South Vietnam. Diem was encouraged to allow the Buddhists to place candidates in the upcoming national assembly elections. Most important, the United States placed significant pressure on the government to ship the Nhus out of the country indefinitely (State 1991a:402, 413, 433).

Between May and August the Kennedy administration used diplomatic pressure and constant meetings between embassy staff and Vietnamese government officials to communicate its displeasure. After the August crackdown on the Buddhists, it took the drastic step of pushing for the removal of the Diem regime. An August 24, 1963, cable from the State Department authorized the new ambassador, Henry Cabot Lodge, to indicate to Vietnamese military officers that the United States would support a successor regime emerging from a military coup against Diem (State 1991a:628; see also Newman 1992:345–58). From that point, "We [were] launched on a course of action from which there [was] no longer any respectable turning back, the overthrow of the Diem regime," argued Lodge (State 1991b:21). CIA operatives maintained constant contact with the Vietnamese generals preparing for the coup. As a sign of U.S. support, the "Voice of America" broadcast a news statement from official sources that placed all blame for the crackdown on Nhu and his Special Forces and absolved the army of responsibility (Mecklin 1965:193–96).

When the Vietnamese military backed off from its coup attempt of late August, the Kennedy administration decided to escalate the pressure against the Diem regime regardless of whether that would lead to a coup. Lodge refused to meet with Diem as a sign of U.S. displeasure and granted Tri Quang asylum in the embassy (State 1991b:76). Kennedy communicated the change in policy in an interview with Walter Cronkite when he suggested that the government of Vietnam could not win the war against the Viet Cong unless it broadened its base of popular support with "changes in policy and perhaps in personnel" (State 1991b:93).

The Kennedy administration pressured Diem to adopt a series of proliberalization reforms at this juncture, but rather than focus on the reforms they believed most crucial, they instructed Lodge to pursue the full range of reforms that had been advocated at any time in the previous three years. On September 17, 1963, the White House ordered Lodge to push for a wide range of pro-democratic reforms, including the following initiatives in approximate order of importance:

(a) clear the air— . . . Diem should be broadminded and compassionate in his attitude toward those who have . . . found it difficult fully to support him. [He should adopt] a real spirit of reconciliation [rather than] a punitive, harsh, or autocratic attitude; (b) Buddhists and students—let them out and leave them unmolested; (c) Press— . . . should be allowed full latitude of expression; (d) secret and combat police—[should] abandon operations against non-Communist opposition groups; (e) cabinet changes—to inject new untainted blood, remove targets of popular discontent; (f) Elections— these should be held, should be free, and should be widely observed; (g) Assembly—the government should submit its policies to it [immediately after the elections] and should receive its confidence; (h) Party—Can Lao party should not be covert or semi-covert. . . . This could perhaps be best accomplished by disbanding the party and starting afresh; (i) repeal Decree 10; (j) rehabilitation by ARVN of pagodas; (k) establishment of Ministry of Religious Affairs; (l) liberation of passport issuances and currency restrictions;

(m) acceptance of Buddhist inquiry mission from World Federation. (State 1991b:252–54)[8]

In October the U.S. embassy escalated its pressure against the Diem regime. The United States suspended payments on the commodity import program and on two major AID projects in Saigon. Aid was eliminated for the Special Forces of Colonel Le Quang Tung, which had perpetrated the pagoda raids (State 1991b:371–75). Coup plotting continued throughout the period, with CIA contact Colonel Lucien Conein shuttling between General Tran Van Don, the representative of the conspirators led by General Doung Van "Big" Minh, and Ambassador Lodge (Hammer 1987). Finally, just as Diem appeared ready to capitulate to at least some American demands, the U.S.-supported coup took place on November 1, 1963. Diem and his brother Nhu were assassinated. While Kennedy expressed shock and dismay at the assassinations just three weeks before his own, they were the logical outcome of his administration's support for a coup in South Vietnam.

The reforms demanded of Diem fit the definition of proliberalization policies used in this study. Kennedy's policies did not reflect a full commitment to liberal reforms, however. Elections played a limited role in the array of U.S. policies during this time.[9] In addition, U.S. policymakers had little idea of what kind of government would replace the Diem regime in the wake of a military coup. While many believed that the successor regime would liberalize the political system to a greater extent than had the Diem regime, most believed that it would be replaced by another authoritarian regime. Ambassador Lodge argued that no one expected a

8. Several weeks later the administration called upon Lodge to pressure the Diem regime to pursue the following additional reforms: "(a) resumption of normal university life—Detained students should be released; school and university classes should be universally resumed; (b) specific concessions should be made to Buddhists—Those still jailed should be processed for release. . . . Repair of pagodas should be facilitated. . . . Assembly action should eliminate laws which deny equal status to Buddhists; (c) renewed activity in land reform program; (d) Joint re-emphasis on political aspects of strategic hamlet program; (e) Police techniques— GVN should abandon its present practices of controlling populace by instilling fear through night-time arrests, brutal interrogation (including women) and other police-terrorist methods; (f) civil liberties should be restored—arbitrary arrests should cease and those arrested speedily released or given fair public trial. Religious freedom should be implemented as guaranteed by constitution. Public gatherings should be permitted; (g) refurbishing GVN image; (h) changes in personnel—especially the Nhus and Colonel Tung of the Special Forces; (i) public statements by Diem to National Assembly" (State 1991b:376–77).

9. Diem conducted National Assembly elections during this crisis. While some administration instructions called upon Diem to liberalize the elections process during this period, the administration did not press this point strongly.

Western-style democracy to emerge in Vietnam (Lodge 1973:211–12). Roger Hilsman thought that a Korean-style military regime might replace Diem (State 1991b:6).

Congress and the Shift to Proliberalization Policies in 1963

Significant liberal internationalist congressional concern with Kennedy's policies in Vietnam emerged for the first time in 1963. Two events stood out as especially important in marking this growing liberal concern. In the first months of 1963, Senator Mansfield and three of his liberal Democratic colleagues in the Senate produced a pessimistic report on the situation in Vietnam after a December 1962 visit to that country. Later in the year, in the wake of the repression of the Buddhist protesters, Senator Frank Church (D-Idaho) offered a resolution condemning the Diem regime and calling for a suspension of U.S. aid. The Kennedy administration was aware of this nascent liberal opposition. The available evidence suggests, however, that the liberal current in the Congress did not constrain the president. If anything, liberal Democrats in the Senate were willing instruments of the Kennedy administration.

Mansfield returned from his December 1962 visit to South Vietnam with the pessimistic assessment that after two billion dollars of U.S. aid over seven years, "Vietnam now appears to be . . . only at the beginning of a beginning in coping with its grave inner problems" (Congress 1963:iv). The basic problem was that "after seven years of the Republic, South Vietnam appears less, not more stable, than it was at the outset, that it appears more removed from, rather than closer to, the achievement of popularly responsible and responsive government." While Mansfield expressed continued support for Kennedy's policies, he argued that "there is no interest of the United States in Vietnam which would justify, in present circumstances, the conversion of the war in that country primarily into an American war, to be fought primarily with American lives" (Congress 1963:8). Mansfield publicly repeated these concerns on several occasions, but did not use his position of considerable institutional strength to pressure the president to change his policies. As the leader of Senate Democrats, Mansfield endeavored to serve the Democratic administration of President Kennedy and assured the president that he would actively support whatever policies he decided to pursue. In fact, Mansfield had gone on the fact-finding mission at the president's request and kept his strongest criticisms to private communications with Kennedy (Congress 1963:22; Gibbons 1986:132).[10]

State Department cables to the embassy in Vietnam began mentioning congressional criticism and public opinion as important considerations for U.S. policy beginning in mid-June, after the self-immolation of Quang Duc (State 1991a:381, 402, 443, 494; State 1991b:70, 76, 104, 128). The Kennedy administration did not have significant manifestations of domestic protest to contend with (Zaroulis and Sullivan 1984:7–16). It was worried, however, about critical press coverage emanating from the *New York Times'* David Halberstam, UPI's Neil Sheehan, and other U.S. correspondents based in Saigon.[11] The message of these press accounts was that the United States was backing an incompetent autocratic regime that violated religious freedoms (Halberstam 1965; Mecklin 1965:162–66; Kern, Levering et al. 1983:141–91).[12]

These domestic political pressures seemed to culminate in the offering of a resolution by Senator Frank Church (D-Idaho) on September 12, 1963, which stated: "It is the sense of the Senate that unless the Government of South Vietnam abandons policies of repression against its own people and makes a determined and effective effort to regain their support, military and economic assistance should not be continued" (Gibbons 1986:168). Twenty-two senators, most of them liberal Democrats, cosponsored the resolution. Despite the administration's expressions of concern with domestic opinion and the Church resolution, however, the administration's own analysis of domestic opinion suggested that they had considerable room to maneuver (State 1991b:182).

There is substantial evidence that domestic public opinion and the Church resolution were tools used by the U.S. government against the Diem regime

10. These private criticisms had an impact on Kennedy because he found them persuasive, not because he feared that Mansfield would publicly pressure him to change policy. When Mansfield made his personal report to the president, Kennedy admitted to an aide: "I got angry with Mike for disagreeing with our policy so completely, and I got angry with myself because I found myself agreeing with him" (O'Donnell, Powers, and McCarthy 1972:15).

11. John Mecklin, the public affairs officer in Saigon, provides an excellent view of the press problem from Saigon (Mecklin 1965:99–155). Also see the records of the visit to Vietnam of USIA Assistant Secretary Manning for more examples of concern about negative press (State 1991b:496). Kennedy was more concerned with adverse press coverage than his subordinates. He would often ask government officials to comment on the latest *New York Times* report he had read that morning. Kennedy brought press reports into high-level meetings more than other officials (State 1991a:638, State 1991b:25, 116).

12. Kennedy officials were especially concerned with adverse public opinion generated by Madame Nhu's remarks. Harriman once instructed Nolting in a personal note to do whatever he could to "shut that bitch up" (Nolting 1988:107).

rather than constraints on U.S. policy. The expressions of concern found in State Department instructions to the embassy beginning in mid-June were instructions for approaches the deputy chief of mission should make to Diem. The need to appease U.S. public opinion was an argument to sway Diem (State 1991b:429). These instructions were written by men like Averell Harriman, George Ball, and Roger Hilsman at the State Department who needed no encouragement to put pressure on Diem.[13]

This became part of a full-blown strategy to mobilize congressional sanctions as a means of pressuring Diem after the fizzled coup attempt of late August. Ambassador Lodge explicitly asked for some form of congressional resolution that he could use against Diem (State 1991b:67). When Church indicated to Hilsman that he planned to offer some kind of amendment, he agreed to coordinate with the administration on the wording and timing of the initiative (State 1991b:166–67). As Hilsman explained the logic of administration policy in a memo to McGeorge Bundy: "The important thing is to win the war. It is important to maintain the leverage of U.S. discontent both in our public posture and in our private conversations with Diem. . . . Our sanction is that Congress may force us to suspend aid. . . . Lodge should not say that aid has been suspended, but that suspension is right around the corner and will be forced upon us" (State 1991b:75). At the NSC meetings where the congressional strategy was decided upon, there was widespread agreement on this policy initiative. Only two concerns were raised. Rusk was concerned that congressional action could get beyond the control of the administration and that a coalition of Republican opponents of all foreign aid bills and liberals who wanted to use aid cuts as leverage to force Diem to reform would combine to impose an aid cut that would tie the president's hands (State 1991b:188). The president, on the other hand, thought that the worst outcome would be if the resolution were offered and then failed to pass (State 1991b:192). This is not the likely position of a president who felt compelled to adopt such a policy by congressional pressure.

In the end, Church and Senate Democrats cooperated completely with the administration. They agreed to make the initiative a nonbinding sense of Congress resolution. They agreed not to attach the resolution to the foreign aid bill. They agreed to withhold Senate action until a time of the administration's choosing. Indeed, the resolution never came to a vote before

13. By August 1963 Ball and Harriman were undersecretaries of state who held the top spots in the State Department hierarchy behind Rusk. Hilsman had been named assistant secretary of state for Far-Eastern affairs.

the full Senate. Even the text of the resolution was drafted by the State Department (Gibbons 1986:168–69).

This congressional action was immediately used by Hilsman and Lodge to escalate the pressure on Diem. After Hilsman testified before an executive session of the Far East subcommittee of the Senate Foreign Relations Committee, he immediately sent word to Lodge of congressional concerns and warned that the Church resolution would soon be offered before the Senate. Lodge, in turn, gave a copy of the telegram to Diem and stated that "it was obvious that public opinion could not condone the idea that the American loss of lives and American aid were being expended for the repression of human rights" (State 1991b:141). Lodge returned to this theme each time he spoke with Diem, Nhu, or Thuan. Therefore, it is clear that liberal sentiment did not constrain Kennedy policy. This sentiment was an instrument of Kennedy's policy. Liberals in Congress did not seriously challenge American policy in Vietnam until the end of the Johnson administration, when the United States had a half million combat troops fighting there.

A Realist Explanation for the Change in Policy in 1963

The issue of what to do with Diem was perhaps the most contentious foreign policy issue debated within the Kennedy administration. While Kennedy displayed an extraordinary amount of indecision, in the end he decided to stop supporting Diem because he thought his regime was too autocratic to win the popular support necessary to defeat the Viet Cong. Those pushing the most anti-Diem and most pro-democratic line—like Harriman, Hilsman, Ball, and Lodge at the State Department, and Forrestal of the NSC staff—believed that the government of Vietnam would have to unify all noncommunist Vietnamese behind a popular program if it were to win the war against the Viet Cong. These officials thought that the Diem regime was incapable of achieving this goal because, as George Ball bluntly put it, "we had tied our nation's fortunes to a weak, third-rate, bigot with little support in the countryside and not much even in Saigon" (Ball 1982:370).

The Buddhist crisis convinced the Kennedy administration that the Diem regime could not win the war. Since Buddhists were generally anticommunist and formed a nominal majority of the population of South Vietnam, they were considered an essential part of an anticommunist coalition. Without Buddhist support, U.S.-backed forces could not win (State 1991b:381, 444). This was aggravated by the fact that a majority of the officers and enlisted men in the armed forces were Buddhist. A continuation of the repression of

Buddhist protests was bound to increase coup activity and decrease fighting morale (State 1991b:5).

The significance of the Buddhist protest went beyond the impact of the monks' actions. The Buddhist movement galvanized protest from all sectors of the Vietnamese urban elite. When State's Joseph Mendenhall returned from a fact-finding mission to Vietnam, he reported universal disaffection with the Diem regime among the urban elites he spoke with. The civil government was paralyzed and continued domestic unrest was destabilizing the government (State 1991b:161).

Nhu was the lightning rod for all of this protest and disaffection. The complaints against Nhu were magnified because of his control of the government's police-state apparatus. Nhu's State Department critics blamed him for pushing Diem to take a hard line in negotiations with Buddhist leaders. They held him personally responsible for the crackdown of August 21 because the Special Forces who carried out the raids operated under Nhu's orders. Nhu was the focus of universal protest and the instigator of government repression. He symbolized all of the things about Diem's autocratic regime that U.S. officials thought damaged the war effort.

U.S. officials also viewed Nhu as being virulently anti-American. There were numerous indications throughout 1963 that the Diem regime was beginning to distance itself from the United States. In the spring, the Vietnamese government attempted to abrogate an agreement that gave the United States some control over the Vietnamese budget. A month later, Nhu stated in a press interview that the U.S. advisory mission should be cut in half (Hammer 1987:122–24). These statements deeply concerned U.S. officials who wanted to maintain as much control over the war effort as possible. During the height of the Buddhist crisis, Nhu argued that the United States should treat South Vietnam more like it treated Yugoslavia or the Soviet Union during World War II. It should give aid without strings attached, or better yet, loans, because there would be no need for the United States to be concerned with the moral character of its ally. Comparing the Diem government with various communist regimes certainly added to the U.S. government's suspicions of Nhu.

Finally, Nhu began making contacts with representatives of the communist government of North Vietnam during the summer of 1963. American officials thought that Nhu would work out some sort of deal with the North to expel the Americans from Vietnam (State 1991b:204). This, they believed, would eventually lead to a communist victory in the south. The Diem regime's strongest opponents in Washington would have argued for a more pro-democratic policy and for the removal of Nhu from the government regardless of these overtures to the North. For many others, this was the last straw. By August 1963 most U.S. officials believed that Nhu's removal was essential to a successful prosecution of the war (State 1991b:212–15).

On the other side of this debate, there were many important figures in the government, including Secretary of Defense McNamara, CIA Director Mc-Cone, JCS Chair Taylor, the U.S. military commander in Vietnam, General Paul Harkins, and Ambassador Nolting, who argued that it was unwise to place too much pressure on Diem, let alone try to overthrow his regime. They argued that a military coup or aid cutoff would disrupt a war effort that was still proceeding well.[14] Advocates of this position, such as the JCS's special assistant for counterinsurgency, Marine General Victor Krulak, argued that disturbances in the cities were irrelevant for the furtherance of the war effort in the countryside (State 1991b:161). The Buddhist crisis was, at best, the action of a few extremists, and, at worst, inspired by the Viet Cong. Harkins argued that Tri Quang, who was granted asylum in the U.S. embassy, and the leaders of the student protest movement were agents of the Viet Cong (State 1991b:194). Instead of focusing on the need for popular support as a prerequisite for an effective government, advocates of nonliberalization policies focused on the disruptive results likely to occur with a change in government through a military coup. McNamara believed there was no alternative to Diem (State 1991b:27; McNamara 1995:52). Nolting argued that "no stable government would result from a military coup. Only Diem could hold Vietnam together" (State 1991b:6). As CIA operative Edward Lansdale later explained:

> I thought it was a terrible stupid thing. . . . The action didn't make military sense to me. We divided our forces in the face of the enemy—a military no-no. . . . The governmental structure was destroyed—the province chiefs and the district chiefs and so forth. The whole structure went down. And from then on as they kept on having more and more coups and new generals would take over, they'd destroy the whole structure of government again. (Gibbons 1986:203)

14. Harkins's reports were uniformly optimistic and positive (and according to Newman 1992, uniformly false.) Harkins's misrepresentations were accepted in Washington through most of 1962. The battle at Ap Bac, however, where a Viet Cong battalion stood its ground and fought a much larger and better-equipped ARVN force to a standstill, convinced many in the United States that the war was going much more poorly than had been reported (Sheehan 1988:201–65). In addition, doubts were raised about the strategic hamlet program. Hilsman, for example, argued that the program was overexpanded; lacked sufficient political action to build popular support; lacked sufficient coordination between military, political, and economic aspects of the program; and served primarily as a mechanism for control by Nhu (Hilsman 1967:440–67).

For the most part, representatives of the State Department and middle-level embassy personnel in all agencies advocated the adoption of pro-liberalization policies, while representatives of the Department of Defense and military argued for nonliberalization policies. The differences were so profound that when Kennedy sent General Krulak and Assistant Secretary Mendenhall to report on Vietnam they came back with such diametrically opposed positions that Kennedy asked, "Did you two visit the same country?" (State 1991b:161). At first glance, it would appear that bureaucratic politics rather than realist calculations determined the outcome. Strong State Department bureaucratic players, like Averell "the Crocodile" Harriman and Henry Cabot Lodge, achieved positions of greater power and influence. Ambassador Nolting was out of the country at a crucial stage of the Buddhist crisis and Defense Department personnel were outmaneuvered when debating political questions, which were the purview of the State Department.

Although there is substantial evidence of bureaucratic disagreement, it does not appear that these debates reflected parochial bureaucratic interests. Rather, they reflected sincerely held and opposed realist conceptions of appropriate policy. Michael Forrestal illuminated the basic difference in perspective that divided Washington on this issue in a memoranda to his superior, McGeorge Bundy, after a week of stalemate in NSC debates:

> On the one hand, Averell [Harriman] sees a world in which the only successful way to resist the Communist menace is to provide the people concerned with an alternative worth fighting for. On the other hand, to Bob McNamara, the issue is more mechanical: if enough of the enemy can be identified and killed by methods his Department has been so successful in developing, there will be time to concentrate on the political and social welfare of people in the countries where an insurgency exists. Each fundamentally views the other's position as an impractical one. (State 1991b:235)

These camps fought bitterly about the wisdom of supporting a coup, but there did emerge a basic consensus that the Diem regime would have to change in a more democratic direction if the war was to be won. General Harkins, who disagreed strongly with talk of a coup, agreed that Nhu had to go and that the United States should pressure Diem to reform (State 1991b:10–12). When Taylor and McNamara went to Vietnam for a fact-finding mission, these leaders of the anticoup faction in Washington were convinced that change needed to take place to avoid future deterioration of the war effort. Eventually, all major bureaucratic players agreed on the need for proliberalization policies to meet U.S. security goals, even if they never came to a final agreement on the wisdom of a coup (State 1991b:336–46).

In the end, the debate over appropriate strategy was so intense and inconclusive because both sides in the debate were probably correct. Those who argued that the United States could not win with Diem and those who said the United States could not win without Diem were probably both right. The participants in this debate were seeking the best strategy for winning a war that may not have been winnable at an acceptable cost. Only one low-ranking participant in these policy debates, State Department Vietnam desk officer Paul Kattenburg, voiced this opinion by suggesting that the United States should prepare to withdraw with honor. He was quickly overruled by his superiors and was not invited to speak in future debates (Kattenburg 1980:119–20).

The Threat of Hard-Line Anticommunist Partisan Attacks

Throughout this period, congressional Republicans remained surprisingly quiet on the issue of Vietnam. Yet President Kennedy believed that if he had withdrawn forces from Vietnam he would have been blamed by congressional Republicans for its fall. This explains part of the reason for his appointment of Lodge as ambassador to South Vietnam in 1963. Lodge, who had been defeated by Kennedy in the 1952 senatorial election in Massachusetts and again in 1960, when Lodge had been Nixon's vice presidential nominee, was one of the most influential leaders of the Republican Party. His father had been a loyal supporter of McKinley's imperial policies in the Senate. Enlisting Lodge's participation in and support for his policy toward Vietnam would help protect Kennedy from partisan attacks.

Even though there was very little visible anticommunist opposition to his Vietnam policy, Kennedy knew that this was only because he had not wavered from his commitment to contain communism there. As presidential aides Kenneth O'Donnell and David Powers report, the president told Senator Mansfield that he was having serious thoughts about withdrawing from Vietnam, "but I can't do it until 1965—after I'm re-elected. . . . In 1965, I'll become one of the most unpopular presidents in American history. I'll be dammed everywhere as a Communist appeaser. But I don't care. If I tried to pull out completely now from Vietnam we would have another Joe McCarthy red scare on our hands, but I can do it after I'm re-elected. So we had better make damned sure I am re-elected" (O'Donnell, Powers, and McCarthy 1972:16).[15] In the meantime the domestic political threat of hard-line anticommunist partisan attacks reinforced the realist need to find the best available strategy for winning the war in Vietnam.

Conclusion

Kennedy policy toward South Vietnam demonstrates how the presidential path to the adoption of proliberalization policies differs from the congressional path. Compromises crafted during the Democratic presidential nomination process did play a role in shaping Kennedy's initial policies on the question of democracy promotion, as expected by the domestic liberal argument. This placed no long-term constraint on his policy, however, as was shown by the frequent shifts in policy between pressuring Diem to adopt political reforms at some times, while abandoning such pressure at other times.

These shifts can be accounted for by the Kennedy administration's search for the most appropriate policies for the service of U.S. security interests as suggested by the realist approach. Kennedy's long-term vision, which was shaped in part by his affiliation with the Democratic Party, suggested that Diem lacked the popular support necessary to win the war against the Viet Cong. Short-term realist calculations, however, often pushed Kennedy toward the conclusion that the application of effective pressure on Diem would harm the war effort.

The Kennedy case also indicates some important findings about the relationship between partisanship and congressional challenges to a president's policy. There were powerful liberals in Congress who had grave concerns about Kennedy's policies toward Vietnam. Because they were Democrats, however, they gave their party's president the benefit of the doubt and co-operated with the executive. The congressional threat that Kennedy worried about was the threat from anticommunists inspired by a different element of America's liberal culture than the liberal internationalists. He worried about this threat because it was the most likely political attack to be wielded by congressional Republicans. Concern for this kind of domestic political pressure did not shape how Kennedy fought the war, however. It only reinforced his search for the best method for winning the war.

15. Newman argues that Kennedy fully intended to withdraw from Vietnam after the 1964 elections and had allowed the deceptive reporting from the U.S. military in Vietnam to continue because he wanted to use the favorable reports of the war effort as a pretext for withdrawing U.S. advisers (Newman 1992:319–27).

The Kennedy administration was perhaps the last one to face little or no liberal internationalist constraints from Congress. As Kennedy's successor, Johnson committed a half million U.S. soldiers to Vietnam in a war that seemed to defy the expectations of both the realist and domestic liberal arguments, and liberal pressure from Congress intensified. Johnson responded by promoting free and fair elections in Vietnam. His Republican successors, Nixon and Ford, responded to increasing liberal pressure from Congress by slowly withdrawing U.S. troops from Indochina. During the 1970s, Congress enacted a wide range of legislation that enhanced its ability to constrain the war powers of the president. These constraints played a crucial role in shaping the Reagan administration's interventions in the Third World. As the experiences of the Reagan administration attest, however, the Vietnam War and its aftermath helped strengthen those elements of American political institutions and culture that make the United States behave more like a liberal state on the world scene than it has in the past.

5

The Duarte Solution

Congressional Pressure and Reagan's Policy Toward El Salvador, 1981–1984

The Reagan administration adopted an unambiguously hard-line policy toward El Salvador when it took office in January 1981. Reagan increased military aid fivefold, removed all human rights conditions on that aid, and embraced the armed forces and oligarchy as allies in a full-scale military effort to destroy the Farabundo Martí National Liberation Front (FMLN). Six months later, however, the administration announced its support for elections for a Constituent Assembly. By 1984, the administration had committed itself to a fuller range of proliberalization policies, including support for elections, José Napoleón Duarte and the centrist Christian Democratic Party (PDC), and a reduction in human rights abuses by the Salvadoran military.

Realist considerations provide a good explanation for the initial choices of the Reagan administration. Reagan abandoned Carter's emphasis on human rights because he thought it would undermine a U.S.-allied government facing a Soviet-backed communist insurgency. Republican Reagan's embrace of the anticommunist tradition in America's liberal culture reinforced and intensified his commitment to nonliberalization policies in El Salvador.

Reagan was compelled to shift to proliberalization policies, however, in order to convince Congress to pay for the Salvadoran military's counterinsurgency war against the FMLN, as expected by the domestic liberal approach. Both committees (and subcommittees) and party institutions provided important avenues for members of Congress to launch liberal attacks on administration policy. Therefore, liberal internationalists on congressional committees and subcommittees with jurisdiction over U.S. policy in El Salvador were able to use their positions of institutional strength to condemn American support for that country's repressive regime. Congressional liberals were assisted by a number of like-minded public interest groups who provided the members valuable information, expertise, and a domestic constituency.

The success of these liberal attacks was guaranteed by partisan division between the Congress and the president. Democrats controlled the House of Representatives and used El Salvador as a convenient issue for making partisan attacks against a Republican administration. This liberal internationalist coalition constrained Reagan's hard-line policies in two important ways; through cuts in the appropriations desired by the administration and through the placement of human rights conditions on the provision of that aid.

This chapter develops this argument by examining three critical choices in Reagan policy. The first choice occurred in mid-1981, when Reagan shifted from nonliberalization policies to support for Constituent Assembly elections. The second took place in mid-1982, when his administration decided to foster a government of national unity rather than support the ascension of hard-line rightist Roberto D'Aubuisson to the Salvadoran presidency. The third happened in late-1983, when Reagan abandoned a renewed hard-line policy and moved toward a more comprehensive set of proliberalization policies in connection with the 1984 Salvadoran presidential elections.

Realism, Anticommunism, and Reagan's Initial Hard Line

Reagan's initial hard-line policies in El Salvador can be explained to a large degree by that country's status as a least-likely case for the adoption of proliberalization policies according to the realist argument. The Soviet intervention in Afghanistan and the Sandinista revolution in Nicaragua intensified the competition between the United States and U.S.S.R. in the Third World and increased the level of threat faced by the United States in the international environment. Internally, the existence of a civil war in

El Salvador increased the risks associated with the promotion of democracy, while the indirect character of U.S. intervention reduced the leverage of U.S. policymakers to force local officials to adopt liberal reforms.

Reagan's policies were not driven solely by rational calculations of power and security interests, however. From the era of Joseph McCarthy through the 1980s, the Republican Party had become the home of those Americans who adhered to the extreme anticommunist tradition of America's liberal ideal. Ronald Reagan appealed to this sentiment within the party and represented those who believed that the central international expression of American liberalism should be an unflagging opposition to communism. Reagan had almost won the 1976 Republican nomination by attacking the détente policies of Gerald Ford and Henry Kissinger as a violation of America's liberal values. Reagan had beaten the more moderate George Bush in the 1980 race for the Republican nomination, in part because Republican voters thought he would be a more implacable foe of the Soviet Union. Reagan's opposition to Soviet-backed governments and insurgencies, therefore, represented both realist calculation and ideological commitment. In practice, each of these elements of Reagan's approach reinforced his administration's search for the policies most likely to achieve victory over the leftist guerrillas in El Salvador.

The Reagan administration did not accept the logic of Kennedy's Alliance for Progress, which argued that the promotion of democracy was the best way to thwart communist insurgencies. Instead, it viewed the situation in El Salvador as a "textbook case of indirect armed aggression by Communist powers acting through Cuba." The administration produced a White Paper in its first days in office, providing evidence of substantial international arms shipments to the FMLN through Nicaragua (State 1981:2; State 1982:1274). To stop this external support, Secretary of State Alexander Haig pledged to go to the Cuban and Nicaraguan sources of the Salvadoran insurgency, a policy which led to the contra war in Nicaragua (and almost to a blockade of Cuba) (Haig 1984:122; Gutman 1988; Walker 1987). Reagan's principal advisers were convinced that Carter's failure to support the U.S.-allied, "mildly repressive" Somoza regime against Cuban-backed insurgents had contributed to the success of the Sandinista Revolution in Nicaragua. They believed that a similar outcome could be expected in El Salvador unless Carter's policies were abandoned.[1]

1. See the preelection publications of Jeane Kirkpatrick, who became Reagan's ambassador to the United Nations (Kirkpatrick 1979; 1984) and Roger Fontaine, who was appointed the Latin Americanist on Reagan's National Security Council (DiGiovanni and Fontaine 1980; Tambs 1980).

Reagan felt confident in drawing the line against communist expansion in El Salvador, however, because he believed that without external support the Salvadoran insurgents could be easily contained and defeated (NSA:NSC Document 16; State 1982:1255).[2] Reagan officials attributed the failure of the FMLN's January 1981 "final offensive" to the insurgents' fundamental weakness and lack of popular support. Following this analysis, the Reagan administration immediately distanced itself from Carter's policies by (1) removing human rights conditions from military aid, (2) embracing right-wing military officers and oligarchs as allies rather than the PDC, and (3) opposing the Salvadoran agrarian reform.

The Reagan administration, therefore, refused to place any human rights conditions on the $25 million in "emergency" military aid it delivered on March 2, 1981, even though this reflected a fivefold increase in the level of military aid in the context of more than 10,000 political killings in El Salvador during 1980 alone (Congress 1981b). Secretary Haig expressed the new administration's approach to human rights issues in his first press conference, when he announced that the United States would replace Carter's emphasis on human rights with an emphasis on combating Soviet-sponsored international terrorism. Ambassador Kirkpatrick and Haig underlined the lack of concern for the human rights performance of the Salvadoran military in a series of callous public remarks about the November 1980 murders of six leaders of the Revolutionary Democratic Front (FDR) and the December 1980 rapes and murders of four American churchwomen.[3] A senior embassy official aptly characterized the human rights approach of the new administration by saying: "You've really got two choices when you get into a nasty human rights situation. You can say, 'Oh Jesus, these guys are real pricks, we can't have anything to do with these people, we're going home.' . . . Or you can say 'All right, it's terrible, it's lousy, it's horrendous;

2. This chapter relies on the declassified government document collections of the National Security Archives (NSA) for evidence of U.S. policy toward El Salvador during this era. In-text citations refer to the source of the document, the identifying number, and the date of the document, if available. (NSC = National Security Council; ST = State Department, SS = the U.S. embassy in San Salvador, and TG = the U.S. embassy in Tegucigalpa Honduras.)

3. In December 1980 Kirkpatrick signaled that the assassinations of the leaders of the FDR were acceptable by telling the New York Times: "I must say that I found myself thinking that it's a reminder that people who choose to live by the sword can expect to die by it." Kirkpatrick later suggested on Meet the Press that the churchwomen were killed because they were "political activists on behalf of the Frente" (Bonner 1984:217). Haig suggested that the churchwomen had been killed in an "exchange" of gunfire while "running a roadblock." He compounded his error with a clarification that the nuns probably had not attempted to run the roadblock given that he had not "met any pistol packing nuns" in his day (Congress 1981d:37).

what are we going to do about it.' . . . You just have to decide who your pricks are and go with them" (Bonner 1984:231–32). In sum, Reagan administration officials believed that human rights had to be subordinated to more important security considerations. Administration officials were concerned with the human rights question only because they were convinced that the issue was being used as a communist propaganda tool to weaken American resolve.[4]

The Reagan administration also instituted important shifts in the pattern of alliances between the U.S. government and groups within El Salvador. The Carter administration had placed its full support behind the Christian Democrats in the period following the October 1979 military coup. Carter officials helped forge the uneasy alliance between the PDC and the military. This soon led to the formation of a junta, in which PDC leaders José Napoleón Duarte and José Antonio Morales Ehrlich joined military members Cols. Jaime Abdul Gutiérrez and Adolfo Majano (Baloyra 1982; Montgomery 1982; Bonner 1984; Stanley 1996:178–217). Carter's ambassador to El Salvador, Robert White, targeted right-wing military officers and members of the Salvadoran coffee oligarchy as important opponents of U.S. interests.

In contrast, the Reagan administration embraced the right and distanced itself from the PDC. These changing alliance patterns became evident during the transition period between the two administrations. In November 1980, members of Reagan's transition team—Jeane Kirkpatrick, Roger Fontaine, and James Theberge—had a cordial meeting in Washington with members of the Productive Alliance, an organization representing the oligarchy. The Reagan team informed the Salvadorans that they would provide whatever military aid was needed to defeat the FMLN. No human rights strings would be attached.[5] This same message was taken to El Salvador by transition team member Cleto DiGiovanni after the election (Bonner 1984:217–18).

4. A cable from Haig to all embassies suggested that combating "a major worldwide propaganda campaign . . . reflect(ing) a major drive by the U.S.S.R., Cuba and others to exploit the support and views of the Socialist International, assorted left-of center political groupings and several religious groups—particularly liberal Catholics" was one of the principal problems in U.S. policy toward El Salvador (NSA:ST 032133, 2/7/81). Haig still referred to the human rights problem as a public relations problem of combating international communist propaganda in a 1982 meeting with Junta member Colonel Gutiérrez (NSA:ST 60508, 3/8/82).

5. In an interesting twist, the Productive Alliance representatives actually announced their support for early elections in El Salvador at this meeting because they considered the PDC-Military junta to be a serious threat to their interests and hoped that it could be unseated in such elections (Stanley 1996:231–32).

Duarte, on the other hand, received a "rude and skeptical interrogation" at the hands of Kirkpatrick, Richard Allen (Reagan's first national security adviser), and Constantine Menges (who served Reagan in the NSC and CIA) in another November meeting (Duarte 1986:159). Reagan's transition team targeted White for immediate replacement, signaling an abandonment of Carter's allies in El Salvador. Indeed, the entire leadership of the inter-American affairs and human rights bureaus at the State Department were purged by Reagan in a housecleaning comparable to the McCarthy-era purge of China experts (Sullivan 1995:120–26).

Reagan fired White and gave Duarte a skeptical welcome in part because of the "socialistic" agrarian reforms they supported.[6] The Carter adminis-tration viewed the March 1980 agrarian reform as the most critical compo-nent of their counterinsurgency strategy to stop a socialist revolution in El Salvador by building a viable alternative to the political project offered by the FDR-FMLN (Prosterman 1981; Pastor 1984; Vaky 1987). The agrarian reform, however, which nationalized banking and export industries and called for the expropriation of substantial quantities of agricultural land, violated Reagan's commitment to free-market economic policies. Further-more, the Reagan administration believed that the agrarian reform would lead to a collapse of the Salvadoran economy because business leaders would no longer invest their capital in El Salvador (NSA:SS 3347, 4/13/81). The Reagan administration wanted to rebuild U.S. alliances with precisely the forces that would be most adversely affected by a full implementation of the agrarian reform: the Salvadoran coffee oligarchy.

In sum, Reagan officials did not believe that the adoption of proliber-alization policies was necessary for achieving U.S. security interests in El Salvador. Because they viewed the basic cause of the security problem as externally sponsored subversion, Reagan officials behaved in accordance with the expectations of the realist hypothesis that the existence of war makes policymakers reluctant to run the risks associated with the promotion of liberal reforms. As Reagan put it, "you do not try to fight a civil war and institute reforms at the same time. Get rid of the war. Then go forward with reforms" (Gutman 1988:27). These beliefs were reinforced by Reagan's ideological commitment to anticommunism.

6. DiGiovanni and Fontaine highlighted this problem in their 1980 critique of the Carter policy, writing: "A pro-U.S. military government in El Salvador which had been economically viable has been replaced by a center-left government supported by the U.S. Embassy. That government, having brought the country to near economic ruin by desperate and sweeping reforms, might fall to Marxist guerrillas" (1980:26).

Congressional Pressure and Reagan's 1981 Decision to Support Elections for a Constituent Assembly

Despite its strong commitment to pursue nonliberalization policies, the Reagan administration shifted to proliberalization policies less than six months later. In a major speech on July 16, 1981, the new assistant secretary of state for inter-American affairs, Thomas Enders, announced that the United States would support "prompt, free, and open" elections for a Constituent Assembly in El Salvador (State 1982:1326–30). This was the first time a senior Reagan official had emphasized elections as a key part of U.S. policy there. Deane Hinton, the new U.S. ambassador to El Salvador, was charged with the implementation of this electoral policy. The United States paid for the Salvadoran government's electoral machinery. U.S. advisers helped modify the existing electoral law. Hinton helped negotiate agreements among the parties involved in the elections. Finally, the United States sent an official election observer team led by Senator Nancy Kassebaum (R-Kan.) to monitor the vote (Congress 1982b). The administration still opposed the placement of human rights conditions on military aid as well as the agrarian reform. The embrace of an electoral solution, however, represented a significant change in policy.

As expected by the domestic liberal argument, congressional pressure compelled Reagan to adopt proliberalization policies in 1981. Reagan's advisers continued to believe that the existing regime could achieve victory over the FMLN if it were provided sufficient resources, but they expected that it would cost more and take longer than originally anticipated. They worried that there might be "no military end in sight to the war of attrition in El Salvador" without vast increases in military aid and intensive training in counterinsurgency techniques (NSA:SS 4455, 6/12/81). This consensus was solidified by a special report prepared by General Fred Woerner in late 1981 that exposed the incompetence, corruption, inadequate training and equipment of the Salvadoran armed forces, as well as its unwillingness to pursue the military strategies necessary to defeat the FMLN (NSA 1981; Stanley 1996:220–27). Reagan modified his policies in order to convince Congress to pay the substantial military and economic aid bill necessary to fund the Salvadoran military's counterinsurgency war against the FMLN.

The first congressional attacks came from committees and subcommittees with jurisdiction over U.S. policy toward El Salvador. On February 25, 1981, the Subcommittee on Foreign Operations of the House Appropriations Committee held hearings on the administration's request to reprogram $25 million in military aid, approving the request by a slim 8–7 margin

(Congress 1981b). The Western Hemisphere Subcommittee of the House Foreign Affairs Committee and the Republican-controlled Senate Foreign Relations Committee held March 1981 hearings on U.S. policy (Congress 1981c; Congress 1981d).

In April, Representative Gerry Studds (D-Mass.) offered a bill before the Foreign Affairs Committee that would cut off all military aid to El Salvador. While Studds's bill was voted down, a compromise measure submitted by liberal Reps. Steven Solarz (D-N.Y.) and Jonathan Bingham (D-N.Y.) was approved. This compromise provided aid to El Salvador, but only after the president certified every six months that the Salvadoran government was making improvements in six areas: human rights, control of security forces, economic reforms, the holding of elections, negotiations toward a political settlement, and investigations of the murders of U.S. citizens (Congress 1981e:38–81). The Senate Foreign Relations Committee backed similar language several weeks later. The certification requirement was enacted into law in December 1981 and the administration filed its first report in January 1982.

Congress delegated to the president the decision of whether or not to stop aid, thus guaranteeing that aid would continue. As Studds's aide, Bill Woodward admitted: "Congress knew that the administration was not going to abide by the certification. In this sense it was hypocrisy. It was a device to let military aid go forward without Congress getting its hands or conscience dirty" (Sullivan 1995:33). Despite the weakness of the constraint imposed by the certification requirement, Reagan's critics were guaranteed a forum every six months to debate his policies. They could keep a "low fire" under the administration, threatening to impose more restrictive legislation if the president did not commit to proliberalization policies. When the administration tried to evade the intent of the certification requirement, as occurred in January 1982, liberals in the foreign policy committees could use the certification hearings to condemn it (Congress 1982a). This bill was a perfect compromise for most members of Congress because it allowed them to register their concern about human rights without taking responsibility for any harm to U.S. security interests (Arnson 1989:69). This is precisely the kind of "position taking" behavior to be expected of members of Congress (Mayhew 1974).

Ideology, Partisanship, and the 1981 Certification Requirement

The ideological goals of members were the most important determinants of this initial congressional action. Many members argued that the United States should stay out of Central America to avoid stumbling down a "slippery slope" toward another Vietnam (Congress 1981b:261–62; Arnson 1989:56). Congressional pressure did encourage the Reagan administration to promise to limit the number of U.S. military advisers in El Salvador to fifty-five in response to these fears (Sullivan 1995:192). Equally prominent in congressional deliberations, however, were the attacks of liberals like Gerry Studds, who argued that the Salvadoran government was simply too brutal and repressive to warrant U.S. support. After a visit to Central America, Studds and two liberal colleagues bitterly attacked U.S. aid to El Salvador in a letter to President Reagan:

> During our trip to Central America we have visited with refugees along the Salvadoran-Honduran border. We are convinced and have collected eyewitness evidence that atrocities are regularly being committed by the security forces of the Salvadoran government. Murder, rape, torture, and burning of crops are being inflicted upon the Salvadoran people by the very troops now receiving U.S. military aid. . . . In the name of justice and humanity and to further the long term best interests of the U.S. government, we appeal to you in the first days of your presidency to halt immediately military aid to El Salvador. (NSA:TG 12065, 1/18/81; Congress 1981a)

They sent a nearly identical letter to Jimmy Carter, suggesting that they were willing to attack the policies of their own party's president on ideological grounds.

The significant variation in the responses of congressional committees and subcommittees also suggests that liberal ideology was the primary factor shaping congressional action in 1981. Opposition to Reagan policy in the House was heard most strongly in the Foreign Operations and Western Hemisphere subcommittees, which were more liberal than the full committees of which they were a part (Arnson 1989:56–57). A handful of liberal members of the House developed an expertise on U.S. policy in Central America and used their positions in these subcommittees to hold a constant stream of critical hearings that helped set the tone and substance of policy debates. Indeed, liberals on the Western Hemisphere subcommittee ousted chair Gus Yatron (D-Pa.) in favor of Michael Barnes (D-Md.) precisely because they suspected that Yatron "was not going to make an issue out of Central America and we needed to counterbalance (Republican Senator Jesse) Helms," according to congressional aide Rob Kurz (Sullivan 1995:191).

The behavior of the Senate Foreign Relations Committee provides more significant evidence for the importance of ideology. Despite Republicans'

control of the Senate during the Ninety-seventh Congress, the Foreign Relations Committee held hearings emphasizing liberal themes and voted to
support the certification requirement proposed by House Democrats. This
anomaly can be explained by the liberal inclinations of the committee's
chair, Senator Charles Percy (R-Ill.), and of other Republican members of
the committee.

That ideological concerns would be most important in 1981 is not surprising, given that committees and subcommittees dominated congressional
decision-making at this time. This maximized the power of strategically
placed liberal minorities to obstruct administration initiatives. The Foreign
Operations Subcommittee possessed the institutional authority to vote on
reprogramming requests. Liberals on that subcommittee were poised to vote
down the administration's initial request for military aid until the unusual
intervention of the two senior members of the full Appropriations Committee, Committee Chair Jamie Whitten (D-Miss.) and ranking Republican
Silvio Conte (R-Mass.), swung the vote in Reagan's favor. The certification
requirement had been hammered out in the Foreign Affairs and Foreign
Relations Committees, which had higher concentration of liberals than the
full House and Senate. Because the work of these committees was respected
on the floors of the House and Senate, the work of liberals within those
committees had a critical impact on the final congressional action.

Partisan considerations were also important. Although Senator Percy sym-
pathized with a liberal internationalist approach to U.S. policy, he was also
careful to combine these concerns with an acceptance of the security premises
of the Reagan administration.[7] As a congressional leader from the president's
own party, Percy was under considerable partisan pressure to support Reagan policy. The Republican-controlled Senate, therefore, was generally more
supportive of the president than was the Democrat-controlled House. In a
similar vein, Representative Conte voted for the administration's February
1981 reprogramming request despite his extreme discomfort at expressing
support for the repressive government of El Salvador (Congress 1981b:301).
Percy and Conte reconciled ideological commitments with partisan loyalties
by embracing the certification requirement as a workable compromise. As

7. Percy began the March 1981 hearings, for example, by stating: "In a situation in which
our direct security interests are readily apparent, we should not allow our tragic Vietnam
experience to inhibit us from acting to protect those interests. . . . But, El Salvador is a country
in the initial throes of a revolution. It is still possible for an enlightened government to win the
support of the Salvadoran population by taking the lead in implementing social and economic
changes needed to bring about a more equitable distribution of prosperity in that country. It is
in the United States' interest to support that process" (Congress 1981d:1–2).

during the Spanish-American War, liberal Republicans tried to forge centrist compromises in cooperation with the administration.

Leading liberal Democrats in the House followed a similar approach when a president from their party, Jimmy Carter, had decided to provide military aid to El Salvador. Liberal Democrats Matthew McHugh (D-N.Y.) and David Obey (D-Wis.) of the Foreign Operations Subcommittee provided the critical votes in support of Carter's $5.7 million "nonlethal" military aid package in 1980. They were willing to give the "benefit of the doubt" to their party's president (Congress 1980:430–31). When Reagan took office, they helped lead the attack against Reagan's policies in El Salvador. The Democrats who led the charge against Reagan policy were guided by their ideological preferences, but House leaders encouraged them to take a leadership role in the debate because this was an issue on which the Republican president was vulnerable.

During 1981, Reagan mobilized significant popular support for his program of income tax cuts, social spending cuts, and increases in defense spending. He threatened to overwhelm the House Democratic leadership on these issues. Democrats thought they could achieve a victory against the popular president on El Salvador, however. Public opinion polls showed widespread opposition to Reagan's policy in Central America because many Americans feared that he was going to get the United States into a war. According to a March 1981 Gallup Poll, two-thirds of all informed respondents were concerned that El Salvador would become another Vietnam, while only 2 percent were willing to send U.S. troops there (Arnson 1989:64). An ABC/*Washington Post* poll in March 1982 found that only 22 percent of the American public was willing to send U.S. troops even if the government was on the verge of defeat. A CBS/*New York Times* poll found that 63 percent of the public thought the United States should stay out altogether. Only 6 percent thought that the United States should even send military advisers (Schneider 1983:57–58). This polling data was reinforced by a rising tide of popular protest against Reagan policy mobilized by the Central America movement.

Anti-intervention groups worked to reinforce congressional opposition to Reagan policy in two ways. First, they provided like-minded members of Congress with a source of authoritative information and expert opinion that members could use to bolster their arguments against administration policy. Second, these groups also mobilized thousands of people to demonstrate against U.S. policy and to lobby their congressional representatives to change that policy. Although these direct lobbying efforts probably had only a limited impact on the voting decisions of members, these public protests did convince congressional Democrats that this was an issue on which they could score partisan points versus the president.

Elements of the U.S. Catholic Church combined both of these roles and provided one of the most powerful sources of opposition in the anti-interventionist movement. Church groups were especially important in focusing the debate on the liberal internationalist argument that the United States should not support the government of El Salvador because of its role in the killings of tens of thousands of its own citizens. Catholic organizations had lobbied against U.S. support for various Salvadoran governments because of the official repression wielded against the Salvadoran Catholic Church (Congress 1977). Pressure from American Catholics intensified in the wake of the 1980 murders of archbishop of San Salvador, Oscar Romero, and the American nuns and pastoral workers at the hands of members of Salvadoran security forces.

Liberal internationalists in Congress clearly viewed the Church as a valuable source of authoritative information to support their cause. In the debate over the extent of and responsibility for human rights abuses in El Salvador, congressional liberals were able to rely on the statistics compiled by the Catholic Archdiocese of San Salvador. When these statistics were presented to congressional committees by bishops and other leaders of the American Church, this gave them added weight in the minds of many members.[8]

Church representatives were joined in this mission and later superseded by groups like America's Watch and Amnesty International, which used careful research to demonstrate that the vast majority of political killings could be attributed either to security forces or to right-wing death squads connected to the Salvadoran security forces. By the end of 1981, these groups were publishing reports every six months to coincide with presidential certifications. These reports placed strong emphasis on liberal internationalist themes, in part because they focused strongly on the issues highlighted in the certification requirements. They also emphasized violations of international law such as the Geneva Conventions on War. By carefully documenting violations of human rights in El Salvador, and the inaccuracy of administration claims that the situation was improving, these reports proved an invaluable resource for liberal members of Congress (Congress 1982a:13–14).

Catholic groups also played a crucial role in lobbying Congress to stop aid to El Salvador. Catholics throughout the country commemorated the

---

8. Archbishop James Hickey of Washington, D.C.; Thomas Quigley and Father Bryan Hehir, S.J., of the Peace and Justice Commission of the U.S. Catholic Conference of Bishops; and Sister Melinda Roper of the Maryknoll Order all testified in the hearings of early 1981.

March assassination of Archbishop Romero and the December murders of the American churchwomen with special masses and demonstrations. On March 24, 1981, 50,000 people turned out nationwide to commemorate the first anniversary of Romero's assassination in candlelight vigils, masses, and memorial rallies (CISPES 1981). Thousands more did the same to commemorate the December killings of the American churchwomen. Catholics organized a Religious Task Force on Central America, which mobilized and educated Catholics throughout the country against U.S. policy. The Catholic Conference of Bishops distributed pastoral letters announcing their opposition to military aid. Parishes throughout the country offered sanctuary to refugees fleeing the violence in Central America.

Catholics were soon joined in opposition to Reagan policy by a wide range of liberal Protestant congregations across the country that also lobbied Congress and granted sanctuary to refugees. National groups like the World Council of Churches and the Quakers' American Friends Service Committee joined in the protests and worked closely with Washington-based liberal think-tank and lobbyist organizations like the Washington Office on Latin America and the Coalition for a New Foreign and Military Policy. These groups may not have played a crucial direct role in shaping congressional action, but their strong liberal internationalist attacks on Reagan policy strengthened the hands of the congressional liberals who were leading the campaign against Reagan's policy toward El Salvador.

One of the groups mobilizing opposition to Reagan policy in El Salvador, the Committee in Solidarity with the People of El Salvador (CISPES), worked from an explicitly illiberal premise. CISPES did not oppose U.S. policy because that policy violated American ideals. It opposed U.S. policy because America stood in the way of a revolutionary victory for the FMLN. Despite this, CISPES emphasized the human rights issue even though it believed that a more pro-democratic intervention should be opposed. A CISPES editorial explained in 1984:

> While "conditioning" is not definitive, neither is it *insignificant*. The death squads in El Salvador are once again on the march. . . . Many sectors of the Democratic, and even Republican, parties are getting uncomfortable about sponsoring such open terror. . . . The public, for its part, clearly wants nothing to do with D'Aubuisson and Company. By itself, this contradiction will not stop U.S. intervention. But it is quite possible that at some future point, combined with a direct challenge from the FMLN, an international anti-intervention consensus, and a strong mass movement here at home, the contradictions created

by revulsion from government terror . . . will open the door through which the people of El Salvador will pass to seize control over their lives. Thus, while the solidarity movement cannot embrace conditioning as a position of our own, we must seize the issue, hammering away at it, *make human rights once again a primary issue of national debate*—do our part to help the Salvadoran people open that door. (CISPES 1983–84:2)

Thus, in an unexpected twist on the domestic liberal argument, even those who do not accept America's liberal culture use liberal appeals to accomplish their political objectives, which leads to the adoption of proliberalization policies.

Reagan Responds to Domestic Pressure

Reagan strongly opposed the proposed certification requirement as a formula for undermining the U.S.-allied government in El Salvador. His administration was even more concerned by the liberals' call for efforts to reach a negotiated settlement between the FDR-FMLN and the junta in El Salvador, a call echoed by America's European allies. The Reagan administration did not wish to allow the FMLN to, as Enders put it, "obtain what they have been unable to win on the battlefield and what they are unwilling to compete for at the polls" (State 1982:1347). Reagan wanted to squash talks of a negotiated settlement on any grounds other than the surrender of the left (Baloyra 1982:154–60; Bonner 1984:270–89).

Members of Reagan's domestic policy team, including Chiefs of Staff Jim Baker and Ed Meese, Treasury Secretary Don Regan, and Management and Budget Director David Stockman, were concerned, however, that congressional attacks against the administration's policy in El Salvador could threaten passage of the administration's tax and domestic spending cuts. Defense Secretary Caspar Weinberger believed that Haig's plans for military action would threaten congressional support for Reagan's defense build-up (Weinberger 1990:30–32). Advisers like Meese and Weinberger were long-time confidants of Reagan and easily won the president's support in their efforts to modify policy to protect the president's more important initiatives.

Therefore, when Enders and Hinton assumed their posts in mid-1981, they were under instructions to defuse the Salvadoran issue. They began by discouraging potential right-wing coups, because this would "greatly complicate the already difficult problem of mobilizing U.S. and international support for measures necessary to avoid power passing to Leninist-Castroite forces" (NSA:SS 4455, 6/12/81). Their principal initiative to accomplish this task, however, was to support the March 1982 "demonstration elections" for a Constituent Assembly in hopes that they would unlock the congressional coffers to fund the war (Herman and Brodhead 1984:93–152).

In connection with this initiative, they publicized U.S. ties with Duarte as evidence of Reagan's commitment to the promotion of democracy and worked for a PDC victory in the elections. El Salvador's foreign minister, PDC member Fidel Chávez Mena, visited Washington in July 1981, according to a confidential State Department memo, "to fully explain to members of Congress the role of elections in developing a political solution for El Salvador" (NSA:ST 7/7/81). Duarte visited in September to use his democratic credentials and promise of elections to convince Congress to provide more money for his government. A confidential briefing paper from Enders to Haig suggests that "we want Duarte's visit to neutralize emotional and irrational concern over U.S. policy in El Salvador. . . . We expect President Duarte to be an effective spokesman for his cause and to that end we have encouraged efforts to give him maximum exposure personally." Duarte's fluent English, Notre Dame education, and apparent victory in the 1972 presidential election, which was taken from him through military intervention, would enhance his credibility in the United States (NSA:ST 9/18/81). Haig put it even more bluntly in a memo to Reagan:

> There are major problems with Congress which we hope his presence will ameliorate. We are not winning the struggle to convince a clear majority within the Congress that the government of El Salvador deserves U.S. assistance. Clear indications that the government of El Salvador is taking firm steps to control acts of violence against noncombatants by right-wing death squads and the security forces would strengthen our hand with the Congress. (NSA:ST 9/19/81)

The administration also hoped the elections would lead to a restructuring of U.S. relations with its "domestically repugnant allies" on the right of the Salvadoran political spectrum. By forcing the coffee oligarchs, right-wing military, and death squads to participate in the elections, policymakers hoped to coax the right into abandoning death squad violence in favor of less violent forms of political action more acceptable to the Congress (Karl 1986:17–18).

State Department personnel often explained their support for democracy in realist terms rather than as a response to congressional pressure. Enders's successor, Langhorne Motley, dismissed the certification process as serving only "to make Congress feel good about itself and to give them a good public relations bit" (Sullivan 1995:33). Enders and Hinton supported elections because they could potentially establish a center-right consensus between the PDC and the oligarchs. Furthermore, "only a genuinely pluralistic approach can enable a profoundly divided society to live with itself" (Baloyra 1982:143–53; State 1982:1328). They also believed that elections might help seize the political initiative from the FMLN. If the FDR chose to participate in the elections, this could shatter the revolutionary coalition and demonstrate the assumed political weakness of the left. If the left did not participate, it could be branded as antidemocratic. Despite these realist rationales, even the most enthusiastic proponents of proliberalization policies realized that elections in the Salvadoran context involved significant security risks, as Hinton's July 1981 memo on the political barriers to successful elections indicates:

> There are three interlocking problems around which events in the coming months are going to gather. If elections actually take place, with no miscarriage or provoked abortion along the way, it will be because these problems have been moved a long way toward solution. First, the deep and abiding and amply justified distrust Salvadorans have in their elections must be dissipated. Second, some process must be started so that a reasonably intelligible choice of policies and alternatives can be presented to voters. Third, means must be found for assuring the interest groups that the rise of one party or group or sector will not spell the ruin of another. This is perhaps the most important condition and the hardest to satisfy in today's climate of extremism and polarization and in the absence of any well functioning political institutions. (NSA:SS 5494, 7/21/81)

The embassy was not certain that the electoral process could be managed peacefully or that the result of the process would be optimal for U.S. security interests (Bonner 1984:290–91).

Despite the guarded optimism of Enders and Hinton, nearly all of Reagan's principal advisers, including CIA Director William Casey, Defense Secretary Weinberger, National Security Adviser Allen, Ambassador Kirkpatrick, and Secretary of State Haig retained their initial assumptions about appropriate responses to authoritarian regimes facing leftist insurgency. The major policy review conducted in late 1981 concluded that the United States should start funding the contra war in an effort to interdict arms flows from Nicaragua to the FMLN and thus deal with the central problem in El Salvador: external subversion (Gutman 1988). Reagan policymakers, therefore, continued to believe that a forced liberalization of the junta was, at most, an unnecessary and second-best response to U.S. security interests. At the least, these policies could undermine the U.S.-allied government. The fact that the Reagan administration shifted to proliberalization policies despite its expectation that such policies were likely to undermine U.S. security interests bolsters the conclusion that domestic political pressure led to support for the Constituent Assembly elections. As State's Luigi Einaudi suggests, the choices were to "go the Argentine route," a reference to Argentina's "dirty war" of extermination during the mid-1970s, "or bumble along and fight the war and build democracy at the same time. . . . The existence of Congress was crucial. It meant that the Argentine solution had to be ruled out" (Arnson 1989:69).

Reagan Support for a National Unity Government in 1982

Reagan faced a second crucial decision point in the wake of the Constituent Assembly elections. The elections were initially a huge public relations success. "Voter turnout was massive everywhere. Complaints of fraud and intimidation are few. . . . Official observers, unofficial observers and the press have expressed amazement at the turnout" (NSA:SS 2704, 3/28/82). The press and the official congressional observer team declared the long lines of *campesinos* waiting to vote a triumph for democracy (Congress 1982b). The vote total may have been inflated to make precisely this impression on American observers.[9] The elections left the anti-intervention movement in disarray as CISPES, for example, mobilized 70,000 for a march on the

9. Soon after the vote, the journal of the Catholic University in San Salvador claimed that although the distribution of votes between parties was not tampered with, the overall vote total was inflated by up to 50 percent in an effort to appeal to U.S. public opinion (ECA 1982). The Central Elections Council (CCE) said that 1.5 million Salvadorans voted in the elections, whereas perhaps only 1 million made it to the polls. Bonner (1984:302–5) reports corroborating evidence, including a statement from the head of the CCE, Jorge Bustamante, who suggested that vote totals may have been inflated by 10 percent. Karl (1986:19) reports that high officials of the ARENA and PDC admitted in interviews that the vote count was inflated. The available documentation, on the other hand, vigorously denies any vote inflation (NSA: "El Salvador Election Wrap-Up," undated). The high turnout may have been related to the fact that voting was mandatory and nonvoters might face government repression. Embassy documents also note, however, that U.S. preelection estimates of the total pool of eligible voters was only 1.4 million (NSA:SS 3/26/82). Furthermore, the early embassy election situation reports that boasted of "massive turnout" estimated that turnout at 1 million voters (NSA:SS 2709, 3/29/82). Voter turnout in the 1984 and 1985 elections was reported to be between 1.3 and 1.4 million, roughly comparable to the 1982 vote.

White House on March 27, 1982, but subsequently suffered from a "big lull," from which it escaped only a year later (Ostertag 1983:8). Interest groups, therefore, played a less important role in the intense congressional pressure that greeted Reagan policy after the 1982 elections.

Early enthusiasm in Congress died down when it became apparent that parties of the "disloyal right" had won the election and threatened to reimpose the kind of "reactionary despotism" that had existed in El Salvador during much of its modern history (Baloyra 1982:105–24). The oligarch-dominated Nationalist Republican Alliance (ARENA) earned 19 seats in the 60-person assembly, while the traditional party of the military, the Party of National Conciliation (PCN), took 14 seats. These two parties possessed the votes to elevate right-wing death-squad leader and ARENA candidate Maj. Roberto D'Aubuisson to the presidency.

Congress members who supported a "pro-democratic" policy wanted the United States to pursue a package of reforms that included not only support for free and fair elections, but also for human rights, moderate political parties, and agrarian reform. When the election results threatened this broader agenda, a high-powered congressional delegation led by the House majority leader, Representative Jim Wright (D-Tex.), and the chair of the Western Hemisphere Subcommittee, Michael Barnes (D-Md.), traveled to El Salvador to demand that the right-wing parties include the PDC in a coalition government of national unity.[10] Wright threatened a cut-off of aid unless a moderate compromise coalition government continued the agrarian reform process, lessened human rights abuses, and held early presidential elections. While Wright partially undercut the impact of his message with conciliatory public statements about D'Aubuisson (Bonner 1984:311), an embassy cable depicting Wright's private meetings with ARENA party leaders suggested that the bluntness of congressional demands meant that "if the Salvadorans did not get the message, then they are unlikely to receive the word ever" (NSA:SS 3088, 4/9/82). This incident was the most significant intrusion of the Democratic Party leadership on the issue of El Salvador to that date and reflected the growing influence of partisanship in the congressional debate.

When the Constituent Assembly voted on May 18, 1982, to suspend the land-to-the-tiller portion of the agrarian reform, congressional committees responded by slashing the Reagan administration's economic and military aid

---

10. Wright was more conservative than most of his Democratic colleagues. He believed that U.S. intervention to keep the FMLN out of power and support for Duarte and the reform process were necessary to serve U.S. security interests. As majority leader, Wright also had to deal with his party's congressional representatives who favored a more liberal internationalist policy in El Salvador. Wright's attempts to balance these two stances within the party would be a continuing theme in congressional reactions to Reagan policy in Central America.

requests for El Salvador. Several congressional committees voted to cut the president's request for FY82 supplemental funds by more than half.[11] Senator Percy stated bluntly: "If the Salvadoran government is reneging on the land-reform program, then . . . not one cent of funds shall go to the government of El Salvador" (Arnson 1989:95). Reagan made no significant effort to reinforce this congressional initiative. When the assembly reinstated the land-to-the-tiller program during the summer of 1982, therefore, it did so in direct response to congressional pressure. This episode provides more evidence of the importance of Congress in bringing about a pro-democratic emphasis in U.S. foreign policy. The role of Senator Percy in the agrarian reform debate indicates the continuing importance of ideological motivations in shaping the congressional reaction.

Ambassador Hinton seconded Wright's call for a government of national unity. In January 1982, when it became clear that the newly formed ARENA party would be a serious challenger in the elections, he began calls for an all-party "government of national unity." Before this time, he had said that the new Constituent Assembly would have absolute authority to govern in any fashion it chose (NSA:SS 741, 1/29/82). Hinton cooperated with the Wright delegation's efforts by constantly reminding the Salvadorans that continued aid would be dependent on the creation of a moderate government (Arnson 1989:87). When the winners of the election refused to cooperate with the PDC, Hinton, with the help of an ambassador at large, Retired General Vernon Walters, moved to salvage at least the appearance of a moderate regime and pressured the military to keep D'Aubuisson from being elected president (Bonner 1984:311). In concert with the U.S. embassy, the Salvadoran military imposed the selection of banker Alvaro Magaña as the figurehead president.[12] Hinton then helped negotiate the Pact of Apaneca, which distributed government positions evenly between ARENA, the PCN, and the PDC (Karl 1985).

11. The president's FY82 supplemental appropriations request was for $128 million in emergency support funds (ESF) and $35 million in military assistance for El Salvador. On May 27, 1982, Foreign Operations voted 7 to 5 to disallow the entire $35 million request for military aid. The Foreign Relations Committee responded by accepting the administration's request for development assistance, but freezing ESF and military aid for FY83 at the regular 1982 levels, allowing only $40 million in ESF and $26 million in military aid. On July 27, Foreign Affairs followed the lead of the Foreign Operations Subcommittee by voting against the Reagan administration's $35 million request for military aid in the FY82 Supplemental bill. They also voted to limit the administration's ESF authorization to $75 million (Storrs 1983:56–82).

12. NSA:SS 3497, 4/23/82, comes close to admitting that Hinton engineered the deal, but significant excisions obscure the precise nature of the U.S. role. It seems clear that the Salvadoran military took this action implicitly in response to American wishes, even if there was no explicit involvement by Hinton.

Ambassador Hinton worked to keep D'Aubuisson out of the Salvadoran presidency in part because he was concerned about the consequences of an ARENA government for the political situation in El Salvador.[13] The most important consideration, however, was that a D'Aubuisson victory could lead to a cut-off of congressional funding. A mid-1982 State Department briefing paper restated the basic problem of Reagan policy in El Salvador:

> The trend of events in Central America is running in our favor. . . . Assuming that Cuba and Nicaragua do not substantially increase the stakes in Central America, the secret to success will be a steady and sustained effort. . . . Our principal difficulty in pursuing this policy will be to obtain the required Congressional support. Human rights concerns, diminished but still present fears of a Vietnam-style escalation, and other competing concerns are all obstacles. . . . If we are unsuccessful in these [upcoming aid] votes we will face increased chances of a political/military debacle in Central America with grave national security consequences. We have broadened support somewhat, but we must also build a stronger constituency on the Hill if we are to succeed over the long run. (NSA:ST 6/26/82)

Despite the fact that Reagan's support for Constituent Assembly elections and a national unity government had been designed to overcome domestic political constraints, these initiatives failed to provide a lasting solution to the problem of domestic consensus. The Reagan administration found it difficult to build domestic policy legitimacy for U.S. involvement in El Salvador because their "democratic" process had yielded an "undemocratic" outcome. The Congress would not have accepted unconditional U.S. support for Roberto D'Aubuisson and the ARENA party. At the same time, President Magaña and the government of national unity also lacked democratic credentials because they were created to circumvent the outcome of the 1982 elections. Finally, although congressional pressure stopped the Salvadoran government from dismantling the reforms that members of Congress associated with a more democratic set of policies, it was clear that the government did not share a positive commitment to those values.

---

13. Hinton described ARENA's platform as "simplistic, unsophisticated and demagogic" (NSA:SS 2022, 3/10/82). Immediately after the March election, an embassy cable noted that an "ARENA national unity government could be a disaster. . . . ARENA would physically annihilate the PDC" (NSA:SS 2909, 4/2/82). See (NSA:SS 4970, 6/14/82) for the embassy assessment that ARENA was an unpredictable and destabilizing force in Salvadoran politics.

Congress responded by denying the administration the funds it needed to successfully prosecute the war. On September 10, 1982, both houses voted against the president's $35 million request for military aid in the FY82 supplemental. They also voted to limit the administration's ESF authorization to $75 million, which cut the president's FY82 supplemental by more than half. Two continuing resolutions in late 1982 maintained funding for El Salvador for FY83, but at levels approved for FY82. The $191.2 million approved for FY83 reflected a $77 million drop from final 1982 outlays. The $26 million in military aid reflected the same amount as had been approved by Congress in FY82 (Storrs 1983:62–63).

Thus, as the war against the FMLN was expanding, the amount of U.S. resources being appropriated for the effort remained stagnant. In addition, the administration policies designed to secure greater funding levels from Congress helped create a more tenuous security situation than had existed in mid-1981, when Reagan first introduced his proliberalization policies. The government of national unity was perpetually stalemated. Nearly all Salvadoran political actors considered President Magaña an exceptionally weak chief executive. The military spent as much time in political maneuvers as it did on the battlefield. Consequently, it lost whatever initiative it may have had on the battlefield against the FMLN. Finally, by late 1982 the FMLN had recovered from its election disarray to mount a significant offensive.

Congressional Pressure Overcomes a Resurgent Hard Line

The Reagan administration was split about how to respond to the deteriorating situation in late 1982. Moderates in the State Department wanted to maintain the emphasis on the promotion of democracy, while administration hard-liners wanted to emphasize a more purely military solution to the crisis. Reagan sided with the hard-liners during the first months of 1983. This shift in policy is especially important because it represented the first time the president became actively involved in Central America policy, and thus can be taken as a clear indication of his preferences. The fact that Congress was able to force a shift back toward proliberalization policies in late 1983, even after the president had committed himself fully to nonliberalization policies, demonstrates the strength of the congressional constraint on the president and of the domestic liberal approach over realism in explaining final presidential choices.

In late 1982 Hinton and Enders moved further toward the center of the domestic debate. Their revised approach mixed increased concern for human rights abuses with tentative initiatives to negotiate with the FMLN. On October 29, 1982, Hinton delivered his strongest rebuke to the Salvadoran government for its human rights record in a speech before the American Chamber of Commerce of El Salvador.[14] Then he explicitly threatened a cut-off of American aid if the Salvadorans did not improve their human rights record and prosecute the killers of American citizens (Arnson 1989:99). Hard-line National Security Adviser William Clark (who replaced Allen in early 1982) repudiated Hinton's October speech in a press interview and instructed him to refrain from making public criticisms of human rights abuses (Bonner 1984:359). Despite this bureaucratic opposition, the State Department's January 1983 certification presented its most candid assessment of the human rights situation in El Salvador and criticized its weak judicial system for its inability to prosecute anyone for political murders. At the same time, Enders drafted a proposal for a "two-track" policy in Central America combining military efforts with tentative attempts to reach negotiated settlements in Nicaragua and El Salvador. There was little likelihood that negotiations could lead to accords consonant with Reagan's objectives. Any effort to negotiate, however, would blunt congressional criticisms that Reagan was not interested in a peaceful settlement of the problems of the region.

The consistent support for democracy promotion among State Department professionals in 1981–82 involved more than a response to congressional pressure (Carothers 1991; Sullivan 1995). State Department professionals generally believed proliberalization policies to be useful for achieving America's security interests. They also had parochial bureaucratic interests in emphasizing "political solutions" rather than "military solutions" to the problem in El Salvador. Enders's relationship with Congress was, therefore, somewhat reminiscent of the State Department's relationship with Congress during the Kennedy administration. Just as Hilsman and Lodge had used congressional resolutions to encourage the Diem regime to adopt reforms, Enders suggested that the certification process had proven useful in gaining compliance from Salvadorans on concerns shared by the administration and Congress. Enders and Hinton used the threat of a congressional cut-off of aid to encourage the Salvadoran government to adopt liberal

---

14. Hinton stated, "Is it any wonder that much of the world is predisposed to believe the worst of a system which almost never brings to justice either those who perpetrate these acts or those who order them? The 'Mafia' must be stopped. . . . If you are not convinced that I am talking about a fundamental and critical problem, consider these facts. Since 1979, perhaps as many as 30,000 Salvadorans have been MURDERED, not killed in battle, MURDERED" (State 1983:1480) (emphasis in original). The official document cited here actually replaced the word MURDERED, used in the speech, with the less harsh phrase "illegally killed" (Arnson 1989:99).

reforms (Carothers 1991:25; Sullivan 1995:158–97). As Elliot Abrams, assistant secretary of state for human rights from 1981 to 1984, put it, Congress allowed the State Department "to play good cop, bad cop," both with the Salvadoran armed forces and with hard-liners within the Reagan administration (Sullivan 1995:195–96).

Enders and Hinton were in a much more vulnerable situation than Harriman, Hilsman, and Lodge had been in 1963, however. The State Department's advocates for liberal reform in Vietnam represented the president while Congress played a clearly subordinate and supportive role. In 1981–82 Enders and Hinton did not represent the perspective of the president. They were isolated from the centers of power within the Reagan administration and advocated policies that Reagan's principal advisers thought foolish. Indeed, all of the top officials in the Bureau of Inter-American Affairs had received their positions because Reagan hard-liners had successfully purged their predecessors because of their support for liberal reforms. The State Department needed allies in Congress to compensate for its weakness within the administration. Partisan differences between a Democrat-controlled House and the Republican administration and real ideological differences between congressional liberal internationalists and State Department pragmatic moderates placed significant limits on the explicit cooperation between the two. Thus, it was not a contrived and controlled threat of congressional action which strengthened the State Department's hand, as in 1963; it was a real threat of congressional opposition to Reagan policy that could be reduced only through the genuine adoption of proliberalization policies.

The strength of the congressional threat became clear in 1983. Reagan administration hard-liners like Kirkpatrick, Casey, and Clark battled the State Department because they favored a return to the Cold War themes that had dominated administration policy in early 1981. When Enders made his two-track proposal, the hard-liners condemned it, just as Clark had condemned Hinton's speech. They opposed negotiations with communists because they could never be trusted to negotiate in good faith. Moreover, the thrust of Reagan policy was to defeat communism, not compromise with it. In 1983 hard-liners believed they could roll back communism in Nicaragua (Menges 1988:106–9). They saw no reason to allow communists to "shoot their way into power" in El Salvador (State 1984:1279, 1288). Enders's two-track policy provided the ammunition to have him and Hinton removed from their posts. As Secretary of State George Shultz, who replaced Haig in mid-1982, described the situation, "State [was] not in control of Central American policy. The president was on the hard-line track. . . . Clark was calling the shots in Central America" (Shultz 1993:315–16).

Administration hard-liners won this bureaucratic battle because the president agreed with them. Until this point, Reagan had been preoccupied with the passage of the three central items on his agenda: tax cuts, cuts in domestic spending, and an increase in defense spending. Jeane Kirkpatrick was instrumental in creating the crisis atmosphere necessary to get the president involved in Central America policy (Arnson 1989:111–12). She returned from twelve days of travel in Central America in February 1983 convinced that communist forces were ascendant and would triumph unless the United States drastically increased its involvement in and aid to the region. Weinberger, Casey, and Clark reinforced this message and Reagan agreed to go on the offensive.

In a March 10, 1983, speech, Reagan outlined the renewed hard-line stance, describing the Salvadoran conflict in global terms as a war against Soviet communism:

> The problem is that an aggressive minority has thrown in its lot with the Communists, looking to the Soviets and their own Cuban henchmen to help them pursue political change through violence. . . . Soviet military theorists want to destroy our capacity to resupply Western Europe in case of an emergency. They want to tie down our attention and forces on our own southern border and so limit our capacity to act in more distant places. . . . [A]n important part [of the problem] is external: the availability of training, tactical guidance, and military supplies coming into El Salvador from Marxist Nicaragua . . . much more critical to guerrilla operations are the supplies and munitions that are infiltrated into El Salvador by land, sea and air; by pack mules, by small boats, and by small aircraft. These pipelines fuel the guerrilla offensives and keep alive the conviction of their extremist leaders that power will eventually come from the barrels of their guns. (State 1984:1286–87)

This speech marked a return to an unambiguous military strategy to defeat the FMLN. As Undersecretary of Defense Fred Ikle later emphasized in a September 1983 speech, "We can no more negotiate an acceptable political solution with these people (the FDR-FMLN) than the Social Democrats in revolutionary Russia could have talked Lenin into giving up totalitarian Bolshevism. . . . You have to defeat these 'rule or ruin' forces militarily" (Defense 1983). At this time, Reagan called for a vast increase in U.S. military aid to El Salvador. He asked for the immediate allocation of $110 million in military aid; $60 million to be reprogrammed from funds already appropriated for FY83 and $50 million to be added to the FY83 supplemental appropriations bill. Reagan also announced his request for $86.3 million in military aid for FY84 (NSA:NSC 3/10/83; Storrs 1984:30).[15] These were not merely sums inflated to reach an acceptable compromise with Congress. The administration deemed this package the absolute minimum needed to regain the military initiative (NSA:SS 4411, 5/26/82).

The renewed hard line for El Salvador was matched by a more hard-line approach to dealing with Congress. Administration officials alluded that their opponents were serving the interests of the communists.[16] Reagan created an Office of Public Diplomacy to fight and win the propaganda war against domestic opponents of his policies (NSA:ST 1/93). Although it was placed in the State Department, State officials viewed Otto Reich's OPD as "filled with right-wingers. His staff came from the DOD, CIA and NSC" (Sullivan 1995:174). On April 27, 1983, Reagan spoke before a joint session of the Congress in an attempt to compel it to approve his military aid plan for Central America. He brandished the threat that congressional opponents of his policies would be blamed for the fall of countries to communism.[17] According to Luigi Einaudi:

> Congressional attitudes were a source of major problems within the administration. . . . I would draw the line between one school that believed that congressional restrictions, attitudes and the values they reflected were serious and legitimate parts of the American political system, and any valid policy had to work within them; and opposed to that school of thought were those who thought that those restrictions . . . were typical of what was leading to national failure and the decline in our foreign policy. And therefore instead of being lived with and agreed to, Congress had to be forced to accept its role as a "communist agent." (Arnson 1989:69)

15. Reagan also planned to reprogram $67.1 million in ESF and development assistance funds, raising the total request for economic aid to El Salvador in FY83 to $227.1 million. The request for FY84 was $190 million.

16. In congressional testimony, Shultz denounced U.S. Catholic opponents of Reagan policy as "churchmen who want to see Soviet influence in El Salvador improved." Kirkpatrick launched a similar attack on the patriotism of House Democrats, claiming that "there are people in the U.S. Congress . . . who would actually like to see the Marxist forces take power in [El Salvador]" (Arnson 1989: 115–17).

17. The president concluded his speech by claiming, "The national security of all the Americas is at stake in Central America. If we cannot defend ourselves there, we cannot expect to prevail elsewhere. Our credibility would collapse, our alliances would crumble, and the safety of our homeland would be in jeopardy. We have a vital interest, a moral duty, and a solemn responsibility. . . . It is a duty that falls on all of us—the President, the Congress, and the people. We must perform it together. Who among us would wish to bear responsibility for failing to meet our shared obligation?" (State 1984:1320).

By the end of 1983, however, Reagan had moved away from this hard-line position toward a more comprehensive set of proliberalization policies. In 1983 Reagan's commitment to free and fair elections for the Salvadoran presidency in March 1984 was linked to clear support for Duarte and the PDC. Reagan coupled this electoral initiative with its first significant effort to limit human rights abuses by the government of El Salvador.

Congress Forces the Shift to Proliberalization Policies

The dynamics of the 1983 return to proliberalization policies approximated the dynamics of the first shift. Hard-line rhetoric led to domestic opposition and slashed appropriations, which led to proliberalization policies. In the 1983 shift, the magnitude and comprehensiveness of the administration's switch were greater because Congress threatened, for the first time, to place significant constraints on the Reagan administration.

The administration considered this congressional threat especially dangerous, given that late 1983 witnessed a dramatic increase in the strength of the FMLN and a weakening of Salvadoran government forces. By the end of 1983 the insurgents controlled approximately one-third of the nation's territory. They had reached sufficient military strength to attack units of the Salvadoran military in conventional battles rather than with guerrilla tactics. As in the first shift in policy, however, the military problem was interpreted as one of lack of resources rather than of inappropriate strategy. Change was necessary to get congressional funding. As a December 1983 confidential State Department briefing paper stated:

> Central to any long-term effort to end the stalemate of alternating government and guerrilla offensives will be increased U.S. military assistance. Uncertainty over U.S. support is a demoralizing factor, and the recent congressional cut reinforced ESAF concerns. Our Embassy and SOUTHCOM estimate that a total of $360–370 million is needed in fiscal years 1984 and 1985 if the stalemate is to end. Human rights violations have hurt our efforts to obtain this level of assistance. (NSA:ST 12/2/83)

The harsh attacks launched by the Reagan administration during early 1983 failed to coerce the Congress into voting for the administration's aid requests. In fact, the renewed hard line led to some of the sharpest congressional attacks on Reagan policy to that date. As in 1981, the strongest attacks came from the Foreign Operations Subcommittee and the Foreign

Affairs Committee in the Democrat-controlled House. For the members of these committees, partisan dynamics reinforced ideological commitments to produce a strong reaction to administration policy.

In March 1983 Foreign Operations voted to approve only half of the administration's $60 million reprogramming request for 1983. In May, Foreign Affairs reported out a foreign aid authorizations bill that cut deeply into the administration's requests through the year 1985 and contained the strictest conditions yet on that aid. U.S. military advisers would be legally limited to fifty-five. The president would not be allowed to use his emergency authority to transfer aid to El Salvador as he had in 1982. All aid would be suspended unless the Salvadoran government entered into unconditional negotiations with the FMLN within ninety days of the enactment of the legislation. In addition to regular certifications, the president would be forced to submit a plan on how the United States would push for progress on the agrarian reform, prosecution of the murderers of U.S. citizens, human rights violations, and negotiations. The committee voted to give Congress veto power over the administration's certification. If Congress disagreed with the president's certification, it could halt all aid to El Salvador (Storrs 1984:32–34).

As in 1981, Foreign Relations took a strong stance, suggesting the independent impact of ideology in shaping the congressional reaction to Reagan policy. The committee concurred in the Foreign Operations Subcommittee's decision to cut Reagan's reprogramming request in half. It voted to place significant constraints on administration policy, although its proposals were not as restrictive as those approved in the House and did not include a legislative veto of administration certifications (Storrs 1984:34–35).

Because the conservative, Republican-dominated Senate Appropriations Committee supported the president on all votes, this had a moderating impact on the final outcome. Nevertheless, spurred on by a resurgent Central America movement, Congress cut the administration's requests for 1983 by half and his requests for 1984 by one-third. The president received $30 million of his $60 million request for reprogrammed 1983 funds. His $50 million supplementary request was cut to $25 million. Finally, $64.8 million of the president's $86.3 million request was approved for 1984 (Storrs 1984:40–43, 60). Thirty percent of the military aid for 1984 was withheld pending a decision in the trial of the murders of the American churchwomen.

By mid-1983, Reagan's renewed hard-line project for El Salvador had run into serious trouble in Congress and the White House had to relearn the lesson that the State Department had learned in 1981–82. Some kind of credible proliberalization policy was necessary to build sufficient support in Congress for intervention in El Salvador. Bringing the president to the forefront of administration policy in early 1983 allowed hard-liners to pursue a more straightforward military policy to defeat the FMLN. Yet, even Reagan could not overcome the domestic political barriers to adopting this set of policies. The fact that even the president and his hard-line advisers were compelled to revert to proliberalization policies suggests that it was the need to build domestic political consensus rather than the realist calculations of specific policymakers that compelled the Reagan administration to adopt proliberalization policies in 1983.

The 1983 Move to More Comprehensive Proliberalization Policies

As in 1981, the shift to a more pro-democratic strategy began with a commitment to the electoral process in El Salvador. In May 1983, in accord with congressional demands, Reagan appointed former Senator Richard Stone as special presidential envoy to the region. Stone's first initiative was to ask the Salvadoran Central Elections Council to move up the timetable for their presidential elections, from March 1984 to December 1983, suggesting that, according to CCE member Ricardo Meza, "if you do the elections this year, we will give you all the money you need" (Karl 1986:25). President Magaña agreed to move the elections, but logistical problems made it impossible to change the date (NSA:ST 143245, 2/17/83).

After having raised the political stakes so high in early 1983, support for free and fair elections would not be sufficient to garner the necessary congressional approval of Reagan policy. The U.S. embassy placed its full support behind the candidacy of Duarte and the Christian Democrats. As one unnamed State Department official stated, "Everyone in the Embassy knew that if Duarte didn't win, that would be the end of Reagan's policy in El Salvador"; Congress would not support a D'Aubuisson presidency (Arnson 1989:149). Having learned from the 1982 elections, the embassy helped make sure that the PDC would win by funneling millions of dollars into the PDC campaign (Karl 1986:25). The Agency for International Development also provided several million dollars to labor unions and *campesino* unions supportive of Duarte's candidacy. Additional funds were given to the PCN in an effort to drain right-wing support from the ARENA party and its candidate, D'Aubuisson.

By placing its support firmly behind Duarte, the administration, at least temporarily, committed itself to his statist and reformist economic program. In preparation for the upcoming elections, Duarte signed a social pact with popular organizations and unions in San Salvador promising social reforms to benefit these constituencies that were reemerging after years of repression (Karl 1986:27–28). By embracing Duarte's candidacy, Reagan was forced to tolerate his social program and constituents, even though he thought the economic programs of questionable wisdom and the popular organizations of questionable loyalty.

Two months before the March 1984 elections, the Reagan administration released the report of the Kissinger Commission, formed in July 1983 at the height of the administration's problems with Congress. The Commission proclaimed that there was "no room for partisanship" and called for support for democracy and reforms in the region in combination with counterinsurgency programs to stop the left (Kissinger 1984). The report prominently proclaimed that, "We have a national interest in strengthening democratic institutions wherever in the hemisphere they are weak" (Kissinger 1984:5). In accordance with existing practice, the report called for vast increases in military and economic aid for El Salvador, with continued conditions on that aid.

The most critical credibility problem facing the administration, however, was the increase in death squad activity in El Salvador during the second half of 1983 and the increased targeting of America's allies in the PDC. In November 1983 the Reagan administration made its first serious effort to control the violence of the Salvadoran military. Fred Ikle and Elliot Abrams delivered the message that the Salvadoran military would have to clean up its human rights record in confidential visits to El Salvador on November 7–8, 1983. The new ambassador to El Salvador, Thomas Pickering, earned a death threat by delivering a public condemnation of the human rights record of the military in a speech before the American Chamber of Commerce on November 25 (State 1984:1379–84). The speech resembled the remarks made by Deane Hinton a year earlier to the same group, but Washington's support for Pickering's speech suggested that the Reagan administration was more serious about the human rights issue than in 1982. On December 11, 1983, Vice President George Bush visited San Salvador to present the harshest demand for a reduction in human rights violations ever delivered by the Reagan administration, stating in his official toast, "Your cause is being undermined by the murderous violence of reactionary minorities. . . . These cowardly death squad terrorists are just as repugnant to me, to President Reagan, to the Congress and to the American people as the terrorists of the left. . . . If these death squad murders continue, you will lose the support of the American people" (State 1984:1389). In private meetings earlier in the day, Bush demanded the removal of several military officers associated with death squad activity and promised a substantial increase in military aid if the armed forces complied with U.S. demands. Even William Casey traveled to San Salvador to reinforce this message (Woodward 1987:291).

The Reagan administration's support for elections, the PDC, and reductions in human rights abuses did not immediately result in positive congressional action. In early 1984 lawmakers were reluctant to accept that the administration had turned over a new leaf. While the administration had made significant strides toward meeting congressional concerns, it also sent conflicting signals. In November 1983 Reagan vetoed Congress' certification requirement. In March 1984, in a maneuver that infuriated many in the House, Reagan attached $93 million in emergency aid for El Salvador to an African famine relief bill that had already passed in the House and was under consideration in the friendlier Senate. When the House postponed consideration of the Senate bill, Reagan lashed out at members of Congress, who acted as if "their only task is to be vocal critics, and not responsible partners. . . . Either we help America's friends defend themselves and give democracy a chance or we abandon our responsibilities and let the Soviet Union and Cuba shape the destiny of our hemisphere." Dante Fascell (D-Fla.), chair of the House Foreign Affairs Committee, responded by saying, "It's difficult to get bipartisan foreign policy if you're reaching out with one hand and punching with the other" (Arnson 1989:148). The House did not take action on the bill. During Congress' Easter recess, Reagan invoked emergency powers to send $32 million. All of these actions contributed to congressional pessimism.

Congressional opposition to aid for El Salvador evaporated, however, when Duarte emerged victorious in the May 1984 runoff election against D'Aubuisson and became president of El Salvador. On May 10, 1984, the House voted to approve the president's aid requests for El Salvador in their entirety, without conditions, instead of a more restrictive bill offered by Fascell (Harper 1985:25–28). During 1984, Congress approved all $110 million in development assistance asked for by the administration in its 1984 supplemental bill and regular FY85 appropriation bill. It also approved all but $15 million of the administration's $300 million in requests for economic support funds. Finally, Congress also approved $198.25 million in military assistance for 1984–85 (Harper 1985:23). Congressional opposition to U.S. policy in El Salvador would remain muted for the remainder of Reagan's presidency.

House Majority Leader Jim Wright was a critical player in turning Duarte's victory into congressional acquiescence. Wright had headed the election observer team to El Salvador and backed unconditional aid in an emotional speech before the House: "This is an agonizing moment for me. And yet, I feel so very strongly that I am impelled to speak out. . . .

We need steady, emphatic commitment to freedom in El Salvador—not a tenuous, tentative, hesitant or begrudging commitment. . . . I have seen this country of El Salvador go through the travail and birth pangs of a democracy. Let us not let that democracy be stillborn or die in its infancy" (Congress 1984:3740). This was an "agonizing" decision for Wright because a vote for unconditional aid meant a vote by the Democratic majority leader for the Republican-sponsored aid package. On the face of it, Wright's position appears to argue for the preeminence of ideological rather than partisan motivations for the support of proliberalization policies. Thus, Congress supported administration policy because democratic elections had produced what members of Congress considered a democratic outcome. "Before 1984, Duarte was seen as a tool of the Colonels. Then he became a major democratic figure, a hero of democracy in the region," according to Representative Michael Barnes (Arnson 1989:143). Duarte's announced program addressed all of the major concerns of members of Congress and they felt compelled to "give Duarte a chance." The most liberal members of Congress continued to doubt whether Duarte's election represented a true movement toward democracy, but a majority of the Congress joined Wright in accepting Duarte's democratic credentials. In addition, with the substantial increase in U.S. military assistance, the Salvadoran military was able to make significant headway against the insurgency in the short term. This eased members' fear that El Salvador would become another Vietnam.

The quiescence of Congress in the wake of Duarte's election also reflected partisan considerations, however. As long as the Reagan administration appeared to be both unconcerned with the pursuit of basic American values in El Salvador and on the verge of getting the United States involved in a war in Central America, the Democrats had an issue that they could use to partisan advantage. The Reagan administration's subsequent support for Duarte appeared to answer these partisan attacks. If the Democrats then opposed the Duarte initiative, they could be in danger of similar partisan attacks from the Republican side of the aisle. Because Duarte reflected a centrist compromise, U.S. policy toward El Salvador became a useless vehicle for partisan politics. It would subsequently play no role in the 1984 American elections for precisely this reason.

Conclusion

As in Cuba at the beginning of the twentieth century, a Republican president, Ronald Reagan, was compelled to shift to proliberalization policies in El

Salvador in order to convince Congress to support his intervention. As in 1898, partisan considerations were important in the shaping of Congress' reaction to administration policy. The strongest opposition to Reagan policy in El Salvador consistently came from the Democrat-controlled House, which used liberal attacks to partisan advantage against a Republican president. As before, liberal Republicans reconciled conflicting ideological and partisan loyalties by working with the administration to shape a workable pro-democratic compromise.

Different tools were used during the two eras, however. In 1898 Congress used an amendment to the declaration of war against Spain. In contrast, Congress hindered Reagan's hard-line policies in two important ways: through cuts in the appropriations desired by the administration and through the placement of human rights conditions on the provision of that aid. Another important difference divides these two cases. In 1898 partisan considerations were overwhelmingly important in determining the outcome. In the Salvadoran case, the liberal ideology of members of Congress played a more significant role. This is not surprising, given that the Congress of the 1980s was institutionally structured to give more authority to committees and subcommittees than was the case at the turn of the century. This allowed ideologically committed minorities to use their positions of strength to launch principled attacks against the Reagan administration for its support of the repressive government of El Salvador.

In any event, the Salvadoran case supports the domestic liberal argument that when a president adopts proliberalization policies in response to congressional pressure, he does so to build domestic policy legitimacy and domestic consensus for policies of intervention. Reagan's experience in El Salvador demonstrated the increasing importance of Congress in constraining presidential interventions in the post–Vietnam era. The United States behaved more like a liberal state in the early 1980s than had been the case twenty years before.

Reagan learned from the Salvadoran experience that the promotion of democracy could provide a powerful ideological tool for building domestic support for an aggressive foreign policy. Soon after, even Reagan hardliners embraced proliberalization policies for the other countries in Central America in order to highlight the "totalitarian" character of Sandinista Nicaragua. Then the Reagan administration supported the removal of its close autocratic allies in the Philippines and Chile and elsewhere in favor of new democratic regimes. Thus, Reagan's experience in El Salvador began the fundamental shift in his policy that culminated in a consistent support for democracy during his second term. Indeed, Reagan subsequently placed democracy promotion at the center of his foreign policy agenda (Carothers 1991; Smith 1994). This shift began well before the demise of the "evil empire," suggesting that the domestic liberal argument provides a better explanation of the Reagan cases than does realism. Reagan's embrace of the promotion of democracy set the stage for the more complete embrace of the promotion of democracy by the Bush and Clinton administrations in the post–Cold War era.

6

Democratic Enlargement in Haiti and Bosnia

In 1993 Bill Clinton proclaimed that "our overriding purpose must be to expand and strengthen the world's community of market-based democracies" (Clinton 1993b:650). In 1994 Clinton tried to implant democracy during a military intervention in the Western Hemisphere's most infertile soil— Haiti. In 1995 Clinton chose an even more forbidding context to practice "democratic enlargement" when he pushed for free and fair elections in Bosnia to bring together people who had spent the previous three years "cleansing" one another from their communities.

Once he intervened, Clinton consistently pursued proliberalization policies, including support for free and fair elections, attempts to moderate local political parties and/or encourage the formation of new centrist parties, and efforts to strengthen democratic institutions in civil society. In both countries, law enforcement responsibilities were taken away from the armed forces and placed in the hands of newly created or enhanced civilian police forces trained and funded by the United States and United Nations. In Bosnia, Clinton made significant efforts to professionalize the local armed forces to reduce their human rights abuses and stop ethnic cleansing. In Haiti the United States helped dismantle a military institution that had been one of the principal obstacles to democracy.

Clinton initially showed extreme reluctance to intervene, however. And once he intervened, his consistent emphasis on proliberalization policies was tempered by an equally consistent timidity. Indeed, his administration has been justly criticized for its vacillating, ineffective, and indecisive use of force abroad. Clinton did not send troops to Haiti until he was relatively certain that those troops would not face combat. Once in place, those troops proved reluctant to dismantle the Haitian armed forces or disarm right-wing death squads. In Bosnia, Clinton constantly promised to launch air strikes against the Bosnian Serbs between 1993 and 1995, only to back off at the last minute, damaging U.S. prestige and the credibility of American commitments. In their implementation of the Dayton Accords, U.S.-led NATO troops made little effort to apprehend war criminals or assist in the repatriation of the victims of ethnic cleansing.

What explains this pattern of behavior? This chapter argues that the present era is the most conducive to the adoption of proliberalization policies in the history of the United States. Realist conditions are extremely favorable for the pursuit of liberal reforms. The end of the Cold War removed the principal international threat to the United States in the global balance of power, opening up new opportunities for the adoption of proliberalization policies. While domestic conditions make countries like Haiti and Bosnia unlikely candidates for successful democratization, their internal conditions allow U.S. policymakers to experiment with liberal reforms with limited risk. Most important, Haiti had not been subject to an ongoing civil war, and the United States did not intervene in Bosnia until the parties in that civil war had agreed to a peace accord.

The Clinton cases also exhibit the conditions most likely to lead to the promotion of democracy according to the domestic liberal argument. These interventions were undertaken by a Democratic administration predisposed to the adoption of proliberalization policies that nevertheless also experienced constant liberal appeals from Congress. In Haiti, liberal internationalists and the black congressional caucus led the chorus for an intervention to reinstate the first democratically elected president in Haitian history, Jean Bertrand Aristide. In Bosnia, congressional liberals were joined by Republicans who used liberal arguments to attack the president's policy, thus ensuring that Clinton would remain committed to the promotion of democracy. The domestic liberal argument also accounts for Clinton's reluctance to intervene initially or to take dramatic measures to disarm right-wing paramilitary forces in either country. Republican institutions of government not only encourage liberal states to pursue liberal goals during their interventions, it also makes them hesitant to pay the potentially high costs associated with efforts to promote those goals.

The Initial Adoption of Proliberalization Policies

The Restoration of Aristide in Haiti

On September 15, 1994, President Clinton announced that "in July, the United Nations Security Council approved a resolution that authorizes the use of all necessary means, including force, to remove the Haitian dictators from power and restore a democratic government. . . . In the face of this continued defiance and with atrocities rising, the United States has agreed to lead a multinational force to carry out the will of the United Nations" (Clinton 1994a:606). The U.S. occupation force that landed in Haiti several days later, therefore, restored Aristide to the presidency that had been stolen from him in a 1991 military coup. General Raoul Cédras, the leader of the junta that had deposed Aristide, was flown to exile in Panama. The United States thus intervened to restore a radical leftist priest and leader of a potentially revolutionary social movement to the presidency of Haiti. No case better illustrates the opportunities available for the promotion of democracy in the post–Cold War security environment. During the Cold War, the United States was more likely to use force to overthrow such leaders rather than support them, as with its covert interventions to depose leftist elected leaders in Guatemala and Chile.

The promotion of free and fair elections was at the core of U.S. political strategy in Haiti. The occupation force began by supervising parliamentary and municipal elections in June and September 1995. In December 1995 Haitians chose a new president, electing Aristide's 1991 prime minister, René Préval, with 88 percent of the vote. In February 1996 one freely elected president replaced another for the first time in Haitian history. In all, U.S. and U.N. officials supervised six rounds of elections, with a large cadre of international observers verifying the free and fair character of each contest. Given Haiti's almost complete lack of democratic institutions and financial resources, international actors were forced to create this new electoral system virtually from scratch while paying nearly the entire cost.

While the United States did not make significant efforts to create new centrist political parties in Haiti, policymakers did try to moderate the stance of President Aristide's Lavalas movement. Before committing itself to intervene in Haiti, the Clinton administration extracted important concessions from Aristide. The Haitian president agreed to step down at the end of his regular term in favor of an elected successor, despite the fact that three years of that term had been spent in exile. He also agreed to make national reconciliation, including an amnesty for coup participants and human rights abusers, the central theme of his remaining time in office. Finally, the Americans pushed Aristide to abandon his radical economic program in favor of an IMF, World Bank, and AID-sponsored commitment to sound money, limited government intervention in the economy, and free trade. American policymakers argued that such a program would both rejuvenate the moribund Haitian economy and build ties between Aristide and the Haitian business elite (Robinson 1996; Dupuy 1997:140–52). To signify his acceptance of this track, Aristide selected the neoliberal economist Smarck Michel as prime minister.

The Clinton administration did not make a clear commitment to the demilitarization of Haiti's armed forces as part of its initial proliberalization policies. Two days after his announcement that war was imminent, Clinton sent former President Jimmy Carter, former Chair of the Joint Chiefs of Staff Colin Powell, and Senator Sam Nunn (D-Ga.) to Haiti in a final diplomatic initiative. "Their mission is to make one last best effort to provide a peaceful, orderly transfer of power, to minimize the loss of life and to maximize the chances of security for all Haitians, and of course, for our own troops in the coalition force" (Clinton 1994b:611).

This mission, backed by a credible threat to use force, succeeded. General Cédras "invited" U.S. troops into Haiti just as the first contingents of the invasion force had become airborne. An important consequence of this permissive occupation was that U.S. troops landed in Haiti as allies of the military that had caused the political and humanitarian crisis in the first place. Only the decision of Haitian troops to fire indiscriminately on civilians celebrating the intervention led to an expansion of the U.S. mission to include disarming the Haitian military. Even at that point the occupation force did not seek to dismantle completely the Haitian armed forces, only to reduce its size, professionalize its conduct, and place police duties into the hands of a new civilian police force funded and trained by the United States and the United Nations. Within a year, however, the Haitian army was formally disbanded. This occurred mostly because of the internal disintegration of the army and the astute political maneuvering of President Aristide in hastening this process. Nevertheless, the United States did acquiesce in and to some extent facilitate this demilitarization process.

The United States consistently pursued a deeper and more comprehensive set of proliberalization policies during its intervention in Haiti than was true of most previous interventions. Throughout the occupation, however, U.S. forces avoided disarming the right-wing elements (many of them demobilized soldiers) who continue to pose a threat to Haitian democracy. The Clinton administration also failed to provide sufficient funds for the ambitious programs of institution building and economic development envisioned by occupation authorities. The United States's desire to retain the Haitian armed forces can be explained in part as a legacy of its traditional realist-inspired strategy of protecting its security interests by forging ties with local militaries. More broadly, however, America's consistent support for democracy in Haiti was marred most by a reluctance to pay the high costs in money and casualties that might be necessary for the success of those proliberalization policies. This is precisely the kind of contradictory behavior anticipated by the domestic liberal argument.

Democracy and the Dayton Accords in Bosnia

The Dayton Accords, signed on November 21, 1995, at Wright-Patterson Air Force Base, provided a blueprint for the subsequent U.S.-led multilateral intervention in Bosnia. Twenty-thousand U.S. troops would lead a 60,000-strong NATO Implementation Force (IFOR) to separate the combatants and patrol the boundary lines between the Muslim-Croat Bosnian Federation and the Srpska Republika of the Bosnian Serbs. Arms control agreements would then equalize the military balance among Serbia, Croatia, and Bosnia, and between the combatants within Bosnia.

The promotion of democracy played a central role in the political strategy of the intervention. As Secretary of State Warren Christopher stated at the signing ceremony, "the agreement is a victory for all of those who believe in a multi-ethnic democracy in Bosnia-Herzegovina" (Christopher 1995). Over the long term, Clinton policymakers saw the creation of a federal republic as the only way to resolve the ethnic hatreds that had brought about the war in the Balkans. Maintenance of the territorial and political integrity of Bosnia would deny victory to the practitioners of ethnic cleansing, while maximum autonomy for the ethnic enclaves would safeguard each community from domination by the others. The constitution agreed upon at Dayton, therefore, separated Bosnia into two entities loosely unified by a weak federal government based in Sarajevo. In what Assistant Secretary of State Richard Holbrooke, principal architect of the Dayton Accords, later described as "the biggest contradiction within the agreements," "national" defense was entrusted to the entities rather than the federal government (Congress 1997b:118). Equal representation of each ethnic group would be mandated in each house of the new parliament and in a three-part collective presidency.

The new constitution enshrined a wide variety of human rights in its text in hopes that protection of individual rights would diminish fears of repression based on religious or ethnic identity. The accords called for the creation of a Human Rights Commission and ombudsman to be controlled by representatives of the Organization of Security and Cooperation in Europe (OSCE). They reaffirmed the parties' commitment to the International War Crimes Tribunal at The Hague and barred indicted war criminals from political office.

International sponsorship of "free, fair, and democratic elections" were crucial for "lay[ing] the foundation for representative government and ensur[ing] the progressive achievement of democratic goals throughout Bosnia and Herzegovina," according to the elections annex of the Dayton Accords (State 1995). The elections, scheduled for September 14, 1996, were the linchpin of the entire political project. As the State Department's William Montgomery noted, "there is absolutely no channel of regular communication between the two entities. . . . There is no regular Parliament or assembly of all the Bosnians. There is no joint Presidency. None of the organizations that were specified by Dayton now exist. They will be created by the elections. Until those elections are held, it is favoring the separatists because there is a growing division between these two entities that only establishing these overreaching government entities will help start to overcome" (Congress 1996b:104–5).

A provisional election commission led by the American head of the OSCE Mission, Robert Frowick, supervised all preparations for the September elections. The commission was charged with: "(a) supervising all aspects of the electoral process to ensure that the structures and institutional framework for free and fair elections are in place; (b) determining voter registration provisions; (c) ensuring compliance with the electoral rules and regulations . . . ; (d) ensuring that action is taken to remedy any violation of any provision of this Agreement . . . including imposing penalties . . . ; and (e) accrediting observers, including personnel from international organizations and foreign and domestic nongovernmental organizations, and ensuring that the Parties grant accredited observers unimpeded access and movement" (State 1995). The elections could not proceed without an OSCE certification that the parties had complied fully with that organization's 1990 Copenhagen Document, which sets standards for free and fair elections.

Policymakers hoped to overcome the threat that the Dayton Accords could lead to ethnic partition by strengthening multiethnic political institutions. The accords contained a provision allowing those who had been evicted from their homes by ethnic cleansing to vote by absentee ballot in the district in which they were registered in 1991. This provision was designed to counteract the effects of ethnic cleansing by encouraging people to use their absentee votes against the extremists that had evicted them. After the elections, Deputy Assistant Secretary of State John Kornblum noted with satisfaction: "The Muslim party will have a substantial bloc of seats in the parliament of Republika Srpska. These were, I'm sure, based mostly on refugee votes. But it shows that the process did, in fact, work; that those people who had been 'cleansed' out of their homes were allowed to vote and did, in fact, elect a good number of seats in the Republika Srpska parliament" (Congress 1997b:98). U.S. policymakers also worked to enhance the electoral fortunes of truly multiethnic parties, former Prime Minister Haris Silajdzic's party foremost among them. In the face of the general expectation that extremist nationalist parties would sweep the September elections, U.S. policymakers held out hope that Silajdzic would win in the Bosnian-Croat Federation. At least one USIA poll in mid-1996 showed Silajdzic and incumbent President Alija Izetbegovic in a dead heat for the Bosnian presidency (Congress 1996b:6). When Silajdzic's party won only 20 percent of the vote, after being repeatedly harassed during the campaign, administration officials still trumpeted this result as a sign of budding pluralism in Bosnia.

In contrast to the Haitian case, the Clinton administration was intent upon strengthening the Bosnian armed forces rather than dismantling them. The arms control agreement in the Dayton Accords called for dismantling part of the arsenal of the Bosnian Serbs. At the same time, it called for increasing the number of heavy weapons controlled by the Bosnian-Croat Federation so that it could deter future attacks by the better-armed Serbs, a strategy consistent with realist balance of power politics. The United States, therefore, planned a $100 million "equip and train" program for the Bosnian army, over the objections of America's European allies. In keeping with the administration's emphasis on proliberalization policies, Clinton sought to professionalize those armed forces and place police functions into the hands of a civilian police force trained, funded, and supervised by a U.N. international police task force (IPTF).

As in the Haitian case, America's consistent support for proliberalization policies was limited most by its reluctance to pay the costs necessary to ensure the success of these policies. Only in July 1997 did NATO troops try to apprehend individuals indicted by the War Crimes Tribunal. For the most part, NATO avoided crossing the paths of indicted war criminals in hopes that they would not have to take the risks associated with bringing them to justice. Radovan Karadzic and Ratko Mladic have continued to control the Bosnian Serb Republic behind the scenes despite their June 1996 agreement to relinquish their posts as president and army commander and leave the public scene. Under their leadership, the Bosnian Serb Republic has systematically refused to participate in Bosnia-wide political and economic institutions and has avoided compliance with the arms control initiatives included in the Dayton Accords. Very few Bosnian refugees have been able to return to their homes in the enclaves controlled by other ethnic groups because NATO forces have proven extremely reluctant to protect returning refugees.

In both Haiti and Bosnia the adoption and maintenance of proliberalization policies reflected Clinton's commitment to the promotion of democracy during the 1992 election, the opportunities provided by a permissive international environment and the liberal attacks from Congress before and during each intervention. The next section addresses how the 1992 elections shaped Clinton's commitment to the promotion of democracy. Subsequent sections examine the importance of security considerations and congressional pressure on Clinton policy.

The 1992 Elections and Democratic Enlargement

Bill Clinton embraced the promotion of democracy abroad in part to gain the Democratic nomination in 1992, as expected by the domestic liberal argument. Most of his principal rivals for the nomination possessed stronger liberal internationalist foreign policy credentials. Tom Harkin (D-Iowa) won election to the House of Representatives in 1974 on an anti–Vietnam War platform. In his first term, Harkin authored landmark human rights legislation. Senator Bob Kerrey (D-Neb.) had been a leader of Vietnam veterans opposed to the war. Even though Paul Tsongas campaigned as a fiscal conservative, he was a strong supporter of human rights legislation while a member of the Senate Foreign Relations Committee. After his victory in the New Hampshire primary, Tsongas had briefly been Clinton's principal opponent for the Democratic nomination. In contrast, as the governor of a small southern state, Bill Clinton was handicapped by his comparative lack of foreign policy experience and liberal internationalist credentials.

By embracing the promotion of democracy, Clinton joined the liberal internationalist consensus in his party and avoided alienating potential allies in the fight for the nomination by shifting too far from the mainstream of the party. There was, therefore, very little debate between these candidates on foreign policy issues because they shared a broad consensus that U.S. policy should reflect a greater emphasis on human rights and democracy than had been present in the Bush administration. Clinton's commitment to liberal internationalist ideas was less important for his nomination by the Democratic Party, however, than was true of Kennedy in 1960. All of the candidates in the 1992 campaign for the Democratic nomination agreed that domestic issues and the health of the U.S. economy should take precedence over foreign policy issues. Clinton's strategy to win the nomination focused on how his "New Democrat" policies would make him more electable in November than traditional liberals, like Tom Harkin, while remaining true to the central ideals of the Democratic Party. Clinton's opponents, in contrast, hoped in vain that character issues, such as charges of marital infidelity, financial irregularities, draft dodging, and pot smoking would upend Clinton's candidacy.

During the general election campaign, Clinton emphasized domestic rather than foreign policy. He attacked Bush as a foreign policy president unconcerned with the domestic economic hardships suffered by many Americans. Clinton took advantage of the less threatening post–Cold War environment to focus on domestic needs. At the same time, he did not want to cede foreign policy completely to the incumbent. Therefore, Clinton emphasized the liberal argument more in the general election campaign than in the primaries, because it allowed him to look presidential while attacking Bush's foreign policies as violating America's liberal ideals.

In his acceptance speech at the Democratic convention, candidate Clinton proclaimed that a Clinton administration would fight tyranny from "Baghdad to Beijing" and "Haiti to Havana" (Clinton 1992a). This phrasing neatly combined a bit of traditional anticommunism with liberal concern for human rights, while also providing a basis for attacking Bush in these and other locations for "coddling dictators." In a major foreign policy speech on October 1, 1992, drafted by the campaign's foreign policy adviser, Anthony Lake, Clinton used liberal rhetoric to charge that "President Bush seems too often to prefer a foreign policy that embraces stability at the expense of freedom; a foreign policy built more on personal relationships with foreign leaders than on consideration of how those leaders acquired and maintained their power" (Clinton 1992b:4).

Clinton's specific campaign attacks on Bush policy toward Haiti and Bosnia placed the strongest constraints on his later policy toward these countries. Clinton attacked Bush's policy of forced repatriation of Haitian immigrants, saying, "I am appalled by the decision of the Bush administration to pick up fleeing Haitians on the high seas and forcibly return them to Haiti before considering their claim to political asylum. This process must not stand" (Lewis 1993). By focusing on the Haitian case, Clinton could argue that Bush had been insufficiently vigorous in his attempt to restore Aristide to office, as well as implicitly suggest to African Americans that his administration was not interested in the plight of refugees who happened to be black. In contrast, Clinton claimed that the restoration of democracy and the protection of the human rights of Haitian refugees would be central to his policy toward Haiti. In his October 1992 speech Clinton also implied that Bush was at least partly responsible for the genocidal policies of ethnic cleansing in the former Yugoslavia: "Bush sent his Secretary of State to Belgrade, where in the name of stability, he urged the members of the dying Yugoslav Federation to resist dissolution. This would have required the peoples of Bosnia, Croatia and Slovenia to knuckle under to Europe's last Communist strongman. When instead these new republics asserted their independence, the emboldened Milosevic regime launched the bloodiest war in Europe in over 40 years" (Clinton 1992b:5).

Thus, in keeping with the domestic liberal argument, Clinton entered office in January 1993 committed to a liberal internationalist foreign policy because of the way he had used liberal cultural appeals to achieve the nomination of the Democratic Party and later to win the general election. As the domestic liberal argument emphasizes, however, the direct constraints placed on presidents by the presidential selection process are limited. Clinton did fill his foreign policy positions with liberals who had served in the Carter administration twelve years before, but with the exception of U.N. Ambassador Madeleine Albright, not with the strongest proponents of an active liberal foreign policy. The most consistent supporter of liberal internationalism among Clinton's principal advisers, National Security Adviser Anthony Lake, styled himself a "pragmatic Wilsonian." Defense Secretary Les Aspin had nearly been deposed as Chair of the House Armed Services Committee during the 1980s because his Democratic colleagues on the committee did not find him sufficiently liberal. Secretary of State Warren Christopher had been selected because he was deeply cautious and unlikely to push for dramatic foreign policy initiatives. Clinton charged Christopher with keeping foreign policy off of his desk so that he could focus "like a laser beam" on the economy in his first year in office (Drew 1994:28; Woodward 1994).

The domestic liberal argument about the presidential selection process is not only about tactical promises made to win votes. Democrats simply tend to nominate candidates who possess a genuine commitment to liberal internationalism, which continues after the constraints of electoral contests fade away. Thus, Clinton maintained his liberal internationalism because he genuinely believed in it. Indeed, he was passionate in his commitment to one portion of the liberal canon—free trade. His administration made the economic rejuvenation of the United States a centerpiece of its policy of "democratic enlargement." It pursued a vigorous and well-crafted foreign economic policy, simultaneously pushing global free-trade agreements and aggressive commercial diplomacy in favor of American firms. Thus, bringing the Uruguay round of GATT negotiations to a successful conclusion was the most important component of the Clinton administration's efforts to strengthen the cooperation among the core "free-market democracies" of Western Europe and Japan (Brinkley 1997). As was true of the Kennedy administration, Clinton also embraced the liberal argument because it provided an elegant way of reconciling realist concerns with liberal ideals by emphasizing the security payoffs of the promotion of democracy. In the words of Anthony Lake, the promotion of democracy "protects our interests and security and . . . reflects values that are both American and universal" (Lake 1993:660).

Domestic Liberalism and Clinton Security Policy

The limited constraints imposed on Clinton during the 1992 election were complemented by a genuine belief among many of Clinton's principal foreign policy advisers that the promotion of democracy served U.S. security interests. The administration's acceptance of the security logic of the domestic liberal argument was first codified in a series of four policy speeches delivered by Lake, Christopher, Albright, and Clinton in September 1993 (Lake 1993; Christopher 1993b; Albright 1993b; Clinton 1993b). Clinton spelled out the broad reasons for the promotion of democracy in a speech to the United Nations:

> The habits of democracy are the habits of peace. Democracy is rooted in compromise, not conquest. It rewards tolerance, not hatred. Democracies rarely wage war on one another. They make more reliable partners in trade, in diplomacy, and in the stewardship of our global environment. And democracies, with the rule of law and respect for political, religious, and cultural minorities, are more responsive to their own people and to the protection of human rights. (Clinton 1993b:650)

Clinton and his subordinates laid out a four-part strategy that flowed from this liberal premise. As Lake summarized the strategy:

> First, we should strengthen the community of major market democracies—including our own—which constitutes the core from which enlargement is proceeding. Second, we should help foster and consolidate new democracies and market economies, where possible, especially in states of special significance and opportunity. Third, we must counter the aggression—and support the liberalization—of states hostile to democracy and markets. Fourth, we need to pursue our humanitarian agenda not only by providing aid but also by working to help democracy and market economics take root in regions of greatest humanitarian concern. (Lake 1993:660)

Like Kennedy, Clinton's foreign policy team saw free-market democracy as the antidote to the poverty, tyranny, and ethnic hatred that generated political instability in Third World countries. They were no longer worried about the possibility that Soviet-inspired communist insurgencies would exploit this instability. They were, however, concerned about instability in countries where the United States possessed "strategic interests, such as those with large economies, critical locations, nuclear weapons, or the potential to generate refugee flows into our own nation or into key friends and allies" (Lake 1993:660). One of the new strategic threats that Clinton officials universally acknowledged was the threat of war or of the forging of "backlash" states arising from ethnic and religious identities opposed to the global spread of American liberal culture. Only the toleration of diversity and respect for individual freedom enshrined in liberal democracy, they believed, could overcome ethnic conflicts in places like Bosnia.

More broadly, Clinton's foreign policy team believed the contemporary era offered a historic opportunity to build a liberal world order congenial to American interests and under American leadership. The post–Cold War era "has left the United States with a continuing responsibility—and a unique capacity—to provide leadership," according to Christopher (Christopher 1993b:656). Clinton's advisers saw the United States as the world's indispensable power, facing an unusually friendly international environment because "America's core concepts of democracy and markets" were more widely held than ever before (Lake 1993:658). America would lead the world precisely because its liberal values were universal values (Clinton 1993b; Lake 1993). American leadership of a global liberal community would be secured if the United States could ensure that the Russians and Chinese embraced these "universal" values.

The promotion of democracy in peripheral states enhances this leadership by forging a cooperative and altruistic, rather than imperial, image for the United States on the world scene. Albright made precisely this point in reference to the ceremonies commemorating the Israel-PLO Accord that had been held in Washington earlier that month:

> I will remember, in particular, a comment by Israeli Foreign Minister Shimon Peres about America's purpose. "When the history books are written," he said, "Nobody will understand the United States, really: You have so much force, and you didn't conquer the land of anybody; you have so much power, and you didn't dominate another people; you have problems of your own, and you have never turned your back on the problems of others." We should be proud that so much of the world sees America the way Foreign Minister Peres sees America, for our leadership today rests on the same solid foundation of principles and values—the same enlightened self-interest—that has made service to America from Valley Forge to Desert Storm a badge not only of courage but of honor. (Albright 1993b:666)

Thus, embracing liberalism not only brings whatever benefits might accrue from the democratic peace, it also provides policymakers with a powerful and persuasive rationale for American leadership of the international system. If other states see the United States as the "leader of the free world" rather than as an imperial power, they will follow American leadership without having to be coerced into doing so.

Clinton's foreign policy team viewed domestic constraints on foreign policy as more significant than international ones. The September 1993 speeches concentrated as much energy on convincing the American people of the importance of continuing American "engagement" in the world as on "democratic enlargement." Each speech denigrated the neo-isolationist impulse to say that "the Cold War is over; we won; let's go home and attend to our problems" (Christopher 1993b:656). Each compared the contemporary era to the immediate post–World War II era, when "the internationalists won those debates [with the isolationists], in part, because they could point to a unitary threat to America's interests and because the nation was entering a period of economic security." The task of building a foreign policy consensus for engagement would be more difficult in 1993, according to Lake, because "today's supporters of engagement abroad have neither of those advantages. The threats and opportunities are diffuse, and our people are deeply anxious about their economic fate" (Lake 1993:664).

Because of its deep roots in America's liberal culture, the promotion of democracy could serve as a crucial mechanism for building a domestic consensus in support of American engagement in the world. As Clinton noted during the 1992 campaign: "A pro-democracy foreign policy is neither liberal nor conservative; neither Democrat nor Republican; it is deep American tradition. And this is for good reason. For no foreign policy can long succeed if it does not reflect the enduring values of the American people" (Clinton 1992b:3). By emphasizing that the promotion of democracy also served U.S. interests, Clinton hoped to convince the American people that a liberal foreign policy was both moral and prudent.

Thus, the Clinton administration's embrace of the promotion of democracy as a central principle of its foreign policy reflected security considerations as well as the constraints imposed by the 1992 elections. Part of this security rationale reflected the belief that liberal democracy offered the best response to the political crises that had engulfed countries like Haiti and Bosnia. More broadly, however, the Clinton administration believed in the security logic of the democratic peace and that the spread of liberal democracy could secure the domestic and international bases of American leadership in the international system.

Congressional Pressure and the Adoption of Proliberalization Policies

The presidential elections and the Clinton administration's liberal internationalist security policies predisposed it to adopt proliberalization policies in Haiti and Bosnia. Congressional pressure strongly reinforced this predisposition. Congressional pressure pushed Clinton in two seemingly contradictory directions, however. On the one hand, pressure by some members of Congress impelled him to fight for the liberal causes of the restoration of democracy in Haiti and the abolition of ethnic cleansing in Bosnia. On the other hand, the opposition of a majority of Congress to both interventions rendered America's involvement limited and indecisive.

Democracy Promotion and the Permissive Occupation of Haiti

The flight of tens of thousands of refugees to the United States in the wake of the 1991 military coup in Haiti spurred many liberals to push for action against the military junta in that country. Clinton joined this chorus with his campaign critiques of Bush's policies of repatriating Haitian refugees. When up to 150,000 Haitians prepared to flee the island in hopes of arriving in Florida during the first days of the new Clinton administration, however, the president-elect's transition team cooperated with the Bush administration on an even harsher quarantine policy. In a radio address broadcast throughout Haiti, Clinton warned that "those who leave Haiti by boat for the United States will be intercepted and returned to Haiti by the U.S. Coast Guard. Leaving by boat is not the route to freedom" (Clinton 1993a:133). Clinton violated his campaign promise to defuse a potential crisis that could have left him with the unpalatable choice of either having to deal with tens of thousands of Haitians on the shores of Florida or immediately intervening militarily to resolve the political crisis that had spawned the waves of refugees.

After Clinton reversed his refugee policy, however, he faced severe criticism from liberal activists for violating his campaign promise in the first days of his presidency (French 1993). The Congressional Black Caucus sharply criticized the administration's policy and demanded that Clinton take immediate action to restore Reverend Aristide to office. Representative Major Owens (D-N.Y.) convincingly conveyed the message in Congress:

> The administration has disappointed all of us in its slow movement toward a resolution of the Haitian problem. . . . We are treating Haiti as if the situation was a game. We are treating Aristide as if he were a toy. We are not serious about democracy in Haiti, about using the clout of the international community to return democracy to Haiti. We are not serious about assuming our role in the world as the last superpower to be a force for good in guaranteeing the human rights of human beings everywhere. . . . The Congressional Black Caucus thinks we've had enough. (Congress 1993a:2456–57)

Others accused the Clinton administration of making a mockery of democratic institutions when it tried to convince Reverend Aristide to agree to amnesty for General Cédras and other coup members: "Like Mr. Bush, Clinton seems to have confused democracy in Haiti with a demand that Aristide coexist with terrorist individuals and institutions. But the consolidation of Haitian democracy depends on vindication for the victims of the military terror" (McGillon 1993).

Clinton attempted to mute these charges of hypocrisy by increasing the diplomatic efforts to return Reverend Aristide to power in Haiti and claiming that the repatriation of refugees was only a temporary expedient in what was still a strongly pro-democratic policy. On June 16, 1993, the Clinton administration pushed a ban on arms and oil shipments to Haiti through the U.N. Security Council. Within two weeks, these sanctions helped bring about a set of agreements at Governor's Island in New York that involved the following provisions: (1) the nomination of a new moderate premier by President Aristide, businessman Robert Malval; (2) the adoption of an amnesty law prohibiting prosecution of military officers who had participated in the 1991 coup and in human rights abuses during the period of military rule; (3) the resignation or reassignment of the military and police high commands; and (4) the return of Aristide by October 30, 1993 (State 1993). Upon successful completion of these steps, the United Nations and the United States agreed to suspend the oil embargo, provide up to one billion dollars of development assistance over the course of a decade, and provide military trainers to reform the Haitian military and police forces. This solution perfectly suited Clinton's domestic constraints by allowing him to argue that he had achieved a victory for liberal democracy and human rights without risking U.S. troops in combat.

The Governor's Island Accords unraveled as Aristide's October 30 return date approached. Aristide supporters in the slums of Port au Prince faced increasing repression at the hands of the military, police, and death squads. His new justice minister and other prominent supporters were assassinated. The remaining members of his newly appointed cabinet were confined to their homes in the climate of intensified violence.

What followed was one of the most embarrassing events in Clinton foreign policy. On October 11, 1993, a week after the fire fight in Mogadishu, Somalia, where eighteen U.S. soldiers had died, the USS *Harlan County* arrived at Port au Prince with 200 lightly armed U.S. and Canadian troops sent to "retrain" the Haitian armed forces. When an equal number of armed thugs proclaiming they were going to turn Haiti into "another Somalia" blocked the disembarkation of these troops, the mission was abandoned and the *Harlan County* recalled. Despite the reimposition of U.N. economic sanctions, it was hard to hide the humiliation suffered by the United States. "We lost the confidence of this Congress, we lost the confidence of the American people, and we have lost the confidence of the world because we are a laughingstock when it comes to our creating or supporting democratic institutions, whether in the Western Hemisphere or anywhere else," according to Representative Dan Mica (D-Fla.) (Congress 1993a:8546–47).

The dominant reaction in Congress was to protest against the possibility of U.S. military intervention in Haiti. This call was led by Senate Minority Leader Robert Dole, who developed legislation that would have required Clinton to ask for congressional authorization before using military force in

Haiti. Dole summed up the sentiments of many in Congress by proclaiming: "I wouldn't risk any American lives to put Aristide back in power" (Friedman 1993a). According to Representative Bob Dornan (R-Calif.), "Aristide is not worth one drop of blood from one U.S. soldier. This is just another one of Clinton's feel good missions that is going to end up getting U.S. soldiers killed" (Congress 1993a:8022–23). This strong congressional opposition reflected a general desire to keep U.S. troops out of potentially costly "feel-good" missions for liberal causes. Congressional Republicans also displayed residual anticommunist sentiment in refusing to support a mission to assist the radical leftist Aristide. The Dole Amendment was defeated even after being watered down to a sense of Congress resolution. This defeat had less to do with support for Clinton's Haitian policy than with legislators' reluctance to infringe greatly on the president's constitutional prerogatives (Congress 1993a:13989–91). Perhaps as important, Clinton had gotten the message from Congress and made it very clear that he had no intention of sending troops to Haiti.

The *Harlan County* debacle demonstrated that Clinton was willing to accept substantial humiliation without taking effective military action. As evidenced by the congressional reaction to this incident, the domestic political costs of military intervention were considered greater than the cost of not avenging this humiliation. Despite this, Clinton paid a political price for abandoning his efforts to restore democracy to Haiti. American liberals who had acquiesced in Clinton's repatriation policies because they believed he was making good-faith efforts to change the conditions in Haiti, began again to criticize his policies openly.

Liberal attacks intensified in early 1994 as Clinton tried to push Aristide into accepting a less advantageous diplomatic settlement than the one he reluctantly agreed to at Governor's Island (French 1994; Greenhouse 1994a). Human rights abuses increased dramatically in 1994, and Clinton was attacked in congressional hearings for his failure to address "the worst [human rights situation] in the hemisphere and one of the worst in the world" (Congress 1994a:51–58). Senator Harkin delivered a scathing attack on Clinton's Haitian policy:

The actions of this administration in regard to Haiti are embarrassing and shameful to this country. They must turn around and they must change. If we do not, then I think that we will doom Haiti not only for another long, dark period of repression and military rule, poverty, murders and killings, and violations of human rights, but I think that we will send a strong signal to all of Latin America to those antidemocratic forces . . . that are still there that would like to overturn some of the progress that has been made in the recent past. We will send a signal to them that it is all right. You can go ahead. We may yell and scream about it, but we will not do anything about it. (Congress 1994a:61)

Trans-Africa Director Randall Robinson protested Clinton's "racist" policy toward Haitian refugees with a twenty-seven-day hunger strike. Congressional liberals dramatized their opposition by chaining themselves to the White House gate. House Foreign Operations Chair David Obey (D-WI) called for intervention because "Haitians are being ground up like hamburger meat because the clowns who run that government don't know how to behave like adults" (Congress 1994a:8).

The Congressional Black Caucus sent a letter to Clinton arguing that his "half-hearted" efforts to restore Aristide "must be scrapped" in favor of tougher sanctions. "While our nation makes public pronouncements regarding our commitment to restore democracy in Haiti, there is growing perception throughout the world that the U.S. is actually doing all in its power to prevent this" (Caucus 1994:9). The caucus urged the president to sever air links with Haiti, deny visas to the Haitian military, and impose sanctions against any country that violated the trade embargo. America's Watch and the National Coalition for Refugees accused the president of embracing "a murderous armed force." The letter continued: "Your administration's failure to support and protect the fundamental rights of Haitians has contributed to a human rights disaster that has tarnished your Presidency and discredited your stated commitment to democracy and human rights around the world" (America's Watch 1994:8–9). The letter called on the administration to end the forcible repatriation of Haitian refugees.

Clinton responded to these criticisms by toughening his stance against the Haitian military junta. In April 1994 Clinton fired Lawrence Pezzullo, who had been seen as anti-Aristide, and appointed a prominent African American politician, William Gray, as his new special adviser for Haiti (Dupuy 1997:156–57). The administration announced its support for a "same-day" plan, wherein the military would step down, the parliament would appoint a new prime minister, and a law-granting amnesty would be enacted simultaneously. In early May, at the insistence of the United States, the U.N. Security Council adopted Resolution 916, which tightened sanctions on everything but humanitarian supplies, prevented Haiti's military leaders and their civilian allies from leaving the country, froze Haitian assets worldwide, and banned nonscheduled flights in and out of Haiti.

Clinton imposed additional sanctions to block assets of all nationals residing in Haiti.

Clinton also reversed his refugee policy. The administration announced that instead of forcefully returning ships at sea, the United States would grant Haitian exiles hearings at sea to determine if they qualified for political asylum. After a sharp increase in the number of Haitians seeking asylum, Clinton announced that refugees intercepted at sea would be taken to Panama or other Caribbean countries rather than the United States. Stopping the flow of Haitian refugees to the United States was always a central goal of the Clinton administration. The events of mid-1994 illustrated that liberal pressure within the United States made it difficult for the Clinton administration to continue the proven policies of quarantine and repatriation, policies which were more cost effective and entailed less risk than a military solution to the refugee crisis.

Clinton also began to threaten to restore Haitian democracy by force. Special Envoy Gray delivered the thinly veiled threat in June 1994 by suggesting that "no invasion [is] imminent. However, the military option is on the table" (Gray 1994:13). In July, the Clinton administration convinced the U.N. Security Council to pass a unanimous resolution approving the use of force in Haiti. The intransigence of the Haitian military regime—which responded to the increasing pressure by naming a new president, Emil Jonaissant, and repressing more supporters of the deposed president—pushed Clinton unwillingly toward a military intervention. By staking an extraordinary amount of his prestige on the removal of the military junta in Haiti and the restoration of Aristide, it became increasingly difficult for the president to back down.

There was still substantial domestic opposition to an invasion of Haiti, however. When an invasion seemed imminent, Congress actively opposed the use of force to restore Aristide. Senator Orrin Hatch (R-Utah) expressed the thoughts of many members when he stated:

> We do not have a vital interest in Haiti. . . . I would argue that it is time for this administration to review its current policy options and available alternatives . . . there is simply no way that the administration will be able to establish a viable, functioning democracy in a few short weeks after an invasion. . . . The administration is playing a high stakes game that commits the United States to an invasion of a sovereign nation and that opens up an indefinite stay of U.S. forces on that island. There is no consensus in Congress or among the American people for intervening in Haiti, or for a prolonged occupation of that

country. Before we place our troops in imminent danger, the American people deserve a clear and concise explanation of what we hope to achieve in that country. (Congress 1994a:12877)

These members of Congress reflected the majority sentiment of the American public. In early September an ABC poll revealed that 73 percent of Americans opposed an invasion.

Despite the domestic pressure against a military intervention, Clinton announced on September 15 that negotiations had ended and the only option left was the use of force. Two days later, he sent Carter, Powell, and Nunn to arrange for the "permissive occupation" of Haiti. Only at the last moment was Clinton able to resolve the contradictory impulses of the domestic liberal dynamic. His administration had tried everything short of military intervention and had failed to stop human rights abuses or to restore democracy. With its last-minute diplomatic gambit, it managed to achieve its objectives without having to fight. U.S. troops arrived in Port au Prince only after the local military institution had promised not to shoot at them.

The same pattern of congressional reactions continued throughout the intervention, especially after Republicans emerged victorious in the 1994 mid-term congressional elections. Days after he helped organize the permissive occupation of Haiti, Sam Nunn presided over hearings of the Senate Armed Services Committee, at which virtually the only question asked was "When are U.S. troops going to leave Haiti?" Senators raised concerns first and foremost about the potential for U.S. casualties. As Senator Carl Levin (D-Mich.) stated: "I hope . . . we do not do anything which will increase the risk for our troops or undermine their morale, and that is a great fear of mine" (Congress 1994c:25).

Members of Congress also continued to pressure the administration to live up to its promise to build democracy in Haiti. Democrats like Senator Claiborne Pell (D-R.I.) were willing to give their party's president the benefit of the doubt in accepting that "the Haitian people were able to freely exercise their right to choose their local legislatures and municipal officials [in the June 1995 elections, which] represent an important step in the building of democracy in that country" (Congress 1995b:9). Republicans, however, harshly criticized the June 1995 elections, which were marred by widespread logistical problems. Voter registration lists were incomplete, candidates were left off ballots, some polling places never opened, and many that did ran out of ballots. Senator John McCain (R-Ariz.) argued that "the recent elections in Haiti do not define Haiti's destiny, but the abuses and irregularities that rendered the election, in the words of almost every observer, extremely chaotic, may if not corrected in the next elections, ultimately crush whatever progress Haiti has made toward enlightened self-government" (Congress 1995b:2).

Members of Congress later questioned whether the December 1995 presidential elections were truly free and fair, given that less than 30 percent of the population voted and the winning candidate received 88 percent of the vote. House Republicans invited the former U.S. ambassador to Haiti, Ernest Preeg, to testify that "the election of President Préval last December was seriously flawed in a number of respects. The provisional electoral council was challenged by opposition parties. The media was harassed, with a few members beaten, and they were effectively silenced. It was a very brief election campaign. All of the centrist and conservative parties boycotted the election. They had won a third of the vote 5 years earlier. And the turnout was estimated to range from 15 to 28 percent. It was very low" (Congress 1996a:23). Congressional Republicans also attacked the Clinton administration, according to Senator Bob Dole, Clinton's opponent in the 1996 presidential race, for being "mute in condemning Haitian government death squads" (Congress 1996a:64). They charged Clinton with covering up Haitian government involvement in a number of political killings that had occurred during 1995 (Congress 1996a:1–2, 63–64). This pattern of congressional responses to the intervention in Haiti accounts for Clinton's combination of consistent support for proliberalization policies and equally consistent timidity in carrying out its mandate. A similar pattern was repeated in Bosnia.

From "Lift and Strike" to the Dayton Accords in Bosnia

The pattern of U.S. involvement in Bosnia clearly illustrates how congressional pressure has both compelled Clinton to act, yet constrained him from taking decisive action. Clinton has been pressured by domestic groups both to do something to stop the humanitarian crisis in Bosnia and to avoid sending U.S. troops into combat. These policy dynamics emerged first in Clinton's early 1993 decision to pursue a policy of "lift and strike," lifting the U.N. arms embargo against the Bosnian government and launching air strikes against the Bosnian Serbs.

Bill Clinton was confronted by constant television images detailing the shelling of Sarajevo and the flight of the victims of Serb ethnic cleansing when he entered office in January 1993. A million Bosnians, most of them Muslims, had been driven from their homes by brutal paramilitary gangs during 1992 and more than 100,000 had been killed. Clinton had used these images during the 1992 presidential campaign to attack Bush's inaction in the face of genocide. Clinton also attacked Bush for backing a plan for a negotiated settlement of the conflict offered by David Owen of the European Union and the U.N.'s Cyrus Vance. The Vance-Owen Plan, which called for a constitutional agreement and a political map of the republic that would break the country into ten relatively ethnically homogenous autonomous provinces under a weak central government, was denounced because it "ratified the atrocities of ethnic cleansing" (Friedman 1993b; Sciolino 1993a). In his first days in office, Warren Christopher expressed the reasons why many Americans wanted the United States to play an active role in resolving the Bosnian crisis:

> We cannot ignore the human toll. Serbian ethnic cleansing has been pursued through mass murders, systematic beatings and . . . rapes . . . prolonged shelling of innocents in Sarajevo and elsewhere, forced displacement of entire villages, inhumane treatment of prisoners in detention camps, the blockading of relief to sick and starving citizens. . . . Our conscience revolts at the idea of accepting such brutality. (Christopher 1993a)

Clinton was on the verge of being trapped by his own liberal rhetoric when in his first Bosnian initiative he gave a luke-warm endorsement of the Vance-Owen Plan, which he had attacked during the campaign. In light of this endorsement, Clinton needed to find some way of demonstrating that he was vigorously pursuing liberal goals in Bosnia.

On the other hand, Clinton also faced institutional constraints from both the American public and Congress that made the large-scale involvement of American troops unacceptable. Many members of Congress feared that Bosnia could easily become a Vietnam-style quagmire if U.S. troops intervened (Krauss 1993). Senator Harry Reid (D-Nev.) expressed the fears of many when he stated, "the Balkans are the fountainhead of guerrilla war. . . . The conflict in Bosnia . . . is a civil war. As we know from our own domestic wars, they can be brutal and unforgiving . . . the last thing that the United States needs at this time in its history, or ever again, is another Vietnam, and that is exactly what this would be" (Congress 1993a:5784–85). Therefore, while Clinton needed to respond to the crisis in Bosnia, he could not take the kind of military action that might have been necessary to resolve the crisis at that time.

In May 1993 the Clinton administration settled on two major policy initiatives. First, it would push to lift the arms embargo that had been imposed on Bosnia by the United Nations. Second, it would punish the Bosnian Serbs by launching air strikes against Serb targets.

Clinton's military advisers were skeptical about these military efforts. Lifting the embargo would take months to give the Bosnians a significant advantage in the fighting. In the short term, it would provide the Serbs with a powerful incentive to attempt to wipe out the Bosnian government before the weapons arrived (Engelberg 1993). On the issue of air strikes, Air Force General Michael Ryan testified to Congress: "If you can find the artillery pieces and get the pilots' eyeballs on them, you can probably take them out. But after the first time, they'll go into hiding, camouflage them or move them around. It's really a tough issue. . . . Without the threat of follow-up ground forces, they'll just ride out a bombing strike" (Congress 1993a:4986–87). These sentiments were expressed more strongly by spokesmen from other branches of the armed forces. Strikes limited to attacking artillery pieces near Sarajevo would be especially ineffectual.

The combination of "lift and strike," however, proved effective for meeting Clinton's domestic dilemma of doing something highly visible in support of the Bosnian cause with little risk of U.S. casualties. Calling to lift the embargo allowed Clinton to argue "that justice has been served," according to Senator Richard Lugar (R-Ind.) (Engelberg 1993). If the United States would not fight for the Bosnians, the least it could do was allow the Bosnians to procure the weapons they needed to protect themselves. Senator Joseph Biden (D-Del.), chair of the Foreign Relations Subcommittee on European Affairs, argued that the United States should do even more to support the Bosnian cause, because "the U.S. must lead the west in a decisive response to Serbian aggression" (Congress 1993c:2–8).

While air strikes might not end the war, the president and the Congress were assured by Air Force General Merrill McPeak that the unsophisticated air defenses of the Serb forces posed "virtually no risk" to American warplanes (Congress 1993b:213–14). Thus, air strikes were a domestically effective way to respond to Serb aggression. The strikes served as a highly visible demonstration of U.S. action, with only minimal risk of politically damaging American casualties. At the same time the United States was contemplating military action from the air, Warren Christopher laid out four strict tests for the use of American ground troops: (1) the goal had to be clearly stated to the American people, (2) there had to be a strong likelihood of success, (3) there must be an exit strategy, and (4) the action had to win public support (Sciolino 1993b). These tests were not remotely close to being met in Bosnia in 1993.

Within two weeks of the announcement of the U.S. intention to begin bombing Serb targets, the Clinton administration backed away from its threat. Instead it endorsed a European plan to establish "safe havens" within which Muslim civilians would be protected from Serb attacks. Despite Clinton's strong rhetoric, he backed down from taking decisive action. International protests, rather than domestic constraints, forced Clinton to shelve his plans. When Christopher traveled to Europe to "consult" with America's allies, the French and British rejected the lift and strike plan because, while it may have solved Clinton's own domestic problems, it would have created domestic problems for the two European powers (Sciolino 1993c). Both countries had substantial contingents of peacekeeping troops deployed in Bosnia and did not want to subject their troops to reprisals by Serb forces.

Torn by contradictory domestic and international pressures, the Clinton administration pursued a vacillating policy between mid-1993 and mid-1995 that led to no better than a continued stalemate in Bosnia. On the one hand, the United States supported European-backed plans for negotiated settlements of the conflict that would have ratified the atrocities of ethnic cleansing. The plans offered by the "Contact Group," comprising the U.S., the United Kingdom, Russia, Germany, and France, would have created a hard partition of Bosnia, with 51 percent of Bosnian territory controlled by a Muslim-Croat Federation and 49 percent controlled by the Bosnian Serbs. Punitive action would be taken if either side refused to accept the plan (Cohen 1994). On the other hand, Clinton pushed on several occasions for air strikes against Bosnian Serb forces while the U.S. Congress pushed even more insistently for a lifting of the arms embargo against Bosnia.

The United States pursued no consistent or decisive policy during this period. Its support for the negotiated settlements offered by the Europeans was limited given Clinton's reluctance to participate in initiatives that would have "compelled the Bosnian government to accept Serb ethnic cleansing" (Gordon 1993). America's tilt toward the Bosnian government removed its incentives to accept disadvantageous compromises while also making the proposed settlements unacceptable to the Bosnian Serbs, who rejected all peace plans before the Dayton Accords.

From mid-1993 through mid-1995, U.S. pressure for air strikes generated only painfully limited attacks that had no lasting impact on the Bosnian Serbs. In August 1993, when Bosnian Serb forces captured the strategically crucial Mt. Igman protecting the Bosnian capital, Clinton called for air strikes. Before the threat was carried out, the Bosnian Serbs agreed to a partial withdrawal and a replacement of Bosnian government troops on the mountain with French peacekeepers. In February 1994, when a Serb mortar attack killed sixty-one at Sarajevo's central market, Clinton called again for air strikes. Before the strikes could commence, the Bosnian Serbs agreed to withdraw their heavy artillery from a 20-kilometer radius surrounding Sarajevo.

Only in April 1994, when the Bosnian Serbs had launched an offensive against the safe haven of Gorazde, did NATO warplanes launch an air strike, but then only against a few tanks and artillery pieces. Serb forces accepted a 20-kilometer heavy weapons exclusion zone around Gorazde, but only after they had defeated the local Bosnian government forces. In November, Bosnian Serb forces attacked another U.N. safe haven, Bihac. Once again Clinton convinced his allies to launch a retaliatory air strike, only to have that strike limited to a Serb airstrip. The Serbs ignored the strike and continued to press Bihac. When a Serb offensive, including an artillery attack that killed dozens of civilians in a Tuzla café, shattered a cease-fire negotiated by Jimmy Carter, the United States pushed for a stronger set of air strikes. The Bosnian Serbs responded by taking more than 350 U.N. peacekeepers hostage, which led to a quick suspension of the strikes.

While the Clinton administration failed in its efforts to convince its allies to lift the international arms embargo and abandoned its threats to violate the embargo unilaterally, it did take two limited steps in this direction in 1994. During the summer, it tacitly supported Iranian efforts to smuggle weapons to Bosnia. In November, Clinton ordered U.S. naval vessels to stop participating in the enforcement of the embargo.

The domestic liberal argument can explain why Clinton settled for half-measures that succeeded only in maintaining a stalemate. Clinton initially adopted a policy of lift and strike because it fit within his domestic constraints. It allowed him to demonstrate that he was doing something to respond to the ethnic cleansing that had created a humanitarian crisis in Bosnia. At the same time, launching air strikes against Bosnian Serb targets and lifting the arms embargo on the Bosnian government posed only limited costs to the United States in lives and treasure. Clinton consistently returned to air strikes as his preferred strategy because it continued to meet his domestic political needs.

In 1993 Clinton chose his policies largely in anticipation of the possible negative response in the United States to alternative policies that might have been either more or less aggressive. By 1994, however, Clinton policy in Bosnia was being driven by manifest public pressure, especially from Congress. Major policy initiatives, like the periodic call for air strikes, came in response to visible, televised attacks on Bosnian civilians that generated outrage in the United States. Meanwhile, Congress became the principal advocate of a unilateral lifting of the embargo.

Members of Congress supported an end to the arms embargo for the same reason Clinton initially gave it his support. This policy allowed them to take a principled liberal stand that would impose very limited costs on their constituents. Senator Joseph Lieberman (D-Conn.) illustrated this political logic in a June 1994 speech:

> [We] feel that the United States has an interest in this conflict: first, in standing up against aggression by one nation against another; second, in not standing idly by while genocidal acts occur; and third, in acknowledging that what happens in Europe has twice drawn us into world wars in this century and we have a strategic interest in preserving order there. . . . We also feel that while we have an interest in the Balkans, it is not sufficient to justify sending American soldiers there. (Congress 1994a:8124)

Thus, the day after Clinton announced his support for a revised version of the Contact Group's peace plan, the House passed a measure by a vote of 244 to 178 that would unilaterally lift the embargo (Congress 1994a:4242–43). Representative Henry Hyde (R.-Ill.) convincingly summed up the sentiment on the floor: "We see unspeakable inhumanity, and we're reduced to shrugging our shoulders, furrowing our brows and folding our arms. . . . We can't let timid and paralyzed nations and self important U.N. bureaucrats prevent us from doing what is right and in our own self-interest" (Congress 1994a:4240–41).

In August 1994 the Senate voted for a bill sponsored by Lieberman and Dole that called for a unilateral lifting of the arms embargo by mid-November. The Senate also voted to approve an amendment sponsored by Sam Nunn that called on Clinton to urge the United Nations to lift the arms embargo if the Serbs did not agree to the peace plan by the end of October 1994 (Greenhouse 1994b). The conflicting resolutions allowed Clinton to seize upon the one sponsored by Nunn, which gave him the most flexibility. Nevertheless, in addition to pressing the United Nations to lift the embargo, Clinton also responded to Congress by ending U.S. participation in the enforcement of the embargo. He avoided having to take a more forthright position only by convincing the Bosnian government to ask that the suspension of the embargo be postponed for six months.

During each stage of the crisis, Clinton initially proposed forceful actions, only to back down at the last minute. When air strikes were launched, they were so limited they made Clinton look weak both to domestic critics and the Serbs. These seemingly anomalous responses largely reflected America's consideration for its liberal allies in Europe. By April 1995, 162 U.N. soldiers had been killed and 1,420 injured (Boutros-Ghali 1995). The Bosnian Serb capture of hundreds of U.N. hostages in mid-1995 provided a stark illustration of the reasonableness of European concerns about the negative consequences for their troops on the ground of a more vigorous military policy. Pressure from America's liberal allies—and those like Russia, which the United States hoped would become liberal allies—pushed the Clinton administration not only to drop its insistence on an end to the arms embargo but also to lobby against this measure in Congress (Congress 1994b:74–88). This stalemate was only broken in the summer of 1995.

In July 1995 Bosnian Serb forces overran the U.N. safe havens of Srebrenica and Zepa. The lightly armed Dutch troops in Srebrenica failed to stop the massacre of nearly 17,000 Bosnian Muslim men who had taken refuge in the "safe haven." Clinton called once again for air strikes. This time, the Contact Group agreed to the use of substantial air power to rescue the safe haven of Gorazde. In August and September NATO launched large-scale air attacks against Serb forces surrounding Gorazde and Sarajevo and destroyed important military assets in other parts of Bosnia. Bosnian and Croatian forces took advantage of these strikes by launching an offensive against the Serbs, "liberating" 770 square miles of western Bosnia by mid-September.

In October the Clinton administration brokered a cease-fire in Bosnia and invited the combatants to engage in peace negotiations in Dayton. After nearly a month of talks moderated by Assistant Secretary of State Richard Holbrooke, the participants signed the Dayton Peace Accords on November 21, 1995, and the United States committed itself to sending 20,000 troops to lead a NATO peacekeeping force. What explains this decisive and resolute policy after three years of indecision? In part, the intensification of the humanitarian crisis in Bosnia, represented by the atrocities committed at Srebrenica, helped break the deadlock in the international response to the Bosnian crisis. Ironically, American fears of suffering significant casualties in a military intervention in Bosnia played an even greater role in bringing about decisive U.S. action. Clinton had been steadfast in his refusal to include U.S. troops in the ongoing U.N. military intervention in Bosnia. When the French called for the direct participation of American aircraft, ground crews, and troops in a more vigorous defense of safe havens in the summer of 1995, this posed a risk that, according to a senior Defense Department official, the "U.S. will not take" (Apple 1995a). The French proposal for a rapid reaction force could not have fully succeeded without the active participation of U.S.

troops and probably not without the unpleasant possibility of placing U.S. troops in combat against the Bosnian Serbs.

A more likely scenario for the involvement of U.S. troops revolved around the withdrawal of U.N. troops. Clinton had promised to send American soldiers to participate in the withdrawal of U.N. troops from Bosnia should that become necessary. He backed off of his insistence on a lifting of the arms embargo in part because the British and French had made it clear that they would ask the United States to evacuate their troops from Bosnia in the event that the United States armed the Bosnian government. When he had vetoed a congressional bill to lift the embargo Clinton declared:

> If the United States unilaterally lifts the arms embargo the United States, as the leader of the NATO alliance, would be obliged to send thousands of American troops to assist in that difficult operation. Second, unilaterally lifting the embargo could cause the fighting in Bosnia to escalate. . . . Third, unilaterally lifting the embargo will lead to unilateral American responsibility. If the Bosnian government suffered reverses on the battlefield, we—and not the Europeans— would be expected to fill the void with military and humanitarian aid. (Clinton 1995:36)

By mid-1995, participants in the U.N. operation in Bosnia were "thinking very seriously that [the United Nations] should pull its troops out of the former Yugoslavia," even without a U.S. decision to violate the arms embargo (Boutros-Ghali 1995). Clinton felt bound to follow through on his commitment to extract the troops of his liberal allies from Bosnia. As he stated in June 1995:

> I determined that the role of the United States should be to vigorously support the diplomatic search for peace, and that our vital interests were clear in limiting the spread of the conflict. Furthermore, our interests were in doing what we could short of putting in ground forces to help prevent the multiethnic Bosnian state from being destroyed, and to minimize the loss of life and the ethnic cleansing. . . . If our allies decide to stay, we want to support them, but within the very careful limits I have outlined. I want to make it clear again what I have said about the use of our ground forces. We will use them only, first, if there is a genuine peace with no shooting and no fighting, and the United States is part of that peace. . . . Second, if our allies decide they can no longer continue the U.N. mission and decide to withdraw,

but they cannot withdraw in safety, we should help them with our unique capabilities. (Clinton 1995:29)

The Clinton administration was faced with the possible choice of abandoning its liberal allies in Bosnia or sending U.S. troops to remove thousands of dispersed U.N. troops from a conflict zone, risking domestically damaging casualties in the process.

Clinton once again called for air strikes as a way to avoid adopting more painful courses of action. This time Clinton garnered allied support because the atrocities committed at Srebrenica had been too profound and humiliating for the Europeans to continue with the status quo. More important, the risks associated with air strikes began to look less severe in comparison to the risks involved in a withdrawal from Bosnia. Furthermore, the removal of peacekeepers from the areas where they had been held hostage earlier in 1995 and the expulsion of others from areas acquired by the Serbs in the summer of 1995 rendered them less vulnerable to Serb reprisals.

Substantially increased domestic pressures reinforced this political dynamic as Clinton tried to resolve the Bosnia issue before he began his campaign for reelection in 1996. Congressional resolutions to lift the arms embargo on the Bosnian government became the principal forum for congressional attacks by the new Republican majority against the morality of Clinton's Balkan policy. On June 8, 1995, the House voted 318 to 99 in favor of a resolution that would unilaterally lift the arms embargo upon the request of the Bosnian government, or if the United Nations withdrew its forces. When the Senate passed this resolution 69–29 on July 26, Senate Majority Leader Dole denounced Clinton's inaction: "It is high time the Clinton administration abandon its flimsy excuses for the United Nations' pitiful performance, shed the false mantle of humanitarianism, and face the reality of the U.N. failure in Bosnia. . . . We have an obligation to the Bosnian people and to our principles, to allow a U.N. member state, the victim of aggression, to defend itself" (Congress 1995a:9722). This bill was passed with majorities that could have overridden the president's veto had he not taken the dramatic action of the August air strikes to demonstrate his resolve.

Clinton used the air strikes not to defeat the Bosnian Serbs but to pressure them to negotiate a peace settlement. Clinton decided that the risks posed to U.S. troops as part of a peacekeeping force would be less than the risks posed by either a difficult mission of extraction or the more robust version of the existing U.N. mission proposed by the French. Furthermore, a peace settlement held out the possibility of reaching some resolution to the humanitarian crisis that had compelled the United States to act in the first place. Despite the reduced risks associated with a true peacekeeping mission, the same members of Congress who had pressed Clinton to take decisive action in Bosnia also argued against the deployment of 20,000 troops called for by the Dayton Accords. According to Senator Fred Thompson (R-Tenn.):

> All of us are for peace in Bosnia and for an end to the slaughter. . . . Any time there is a moral imperative to stop slaughter, to stop genocide . . . there is a national interest in seeing that this is stopped. That does not mean in every case that the U.S. should send ground troops or we would have ground troops in possibly 20 or 30 or 40 places on the globe today. . . . So the mere fact that there is a moral imperative in some sense to stop the slaughter, to stop the genocide in different parts of the world, does not automatically mean the U.S. should send ground troops. (Congress 1995a:18397–407)

Just before the Dayton Accords were signed, the House voted to bar any money for the peacekeepers in Bosnia. It then narrowly turned back an amendment that would have halted funds for American peacekeepers, 210 to 218, in a December 13, 1995, vote (Congress 1995a). In nearly derailing the deployment of U.S. troops essential for the successful implementation of the peace accords, the House followed public opinion. Polls indicated that only 36 percent of Americans thought the deployment was the "right thing to do," while 58 percent said that the troops should be kept home (Apple 1995b).

Clinton gained Congress' reluctant approval by assuring the leadership in a November letter that the size of the NATO-led force, the high quality of American and NATO troops and equipment, and the rules of engagement adopted for the mission would create conditions offering the minimum possible risks to American soldiers (Sciolino 1995). The Senate voted down the amendment, which would have cut funds for the peacekeepers by a larger margin than the House, after Clinton promised Dole that the United States would arm and train the Bosnians before it would withdraw its forces (Congress 1995a:18551; Seelye 1995).

Clinton declared that while the United States should not serve as the world's policeman, "we must do what we can do. There are times and places where our leadership can mean the difference between peace and war. . . . In Bosnia this terrible war has challenged our interests and troubled our souls. Thankfully, we can do something about it. . . . The people of Bosnia, our NATO allies and people all around the world are now looking to America for our leadership. That is our responsibility as Americans." Thus, Clinton sent troops to Bosnia to achieve liberal goals. Nevertheless, he also promised "that our mission will be clear, limited, and achievable" and that U.S. troops would leave Bosnia in a year's time (Clinton 1996:47–48).

The same pattern of congressional responses have continued throughout the U.S. intervention in Bosnia. As with Haiti, the initial congressional hearings focused overwhelmingly on the question of when U.S. troops would leave Bosnia so that they could be out of harm's way. Throughout 1996 there was rampant skepticism in Congress about the administration's professed commitment to bring U.S. troops home by December 1996. Republican members of Congress spent an entire year of hearings trying to goad administration representatives into admitting that substantial numbers of American troops would stay in Bosnia beyond December 1996.

As also was the case with Haiti, congressional Republicans challenged the administration on whether it was sufficiently committed to the pursuit of liberal democracy in Bosnia. The House International Relations Committee held a set of hearings on the September 1996 elections in Bosnia, at which committee chair Benjamin Gilman (R-N.Y.) claimed: "These elections have given a mantle of legitimacy to individuals who have no interest in seeing Bosnia reconciled and reintegrated. Moreover, that mantle of legitimacy was conferred by a process where the hard-liners have an insurmountable advantage in terms of the control of media and local police and other institutions of authority which made the elections in many places unfair" (Congress 1997a:7). As with Haiti, these contradictory congressional pressures continued to push the Clinton administration to maintain its commitment to proliberalization policies in Bosnia while systematically avoiding potentially dangerous policy initiatives, such as the capture of indicted war criminals, which might have been necessary for the successful democratization of Bosnia.

The Clinton administration's response to the Bosnian crisis strongly reflected the political dynamics expected by the domestic liberal argument. Simultaneous congressional pressures to do something about the humanitarian crisis in Bosnia, yet not risk the lives of U.S. soldiers, led the administration to call for air strikes as its strategy for addressing the Bosnian crisis. Calling for a lifting of the arms embargo against the Bosnian government also remained a persuasive strategy for doing something consistent with American liberal ideals while putting U.S. troops at limited risk. Clinton was stopped from implementing this strategy of lift and strike only by America's liberal allies whose peacekeeping troops would have been placed at risk by this strategy. The stalemate was not broken until 1995, when Clinton decided that the risks to U.S. troops associated with a real peacekeeping mission in Bosnia would be less than those associated with a mission to extract our allies' forces from the region. Furthermore, a peacekeeping mission held out the possibility of achieving at least some of America's liberal humanitarian goals, while an extraction mission would have illuminated the humiliating failure of the United States to address the humanitarian crisis in Bosnia.

Conclusion

The Clinton administration's military interventions exhibit an important shift in the relative importance of the political dynamics emphasized by the realist and domestic liberal arguments. In most prior U.S. interventions, the United States intervened to serve its material and security interests, as expected by the realist argument. It promoted democracy when that strategy was deemed most likely to win its wars. The domestic liberal argument explained why Democratic presidents might be predisposed to the promotion of democracy to achieve security goals and how liberal pressure from Congress could compel presidents to adopt proliberalization policies to encourage Congress to appropriate the funds necessary for the successful prosecution of the war.

In contrast, the Clinton cases suggest the increasing power of the domestic liberal argument for explaining contemporary U.S. interventions. On the one hand, Clinton appears to have launched interventions primarily to achieve liberal goals, such as the restoration of democracy in Haiti and the abolition of ethnic cleansing in Bosnia. On the other hand, Clinton has generally been vacillating, ineffective, and indecisive in his use of force abroad. He has consistently avoided taking risks that might lead to U.S. casualties. Indeed, Clinton agreed to send U.S. soldiers to Haiti and Bosnia only when he was relatively certain that no one would actually shoot at them.

This is precisely the pattern of interventionist behavior that one should expect of any liberal state. Cultural values cause liberal states such as the United States to intervene in response to humanitarian crises, human rights violations, and political tyranny in states where they lack more concrete national interests. At the same time, however, the political constraints imposed by liberal institutions of governance make these states reluctant to use force or to pay high costs to achieve liberal goals. Thus, liberal values and liberal political institutions have somewhat contradictory impacts on military intervention.

These conflicting political dynamics lead to a distinctive pattern of military intervention. On the one hand, presidents must respond in a manner consistent with American liberal values to the political and humanitarian crises that reach the consciousness of the American people. Failure to do so could open them up to charges of violating liberal values either by callously disregarding a human tragedy or by failing to fight for liberal democracy. These attacks can come from both "liberal" Democrats and "conservative" Republicans and can reflect both genuine commitment to liberal internationalism and/or partisan politics. On the other hand, any presidents who send troops into combat make themselves vulnerable to political charges that they have needlessly sacrificed the lives of U.S. soldiers. While some of these constraints are imposed directly on presidents through the electoral process, it is Congress that plays the crucial role in constraining executive authority.

The logical response of presidents placed in this domestic political bind is to do whatever they can short of war to demonstrate that they are responding to the crisis in the country in question. Presidents do this even if they believe that their limited actions are unlikely to resolve the crisis. If they are fortunate, diplomacy, economic sanctions, and the threat of force might achieve limited progress or preserve a stalemate, even if failing to generate a definitive solution. Having staked U.S. resources and prestige on achieving solutions, however, it becomes much more difficult and costly to disengage from the situation when it appears that a substantial commitment of U.S. military power may be necessary to resolve the crisis.

When the political costs of suffering casualties in war are greater than the cost of violating American principles, as they often are in these cases, presidents are likely to withdraw from the intervention. Knowing that this would be the likely outcome, the wisest choice might be to decide early on not to commit U.S. resources and prestige to a losing battle one is unprepared to fight. However, when the initial choice is to do nothing or to demonstrate commitment to the cause by using diplomacy or sanctions that have a limited chance of success, the politically safest course at that time is to take limited action. Thus, presidents appear doomed to repeat the pattern of gradually escalating U.S. involvement in these crises and then stepping away from the brink when it appears that military force might be necessary to achieve a solution. When military force is used in support of liberal values, it will often be used in a limited, vacillating, and ineffectual manner.

Realism still plays an important role in explaining these cases, but in a broader sense than was true of previous eras. First, the increasing prominence of liberal interventionism could only take place in what is the most secure and permissive international security environment that the United States has ever faced. Second, the Clinton administration's embrace of the liberal approach reflects a conscious strategy to legitimize normatively to both domestic and international audiences America's continued status as "leader of the free world."

7

The Impact of U.S. Intervention on Democratization

Do American efforts to promote democracy during military interventions lead to the democratization of target states? Until recently scholars approached this question with almost unrelieved skepticism, agreeing with Lowenthal that U.S. attempts to export democracy have generally been "negligible, often counterproductive, and only occasionally positive" (1991:243). This negative conclusion has flowed from two sources. First, most contemporary literature on transitions to democracy emphasizes the purely domestic sources and politically contingent nature of contemporary democratization (O'Donnell, Schmitter, and Whitehead 1986; Diamond, Linz, and Lipset 1989). Consequently, many scholars analyzing the failure of U.S. efforts to promote democracy blame local factors beyond the control of American policymakers (Huntington 1984; Lowenthal 1991; Muravchik 1991). Second, scholars who believe that the United States does have a significant impact on political regimes see an antidemocratic bias in U.S. policy because democracy is subordinated to economic and security interests (Herman and Brodhead 1984).

In contrast, this chapter starts from the premise that countries experiencing military intervention should provide the most likely cases for a profound external impact on local politics. In addition, while earlier chapters have established that the promotion of democracy is usually fundamentally tied to U.S. security interests, that does not mean that the commitment to democracy is not genuine. Indeed, policymakers have engaged in a relentless search for ways to reconcile the real democratization of target states with American security concerns. This is most clear for those presidents who adopted proliberalization policies because they were convinced that only the genuine democratization of target states would create stronger and more stable allied regimes. Even when they supported demonstration elections to legitimate ongoing interventions, presidents had to ensure that those elections were minimally free and fair in order to convince a skeptical Congress. As the pattern of U.S. military interventions more closely reflects the expectations of domestic liberalism in the contemporary era, the U.S. commitment to democracy is likely to become even more genuine and the success of American proliberalization policies in building democracy more apparent.

The empirical analysis presented in this chapter demonstrates that states in which the United States adopted proliberalization policies during military interventions were significantly more likely to be democracies in 1993 than states that had not had this experience. Furthermore, U.S. proliberalization policies have helped forge democracy in countries like Cambodia, the Dominican Republic, El Salvador, Grenada, Haiti, Honduras, Nicaragua, Panama, and the Philippines, which present inhospitable domestic conditions for democracy. It is the democratization of these poor, inequitable, conflict-ridden societies that presents the greatest challenge to those who argue either that the United States cannot have a significant impact on democracy or that the pursuit of America's security and economic interests inherently pushes the United States to thwart democracy in target states.

This chapter's analysis builds on recent studies by Hermann and Kegley (1998) and Meernik (1996), which have found that U.S. military interventions generally leave target states more liberal than before intervention, but adds two dimensions not emphasized in their studies. First, while Hermann and Kegley and Meernik examine whether U.S. interventions have led to any liberalization in target regimes, this chapter asks whether they have produced regimes that have surpassed the procedural minimum to be considered democracies, as measured by whether they achieve a score of at least six on the democracy scale of the Polity III data set compiled by Gurr,

Moore, and Jaggers (1995).[1] Second, while the previous studies test whether certain aspects of U.S. intervention have had a positive or negative impact on democratization, neither directly examines whether specific efforts to promote liberal reforms during those interventions have had a positive impact on democratization. This chapter focuses on the impact of proliberalization policies on democracy in target states and finds that it is the adoption of such policies that accounts for the positive relationship between U.S. intervention and democracy, which has been discovered by previous studies.

The United States as a Force for Democracy?

Two projects—O'Donnell, Schmitter, and Whitehead's *Transitions from Authoritarian Rule* (1986) and Diamond, Linz, and Lipset's *Democracy in Developing Countries* (1989)—set the tone for the early literature on the "third wave" of democratization. Both of these major studies argue that recent transitions to democracy can be better explained by domestic rather than international factors. O'Donnell and Schmitter (1986) take this a step further by attacking structural explanations at any level of analysis in favor of an emphasis on elite politics, pact making, and contingent political choice.

As the third wave crests, an increasing number of states with unfavorable domestic conditions for successful democratization are nevertheless joining the democratic camp. The mainstream literature on transitions to democracy is therefore having an increasingly difficult time explaining the global spread of democracy (Remmer 1995). International factors, such as the efforts of the world's most powerful liberal state to promote democracy abroad, offer persuasive alternative explanations for contemporary democratization.

Despite this, even those who have focused exclusively on the impact of the United States on democratization have joined the consensus that domestic political dynamics are primary in explaining democratization. Some argue that U.S. action explains the success stories, while failures can be explained by purely domestic impediments to democratization. Huntington suggests that U.S. intervention accounted for the greatest democratic successes in Central America and the Caribbean during the early part of the century, while local factors spawned the dictatorships that ruled in the aftermath of

1. This chapter uses the May 1996 version of Polity III available by anonymous FTP at isere@colorado.edu.

those interventions. "It had taken American power to impose even the most modest aspects of democracy in these societies. When American intervention ended, democracy ended" (1982:27). Muravchik seconds this conclusion, arguing that U.S. occupation was crucial for the successful democratization of the Axis powers after World War II (1991:91–118). America's failures to build democracy in the Third World, however, "prove, if anyone doubted it, that U.S. military occupation is not a sufficient condition to make a country democratic" (1991:116).

Even critics of U.S. intervention agree that domestic factors overwhelm international ones in explaining democratization. Lowenthal concludes that the central reason for the failure of U.S. efforts to export democracy is that "external factors, including U.S. policy, are usually of secondary or tertiary importance in determining a Latin American nation's prospects for democracy." Furthermore, the United States has never "succeeded in an enduring fashion unless local conditions were propitious" (1991:260). More broadly, critics of U.S. intervention have argued that democracy must be built on foundations of popular sovereignty and the freedom of peoples to determine their own future. It cannot be coercively imposed by outsiders (Herman and Brodhead 1984; Karl 1990; Whitehead 1991). Thus, scholars from diverse and contending theoretical and ideological traditions concur that the failure of U.S. efforts to promote democracy can be best explained by conditions within the target countries.

Scholars who believe that U.S. military intervention does have a profound impact on target societies generally see that impact in negative terms. These scholars argue that the United States often does not attempt to promote democracy during its interventions and even when it does adopt proliberalization policies, such policies are either a fig leaf covering antidemocratic policies or are undermined by other elements of the intervention. Thus, Herman and Brodhead (1984), Karl (1986), Rueschemeyer, Stephens, and Stephens (1992), and others posit that the principal impact of U.S. military intervention on target states has been to strengthen the political power of military institutions relative to other political actors, which can seriously undermine the prospects for democracy in target states.

Military institutions almost always play a crucial role in autocratic regimes, even if the military does not govern directly. As Stepan explains:

> [A] serious examination of the problem of how to manage the military democratically . . . would seem to be fundamental to our analysis of the weakening of authoritarian regimes, of democratic transition, and democratic consolidation for three reasons. First, the military either

heads or provides the core of the coercive state apparatus of most authoritarian regimes. Second, most of the would-be "successor" democratic regimes are immediately faced with major problems as to how to control and redirect the military and intelligence systems they inherit. Third, the military often continues to represent a critical component in politics by offering, implicitly or otherwise, a threatening alternative to democracy. (1988:xx)

For these reasons, scholars of democratization consistently point to the "reserve power" and special prerogatives of military institutions as some of the most significant barriers to the consolidation of democracy (O'Donnell, Schmitter, and Whitehead 1986; Stepan 1988; Stanley 1996).

Because the United States often enhances the power and prerogatives of local military institutions, the combination of democracy promotion and counterinsurgency warfare can lead to the liberalization of authoritarian regimes rather than to genuine democratization (Karl 1990). Elections take place in a context of fear and intimidation. Governments restrict freedom of speech and silence the independent press. They forcibly dismantle labor unions, popular organizations, and other democratic interest groups and exclude opposition parties from electoral participation. Finally, local militaries remain unaccountable to civilian leaders (Herman and Brodhead 1984:11–16).

Military Intervention, Proliberalization Policies, and Democracy

Because of these and other concerns, this chapter does not suggest that any application of U.S. military power is enough to promote the cause of democracy. Huntington, for example, argues that states emulate American democracy because they are impressed by American power. "When American power was clearly predominant . . . no Harkin Amendment was necessary to convey the message of the superiority of liberty. The message was there for all to see in the troop deployments, carrier task forces, foreign aid missions, and intelligence operatives" (1982:34). More broadly, one can argue that most of America's foreign and defense policies are at least partially shaped by America's liberal ideals. Based on this logic, Meernik suggests that it is appropriate to measure whether any type of U.S. military intervention leads to the democratization of target states.

In contrast, this chapter argues that if U.S. military power is used to overthrow elected regimes (Forsythe 1992), support "friendly tyrants" (Kirkpatrick 1979; Pipes and Garfinkle 1991), or bankroll illiberal insurgent movements (Schraeder 1992b), U.S. military intervention has a negative impact on democracy. It is unlikely to have a positive impact on democracy even if the failure to adopt proliberalization policies represents the limited nature of the intervention rather than an active effort to undermine the prospects for democracy in the target state. It is the adoption of proliberalization policies during military intervention that generates democracy, not intervention in and of itself. Because the United States has adopted proliberalization policies only slightly more than a third of the time, and nonliberalization policies almost two-thirds of the time, these two conflicting tendencies should cancel each other out in a broad examination of the impact of U.S. military intervention on democracy. These conflicting tendencies are reinforced by the potential contradictions noted above, which are likely to render proliberalization policies less than completely successful in building democracy. This leads to the first hypothesis examined here.

Hypothesis 7.1: There is no relationship between U.S. military intervention broadly conceived and democracy in target states.

Meernik and Hermann and Kegley recognize the importance of distinguishing those cases that include efforts to promote liberal reforms from those in which no such effort is made, but neither directly examines proliberalization policies. Meernik relies on declaratory policy and finds that target states are more likely to become democratic when presidents proclaim that promoting democracy is an important goal of the intervention (1996:398–99). Relying on Pearson and Baumann's (1994) coding decisions, Hermann and Kegley classify interventions as focusing on "the protection or promotion of democracy in the target" if "they involved military force used either (1) to support a government that was leaning toward or in the liberal democratic community or (2) to oppose an autocratic government" (1998:94). Pearson and Baumann's data, and thus Hermann and Kegley, do not indicate which particular policies, either in support of democratic regimes or in opposition to autocratic regimes, should be considered as evidence of the adoption of proliberalization policies.

This chapter uses the adoption of proliberalization policies, which has been the dependent variable thus far, as an independent variable to explain democratization in target states. It argues that specific efforts to liberalize target regimes can be successful in fostering democratic regimes, as suggested by the second hypothesis:

Hypothesis 7.2: The adoption of proliberalization policies during U.S. military interventions increases the likelihood that target states will become democracies.

The statistical tests in this chapter examine the impact of the entire package of proliberalization policies, as categorized in Table 2.2. The theoretical argument and discussion of specific cases focus on the impacts of U.S. support for free and fair elections and the demilitarization of target states.

Military interventions provide the United States with the power and leverage to compel local actors to accept institutional reforms, such as elections they might have opposed in the absence of U.S. imposition. While the successful inauguration of free and fair elections is not a sufficient condition for democracy, and can lead to a hollow formalism void of democratic content, honest elections are a necessary part of the equation and can serve as a catalyst for a more complete democratization of target countries. As Huntington (1991:174–92) argues, even elections convoked in the most inhospitable political climate for democracy, which is often the case in the context of military interventions, have had a powerful democratizing effect. Even if governments exclude some parties from electoral participation, the convocation of nonfraudulent elections with multiple parties competing for votes can still lead to genuine democratization of the polity. Any loosening of restrictions on rights of association and speech can energize civil society and undermine the legitimacy of autocratic elites, despite the absence of a full commitment to democratic civil liberties. Formal civilian command of the armed forces can transform civil-military relations to some extent, despite the continuing autonomy of military institutions in states making a transition toward democracy. Furthermore, elections can also create a fait accompli, whereby insurgent movements have little choice but to seek incorporation in the democratic arena if they want to have access to political power. Following Huntington (1991), I argue that U.S. support for free and fair elections can lead to genuine democratization despite the potential contradictions associated with promoting democracy during a military intervention.

Critics of U.S. intervention are correct, however, in arguing that the U.S. relationship with local military institutions can have a profound impact on the success of American-sponsored elections. When the United States has intervened as an ally of local militaries, the twining of democracy promotion and counterinsurgency warfare has often created partially democratic "electocracies" or liberalized authoritarian regimes (Karl 1990). Some of these regimes exceed the procedural minimum to be considered democracies, but have difficulty in deepening and consolidating that democracy because the military retains extraordinary autonomy relative to a civilian-elected government, thus placing limits on democratic accountability.

Elections are much more effective in generating democracy if combined with a consistent policy to reduce dramatically the power and autonomy of military institutions in target states. What critics of U.S. intervention miss is that these policies can be, and at times have been, pursued simultaneously by American policymakers. Support for free and fair elections and demilitarization work in tandem when the United States identifies the local armed forces as the enemy of U.S. security interests. If the United States achieves a military victory, its destruction of the adversary's army removes a substantial obstacle to democratization in the target state. In a subtler version of this process, U.S. support for a substantial reduction in the power and influence of allied militaries and insurgent movements as part of the reconciliation of civil wars can have a profoundly positive impact on the democratization of those societies.

Testing for the independent impacts of support for free and fair elections and demilitarization would allow us to understand the complex relationship between these different aspects of U.S. intervention. Unfortunately, the United States has not adopted demilitarization policies in enough of its interventions to allow for a statistical examination of this relationship. There are only a handful of cases in which the United States pursued unambiguous demilitarization policies. The systematic dismantling of the military institutions of the Axis powers after World War II and Panama in 1989 count as clear cases of demilitarization policies. The only other cases that come close to involving conscious demilitarization policies are the Central American cases of the late 1980s and early 1990s, where the United States supported the reduction of the capabilities, prerogatives, and power of local military and paramilitary institutions in El Salvador, Honduras, and Nicaragua as part of the resolution of long-standing civil wars in the region (after spending most of the previous decade building up these forces). Since all of these countries were democracies at the end of their experience with U.S. intervention, for a 100 percent success rate, the demilitarization variable falls out of the statistical equation.

Another aspect of U.S. intervention must be included as a control variable. Support for the government of a target state provides greater opportunities for the adoption of proliberalization policies than when the United States opposes the government. Thus, it was easier for the United States to promote democracy in South Vietnam than in North Vietnam, even though it intervened militarily in both countries. In addition, because the clandestine nature of insurgent movements keeps them from holding elections, U.S. support for insurgencies rarely includes pro-electoral policies. Finally, while the United States has helped topple elected governments, it generally targets illiberal governments (Hermann and Kegley 1996). A third hypothesis is examined to control for this factor.

Hypothesis 7.3: U.S. opposition to the government of the target state decreases the likelihood that target states will become democracies.

One final variable must be included because of the likelihood that it has a strong relationship with both U.S. intervention decisions and the possibilities for democratization: war.[2] A state's participation in either international or civil war increases the power of the chief executive and enhances the size and political power of military and other repressive institutions within the state (Mearsheimer 1990; Thompson 1996). Autocratic regimes threatened by democratic transition often pursue diversionary war strategies to enable them to continue their undemocratic regimes (Lake 1992; Mansfield and Snyder 1995; Stanley 1996). Civil wars are especially damaging to the prospects for democracy, given that the victors are likely to have little sense of common citizenship and identity with those they have just vanquished. Building a civic culture in conflict zones poses daunting challenges.

On the other side of the equation, U.S. military intervention has some definitional relationship to war, although a majority of U.S. interventions have involved the use of force short of full-scale war, according to the 1,000-death battle threshold used by the Correlates of War project (Singer and Small 1994). Nevertheless, even if the United States is not an active participant in a war, the existence of civil war in a target country often encourages the United States to intervene. Furthermore, policymakers often explain their failure to adopt proliberalization policies on the presence of war in the target country (Kirkpatrick 1979). To assess the impact of this variable, this study examines a fourth hypothesis:

Hypothesis 7.4: Participation in either international or civil war decreases the likelihood that states will become democracies.

Measuring Democracy

The dependent variable in this chapter, democracy, is measured using the Polity III data set compiled by Gurr, Moore, and Jaggers (1995). Polity III

2. Meernik (1996) addresses this problem in one of the most creative contributions of his work by comparing countries that have experienced U.S. military intervention with those that have experienced "international crises" in which the U.S. was not a participant.

classifies the regime characteristics of all polities of more than one million inhabitants from 1800 to 1994. Thus, it is the only data set on democracy that allows for consistent comparisons between the U.S. experiences in Cuba and Nicaragua during the first years of the twentieth century, Germany and Japan after World War II, and Panama and the Persian Gulf in the contemporary era. Gurr et al. code each polity along nine dimensions, five of which are used to construct a composite score of the democratic characteristics of political regimes. The first two elements characterize the competitiveness and openness of executive recruitment within states. A third variable codes the political constraints imposed on the executive. The final two components measure the regulation and competitiveness of participation. Polity III, therefore, approximates the more comprehensive definition of democracy offered by Karl, which served as the basis for the concept of proliberalization policies developed in Chapter 2: "(1) contestation over policy and competition for office; (2) participation of the citizenry through partisan, associational, and other forms of collective action; (3) accountability of the rulers to the ruled through mechanisms of representation and the rule of law; and (4) civilian control over the military" (1990:2). The lack of an explicit measurement of civil-military relations in Polity III makes it a less than perfect fit.

Polity III classifies states as institutionalized democracies on an 11-point scale if the executive is chosen in open elections, is subordinated to or significantly constrained by an elected legislature, and political participation is competitive. It classifies states as institutionalized autocracies on a different 11-point scale if the executive is "selected" in a closed process, the executive possesses unlimited decision-making authority, and political participation is restricted and/or suppressed. Since states may have mixed characteristics, or may have unregulated political processes that would cause them to score low on both scales, there is not a perfect correlation between the two scales.

The use of Polity III facilitates direct comparisons between this study and the results reported by Meernik and Hermann and Kegley using the same data. Although both studies claim to be measuring "democratic change" in target states, they actually measure the liberalization of autocratic regimes. Hermann and Kegley create a 20-point scale (−10 to +10) by combining the autocracy and democracy scales. They then compare the mean scores of states on this scale before and after the interventions and use analysis of variance tests to discover whether the change in the mean is statistically significant. They find that states are significantly closer to the democracy side of the scale after an intervention. Among the sixty-four reform interventions they test, they find that the mean score moved from −1.50 to −.62 (Hermann and Kegley 1998:97). This is an important finding that suggests that U.S.

intervention leads at least to the liberalization of target regimes. One problem with this finding, however, is that even after interventions, the mean score for target states is still closer to the autocracy side of the scale than to democracy. As Przeworski et al. point out, "while some democracies are more democratic than others, unless offices are contested, no regime should be considered democratic" (1996:52). Furthermore, as O'Donnell and Schmitter argue, the liberalization and democratization of political regimes are related yet distinct political processes (1986:6–14). It is possible that Hermann and Kegley have captured the liberalization of polities that still fail to surpass the minimum institutional threshold to be considered democracies. This is highly likely to be the case for any regime that receives a negative score on the combined democracy and autocracy scale. It is therefore difficult to know from their results whether U.S. intervention has merely produced less repressive autocratic regimes or genuine democratization.

Meernik's study suffers from similar problems. It presents a simpler, three-part categorization that codes cases as experiencing a positive change, no change, or a negative change in their Polity scores in the wake of an intervention. A regime can move one point on the Polity scale in the wake of an intervention and still be counted as a success or failure of U.S. intervention. This leads to the disconcerting finding that U.S. interventions in Yugoslavia in 1951, Zaire in 1961 and 1964, and Egypt in 1982 are considered successful cases of democratic change even though none of these regimes has ever come close to being considered democratic in Polity III (Meernik 1996:395).[3] Even if these regimes all liberalized in some marginal fashion, it is not clear that this should be termed democratic change. Given that U.S. intervention can liberalize target regimes while restricting their transition to full democracy, it is important to put the record of U.S. intervention to a more demanding test.

This chapter translates Polity III's 11-point democracy scale into a dichotomous variable by coding states as democracies if they score between 6 and 10 on the democracy scale, and as nondemocracies if they score between 0 and 5. To argue that U.S. intervention leads to genuine democratization, it is essential to establish a reasonable minimum threshold for states to be considered democracies. A cut-off point of 6 on the democracy scale accomplishes this by approximating the definition of democracy laid out above. A polity cannot reach 6 on the democracy scale without having free

---

3. Indeed, even Meernik's categorization of the Zairian cases may be in error. The Polity data set measures no change toward democracy in the history of Zaire, although it does measure changes toward democracy in neighboring Congo, which was not a target of U.S. intervention.

and fair elections, but it also cannot reach this point by only having free and fair elections for the chief executive.

It would be possible to create an interval scale of the "level" of democracy by differentiating between states that receive scores of between 6 and 10, but this could generate additional problems. Because the Polity III democracy scale combines evaluations about separate institutional characteristics of states into a single scale, each increment in that scale is not of an identical intensity. It is therefore not appropriate to conceive of it as a continuous variable (Gleditsch and Ward 1997). A state that receives a 7 on the scale is not necessarily more democratic than one that receives a 6. They could simply be different types of democratic regimes with varying institutional characteristics. Indeed, this study uses 6 as a cut-off, in part because the democracy scale exhibits a substantial bias in favor of parliamentary systems and those in which the legislature is a coequal branch with the executive, and a bias against democracies with strong presidents (Gleditsch and Ward 1997). Four of the ten points of the democracy scale involve a measurement of the degree to which the executive is constrained by the legislature. Thus, de Gaulle's France would not be considered an institutionalized democracy by this scale if 7 were used as the cut-off point. Since this study is interested in whether U.S. intervention leads to any kind of democracy, regardless of the specific institutional characteristics of the regime, a dichotomous measure of democracy is most appropriate.

Assessing the Impact of U.S. Military Intervention on Democracy

Does any application of U.S. military might encourage democratization? This section examines the question using the list of cases of U.S. military intervention from the Spanish-American War of 1898 through Bill Clinton's election in 1992, found in Chapter 2 (Table 2.1). The Clinton administration cases are not included because of the lack of Polity scores for the most recent cases. The democracy score of each target state is then measured in the year before the intervention and then one and ten years after the intervention.[4]

---

4. Polity III generally does not code countries occupied by foreign powers or undergoing political transitions. Since this is true for many cases examined here, this study uses the first available scores in the data set to code the democratic status of states before and after U.S. intervention. For the handful of cases that emerged from colonial rule during a U.S. intervention, the pre-intervention regime is classified as nondemocratic. I rely on Meernik's coding decision for Grenada, which does not meet Polity III's minimum population criteria.

Table 7.1 divides the ninety cases of U.S. military intervention based on their democratic status one year before and one year after the intervention. It shows that a large majority of the states that have experienced U.S. military intervention were nondemocracies before the intervention. Most remained nondemocracies after U.S. intervention. Nevertheless, Table 7.1 indicates that twice as many states were democracies one year after being the target of U.S. intervention than were democracies before intervention. Whereas only 12 percent (11 of 90) of the target countries were democratic at the outset of the intervention, 26 percent (23 of 90) were democracies one year after the termination of the intervention. Nearly all the cases that changed after U.S. intervention (14 of 16), changed in the direction of democracy. Only Laos and Syria moved from the democratic to the non-democratic camp within a year of American intervention. Only in the Laotian case does the United States share in the blame for the reversal.

These patterns hold over the longer term. Virtually every state that was a nondemocracy one year after U.S. intervention remained a nondemocracy ten years after the intervention. Virtually every state that was a democracy one year after a U.S. intervention remained a democracy ten years later. Of the seventy-one interventions that ended at least ten years before the end point of this study in 1993, only one country experienced any change in regime between the first and tenth year following that intervention. South Korea experienced a single year of democracy in 1960 in the transition between the Rhee and Park dictatorships. Another target of U.S. intervention, Thailand, experienced a brief interlude of democratic rule from 1973 to 1976 during a U.S. intervention, but had reverted to autocracy before the withdrawal of U.S. troops and maintained its nondemocratic status in the decade after the intervention.

It is too early to measure the long-term impact of interventions that terminated in the late 1980s and early 1990s. Of the nineteen most recent cases, only two have experienced any regime change between the year after the end of U.S. intervention and 1993. The Sudan shifted from democracy to nondemocracy, while Guatemala moved from nondemocracy to democracy. The one case that experienced a breakdown of democracy within ten years of the end of a U.S. intervention involved perhaps the most insignificant intervention in the data set. In 1984 the United States airlifted Egyptian troops to the Sudan to participate in that country's civil war. A negotiated settlement that inaugurated a democratic regime in the Sudan in 1985 broke down in 1987.

The finding that virtually every regime that made a transition to democracy in the immediate aftermath of a U.S. intervention sustained that

Table 7.1   Military intervention and democracy

After Intervention:	Before Intervention	
	Democracy	Nondemocracy
Democracy	Honduras 1924–25 Turkey 1957 Cyprus 1964 Cyprus 1974 Bolivia 1986 (N = 9)	Philippines 1898–1936 Italy 1943–48 Germany 1945–49 Austria 1945–55 Japan 1945–52 Philippines 1949–52 El Salvador 1981–91 Nicaragua 1981–90 Cambodia 1982–91 Honduras 1982–90 Grenada 1983 Sudan 1984* Philippines 1985–88 Panama 1989–92 (N = 14)
Nondemocracy	Syria 1957 Laos 1959–75	Cuba 1898–1902 China 1900 Panama 1903–36 Cuba 1906–9 Nicaragua 1909–33 Mexico 1914 Haiti 1915–34 Dominican Rep. 1916–24 Mexico 1917 Cuba 1917–22 Russia 1918–20 China 1927 China 1945–49 Liberia 1947 S. Korea 1945–49 S. Korea 1950–53* N. Korea 1950–53 S. Vietnam 1950–75 Yugoslavia 1951 Taiwan 1954–55 China 1954–55 Guatemala 1954 Indonesia 1956–58 China 1956–73 Lebanon 1957 Taiwan 1958 China 1958 Lebanon 1958 Jordan 1958 Cuba 1958

continued

Table 7.1 Continued

	Before Intervention	
Democracy		**Nondemocracy**
	Panama 1959	Cuba 1959–60
	Zaire 1960–61	Cuba 1961
	Dominican Rep. 1961	Thailand 1962
	Haiti 1963	S. Korea 1963
	S. Arabia 1963	Panama 1964
	Zaire 1964	N. Vietnam 1964–75
	Cambodia 1964–75	Dominican Rep. 1965–66
	S. Korea 1965–69	Thailand 1966–76
	Zaire 1967	Jordan 1970
	Iraq 1972–75	Angola 1975–76
	Zaire 1978	Guyana 1978
	Iran 1980	Afghanistan 1980–91
	Egypt 1982–92	Lebanon 1982–84
	Chad 1983	S. Arabia 1984
	Angola 1985–91	Libya 1986
	Guatemala 1987*	Kuwait 1987–88
	Iraq 1990–92	Kuwait 1990–92
	S. Arabia 1990–91	
	(N = 65)	
(N = 2)		

*Cases that shifted from democracy to nondemocracy or vice versa within ten years of U.S. military intervention
N = 90.

democracy for many years after the intervention is quite surprising. On the one hand, one might expect that externally imposed institutions might collapse over the longer term, either because domestic conditions were unfavorable or because of contradictory legacies of the U.S. intervention. On the other hand, one also might expect that any positive impact of U.S. intervention might take years to develop.

While this data shows that more states which experienced U.S. intervention were democracies after the intervention than before, and that these regimes sustained democracy over the long term, the information in Table 7.1 does not provide statistical evidence that U.S. intervention was the cause of these democratic transitions. It is unclear whether any application of U.S. military force is likely to have a positive impact on democracy or if the adoption of proliberalization policies during U.S. interventions is the crucial factor. In addition, it is not clear from this table whether the higher percentage of democracies after U.S. intervention merely reflects a secular trend toward democracy caused by domestic factors unrelated to U.S. intervention.

In another important limitation of the data presented in Table 7.1, many readers will be justifiably concerned by the extreme disparities in intensity among the cases. Is it appropriate to compare major wars like Vietnam with minor interventions like the periodic use of U.S. military aircraft to transport Zairian soldiers to combat zones? One would expect that limited interventions would have a less profound impact on the political regimes of target states. The statistical analysis reported in Table 7.3 addresses this concern by operationalizing the "military intervention" variable in terms of the number of months in which the United States intervened in each country from 1945 to 1992. This should more accurately assess the relative impact of lengthy and generally more intense U.S. interventions from the numerous limited interventions included in the comprehensive data set. It should also distinguish between countries that have experienced multiple interventions and those that have only been the target of intervention a single time.

Assessing the Impact of Proliberalization Policies on Democracy

Are specific efforts to promote democracy during U.S. interventions the key to the successful democratization of target countries? Table 7.2 categorizes cases based on whether the United States adopted proliberalization policies during the intervention and then determines whether these countries were democracies one year after the intervention. The data for this test is derived from Table 2.2, but with one important difference. While Chapter 2 codes each administration's policies during an intervention as a separate case, this chapter considers each *intervention* as a separate case. While there are important theoretical reasons for examining each administration as a separate case when explaining presidents' policy choices, it is not clear that it is appropriate to divide long-term interventions into multiple cases when examining the impact of proliberalization policies on democracy.

In many cases, the United States supported proliberalization policies early in the intervention, only to abandon such policies later, often fundamentally undermining whatever liberalizing impact earlier policies might have had. Thus, while the Johnson administration supported elections in South Vietnam in 1967, the Nixon and Ford administrations not only abandoned such policies but undermined previous efforts to liberalize South Vietnam. In an effort to provide a strong test of the impact of U.S.-sponsored proliberalization policies on democracy, Table 7.2 lists all cases in which the United States adopted proliberalization policies at any point during an intervention. This means that six cases in which earlier proliberalization policies were abandoned by the end of the intervention are coded as involving American sponsorship of such policies. As noted in Table 7.2, all six of these cases ended in nondemocracy.

The data in Table 7.2 provide empirical support for hypothesis 7.2, that the promotion of proliberalization policies during a military intervention rather than intervention itself has the most powerful impact on democratization in target states. Only 14 percent (8 of 59) of cases in which the United States did not adopt proliberalization policies were democracies one year after the intervention. Seven of these countries had already been democracies before the intervention. The only case of transition to democracy after a U.S. intervention without American sponsorship of proliberalization policies was the Sudan. As noted above, this is the only case in which a transition to democracy after a U.S. intervention was not sustained over the long term. Of those countries in which the United States promoted elections, 48 percent (15 of 31) were democracies one year after the intervention. Of these, only two—Honduras in 1924 and Greece in 1947—were democracies before the intervention. Thus, thirteen of the fourteen cases of transition from nondemocracy to democracy after U.S. intervention identified in Table 7.1 are cases in which the United States actively supported proliberalization policies. If the six ambiguous cases, in which the United States was no longer supporting proliberalization policies by the end of the intervention, are excluded, the success rate increases to 60 percent (15 of 25). These findings

Table 7.2 Proliberalization policies and democracy

Proliberalization Policies	Democracy	
	Yes	**No**
Yes	Philippines 1898–1936 Italy 1943–48 Austria 1945–55 Greece 1947–49 El Salvador 1981–91 Cambodia 1982–91 Grenada 1983 Panama 1989–92 Honduras 1924–25 Germany 1945–49 Japan 1945–52 Philippines 1949–52 Nicaragua 1981–90 Honduras 1982–90 Philippines 1985–88 (N = 15)	Cuba 1898–1902 Cuba 1906–9 Haiti 1915–34* Cuba 1917–22* S. Korea 1945–49 Lebanon 1958 Dominican Rep. 1965–66 Angola 1985–91 Panama 1903–36* Nicaragua 1909–33 Dominican Rep. 1916–24 China 1945–49* S. Vietnam 1950–75* Laos 1959–75* Lebanon 1982–84 Iraq 1990–92 (N = 16)
No	Turkey 1957 Cyprus 1964 Cyprus 1974 Sudan 1984 India 1962 Trinidad 1970 Ecuador 1981 Bolivia 1986	China 1900 Mexico 1917 China 1927 S. Korea 1950–53 Yugoslavia 1951 Taiwan 1954–55 Indonesia 1956–58 Syria 1957 Taiwan 1958 Jordan 1958 Panama 1959 Zaire 1960–61 Dominican Rep. 1961 Haiti 1963 Mexico 1914 Russia 1918–20 Liberia 1947 N. Korea 1950–53 Guatemala 1954 China 1954–55 China 1956–73 Lebanon 1957 China 1958 Cuba 1958 Cuba 1959–60 Cuba 1961 Thailand 1962 S. Korea 1963

continued

Table 7.2 Continued

Democracy		
Yes	**No**	
	S. Arabia 1963	Panama 1964
	Zaire 1964	N. Vietnam 1964–75
	Cambodia 1964–75	S. Korea 1965–69
	Thailand 1966–76	Zaire 1967
	Jordan 1970	Iraq 1972–75
	Angola 1975–76	Zaire 1978
	Guyana 1978	Iran 1980
	Afghanistan 1980–91	Egypt 1982–92
	Chad 1983	S. Arabia 1984
	Libya 1986	Guatemala 1987
	Kuwait 1987–88	Kuwait 1990–92
	S. Arabia 1990–91	
	(N = 51)	
(N = 8)		

*Proliberalization policies abandoned prior to the end of the intervention.
Chi square: 12.957; p. < .001.
N = 90

are confirmed by the longer-term results. Every state that was a democracy one year after an intervention involving proliberalization policies remained a democracy ten years after the intervention, or until 1993 in the case of more recent interventions.

Table 7.2 illuminates an additional point that speaks to the robustness of the statistical findings throughout the book. To classify cases of the adoption of proliberalization policies, one must make difficult coding decisions about ambiguous, "soft" data. There are several cases coded as involving the adoption of proliberalization policies, such as the Lebanese and Iraqi cases, which other observers might legitimately code as involving nonliberalization policies. There are other ambiguous cases, such as the Thai case, which were coded in Chapter 2 as involving nonliberalization policies, but which could have been classified otherwise.[5] Virtually all of the most ambiguous cases, however, were in countries that were nondemocracies in the aftermath of U.S. intervention. Thus, when ambiguous cases are coded as involving the adoption of nonliberalization policies, this weakens the statistical results in Chapter 2 but strengthens the results in this chapter. When ambiguous cases are coded as involving proliberalization policies, this lends greater support to the theoretical argument of Chapter 2 but lessens the impact of such policies in generating democracy according to the analysis of this chapter. The fact that the statistical analysis of presidential policies in Chapter 2 and of the impact of U.S. proliberalization on democracy in this chapter yield strong results despite this trade-off suggests that these results are robust.

A Multivariate Model of the Impact of U.S. Intervention on Democracy

The data in the tables presented above suggest that states which have experienced U.S. military intervention and/or American-sponsored proliberalization policies were more likely to be democracies after U.S. intervention than

5. The Thai military regime sponsored elections for a reopened parliament in 1969, in which opposition parties were allowed to field candidates. There is evidence to suggest that the Thai military took this initiative to answer U.S. critics of the American commitment to Thailand, which emerged in the context of the Vietnam War. The available evidence also suggests, however, that the U.S. government played virtually no role in the convocation of these elections. Subsequent elections after the 1973 breakdown of the military regime did lead to a brief but genuine democratization of Thailand. This democratic opening, however, was led by opponents of the U.S. military role in Thailand, and the new government negotiated the withdrawal of U.S. troops (Girling 1981).

they were before. Two problems with this data need to be addressed. First, it is not clear from these tables which aspect of U.S. intervention is driving the positive relationship between intervention and democracy. Second, a comparison with control cases and the inclusion of variables like previous democratic experience, U.S. support for or opposition to the government in the target state, and war participation is needed to ensure that the positive relationships noted above are not spurious.

These problems are addressed here in a series of statistical tests that examine all of the countries included in the Polity III data set, thus comparing the intervention cases to all other states in the international system. I use logit to test these relationships because this study dichotomizes the dependent variable, democracy, for the reasons discussed above. I examine the impact of U.S. intervention during two broad historical eras: before and after World War II. For the pre–World War II era, all states are measured in 1897, the year before the Spanish-American War, and in 1936, when the last of the early U.S. interventions in the Caribbean Basin ended.[6] For the post–World War II era, states are measured in 1944 and 1993.[7]

At the beginning of each era, before the first U.S. intervention of that time period, each state is measured using Polity III's democracy scale to determine whether cases that would later experience U.S. intervention are identifiably different from the norm for all other states in the system. This helps control for the historical experiences of target states with democracy before U.S. intervention. These states are again measured at the end of each era to discover whether the intervention cases are more democratic than those not experiencing U.S. intervention.

An examination of the impact of U.S. intervention in the pre–World War II era shows no systematic relationship between U.S. intervention and democratization. The United States failed to promote democracy successfully in virtually all of its interventions during this era. Of the ten countries

6. Only one pre–World War II intervention, the Philippines, continued until World War II. To facilitate the separation of the pre– and post–World War II cases, Filipino democracy will be measured in 1936, just after it achieved its commonwealth status and the Polity data set begins to record data for that country.

7. This part of the study runs into the dilemma of the disintegration of both traditional and colonial empires during each of these time periods. A majority of today's states were not independent entities in 1897 or 1944. The same procedures are followed for these states, as was true for the intervention cases. Any state that was independent at any moment during either of the relevant eras is included. If that state began the era as a colony of another state, it is coded as nondemocratic. If it began the era as an integral part of another state, as in the cases of most of the republics that broke away from the Soviet Union, a state is coded the same as the parent state at the beginning of the relevant era.

that would subsequently experience U.S. intervention during the pre–World War II era, only one, Honduras, was a democracy in 1897. Only one, the Philippines, was a democracy in 1936. The United States adopted proliberalization policies in the Philippines and Honduras, where democracy was replaced by a personalist dictatorship in 1936, after sustaining democracy for ten years following the U.S. intervention of 1924–25. It also pursued these policies in five countries that did not become democracies by 1936. The logit models for this era are not reported because the limited number of instances of intervention and proliberalization policies and the even more limited number of successes rendered the coefficients in the statistical tests unreliable. In general, most countries were nondemocracies in 1897 and remained nondemocracies in 1936. In both years, the intervention countries were less likely to be democracies than the norm. For this reason, it is difficult to know whether the failure to build democracy in these countries resulted from U.S. policy or conditions within the target countries.

An analysis of the post–World War II cases, however, suggests that the promotion of proliberalization policies during U.S. military interventions has had a positive impact on democracy in target states over the past fifty years. To assess this impact, I first examine the democracy scores of all states in 1944 to determine whether countries that would later experience U.S. intervention were identifiably different from the norm for all other states in the system. Logit analyses indicate that those states that would subsequently experience U.S. intervention or the adoption of proliberalization policies during an intervention were generally less democratic than the norm in 1944, although these differences were not statistically significant.[8] This roughly matches the information in Table 7.1, which indicates that 88 percent of

8. The information in the table below does not test a causal argument; it merely sets a baseline for the proportion of democracies among the countries that would later experience intervention or American-sponsored elections in comparison to the proportion of democracies among those states that would not share these experiences.

Post-WWII Interventions and Democracy in 1944

Variable	Coefficient (standard error)	Coefficient (standard error)
Post-WWII intervention	−.012 (.010)	
Post-WWII proliberal policies		−.518 (.781)
Constant	−1.604*** (.231)	−1.680*** (.232)

***p. < .001; one-tailed test.

the countries that would become targets of U.S. military intervention were nondemocracies before the intervention.

The democratic status of all states is evaluated again in 1993, soon after the end of the Cold War, to determine whether states that experienced U.S. intervention and/or American-sponsored proliberalization policies during the post–World War II era were more likely to be democracies than those that did not experience U.S. intervention. The year 1993 is convenient for disentangling the impact of U.S. intervention from the general trend toward democracy in the international system. That year is near the crest of the "third wave" of global democratization that began in the mid-1970s. Since there were more democracies in the international system at this time than ever before, if U.S. intervention and/or American-sponsored proliberalization policies are found to have a statistically significant impact on democracy, this provides strong evidence that the positive relationship between types of American intervention and democracy is not spurious.

Fifty years represents a substantial gap between observations. The continuity of regime type in target states in the ten years following U.S. interventions, however, suggests that this gap should not bias the results substantially. Significant volatility in the regime type of target states during the postintervention period would have rendered the research strategy pursued here less reliable.

Table 7.3 includes four logit models that separately measure the impact of U.S. intervention and American-sponsored proliberalization policies on democracy. It then looks at their joint impact and examines whether the relationships between intervention and proliberalization policies and democracy in target states remain significant in a model controlling for American opposition to the target regime and war participation by the target state. All four models include the democracy scores for all states in 1944 in order to control for the previous democratic experiences of states and to evaluate the change in regime over time. The fact that the democratic status of states in 1944 was the most significant variable for explaining democracy in 1993 suggests that continuity in regime type was the norm for all states, not just those that have experienced U.S. intervention.

As noted above, military intervention is operationalized as the number of months the United States intervened militarily in a target state between 1945 and 1992. American sponsorship of proliberalization policies is coded as a dummy variable, receiving a "1" if the United States actively supported proliberalization policies at any time during any intervention from 1945 to 1992 and a "0" if the United States did not intervene or if it did not adopt proliberalization policies during its intervention in a target country. The variable examining U.S. opposition to the government of the target state is also a dummy variable, receiving a "1" if the United States intervened against a target state and a "0" if the United States did not intervene or if it intervened on the side of the local government. The Pearson and Baumann and Schraeder data sets are used to determine whether the United States opposed the target regime. In those few countries, such as Guatemala, where the United States has intervened both for and against local governments at different times, the most recent intervention is used to code this variable. Finally, the war participation variables are also coded as dummy variables. Any state that participated in a civil or international war between 1945 and 1992 that met the Correlates of War 1,000 –battle death criteria received a "1." Any state that did not participate in a war of this magnitude during this era received a "0." The impact of international and civil wars are examined separately.

Table 7.3 provides support for hypothesis 7.1, confirming that there is no clear relationship between U.S. military intervention broadly conceived and democracy in target states. Model 1, which compares countries that have experienced U.S. military intervention with those that have not experienced intervention, suggests that intervention countries are indistinguishable from nonintervention countries. Model 3, which measures the joint impact of intervention and American-sponsored proliberalization policies suggests that there is a negative and statistically significant relationship between U.S. military intervention broadly conceived and democracy. The coefficient remains negative in model 4, which controls for U.S. opposition to the government in the target state and war participation, but is not significant in the fully specified model. As expected by hypothesis 7.3, the limited opportunities to promote democracy when the United States opposes the government in the target state are reflected in the statistically significant and negative coefficient for the "oppose government" variable in model 4 of Table 7.3. The addition of this variable helps account for the reversion of the military intervention variable from statistical significance in model 3 to insignificance in model 4. These results suggest that the positive and statistically significant relationship found by Meernik and Hermann and Kegley between U.S. military intervention broadly conceived and democracy is an artifact either of the kinds of proliberalization policies they do not measure directly or of the methods they use to measure democratic change.

There is also considerable evidence for hypothesis 7.2 in the results presented in Table 7.3. American-sponsored proliberalization policies have a positive and statistically significant impact on democracy in target states regardless of how the model is specified. Model 2 suggests that those states in which the United States has adopted proliberalization policies during a post–World War II military intervention were significantly more likely to be democracies in 1993 than those that had experienced interventions where such policies were not adopted, or where the United States had not intervened. These countries had been slightly less democratic in 1944 than the control group, yet they had democratized at a faster pace than other countries. Slightly more than half (73 of 140) of the states that had not experienced American-sponsored proliberalization policies during a military intervention were democracies in 1993. Seventy percent (14 of 20) of the states that had experienced such policies were democracies in 1993. In model 3, not only do proliberalization policies have a positive and significant impact on democracy, military intervention broadly conceived has a negative and significant impact on democracy.

The proliberalization variable reaches its greatest statistical significance in the fully specified model. Model 4 indicates that the positive relationship between support for proliberalization policies and democracy remains significant despite the partial confirmation of hypothesis 7.4. States that participated in wars during the post–World War II era were less likely to be democracies in 1993 than the norm. Seventeen of the twenty cases in which the United States sponsored proliberalization policies took place either during an ongoing war, or in the immediate aftermath of war.[9] Thus, American-sponsored proliberalization policies often overcame the substantial impediments that war places in the path of democracy. One of the most interesting findings in Table 7.3 is that civil war exhibits a much more negative impact on democracy than does participation in an international war. This finding merits future research.

How Robust Are These Findings?

How sensitive are these findings to different reasonable decision rules for the coding of the data and the inclusion of cases? This section looks at

---

9. Four of these seventeen cases involved the occupations of the Axis powers after World War II. While Germany, Austria, Italy, and Japan are not coded as participating in a post-1945 war in model 4 of Table 7.3, the United States nevertheless adopted proliberalization policies in these countries in the wake of World War II. These states overcame the authoritarian legacies of the war to emerge from their postwar occupations as democracies. Seven of the thirteen other states in which elections were sponsored in the context of war were democracies by 1993. This record suggests that an interactive variable measuring whether the positive impact of proliberalization policies depends on the presence or absence of war in countries where such policies were pursued would not show a strong relationship. This was confirmed in a logit model that included such an interactive variable with the other variables in model 4 of Table 7.3. The coefficient for this statistically insignificant variable was .283, with a standard error of 1.440.

Table 7.3   U.S. intervention, proliberalization policies, and democracy

Variable	Model 1: Coefficient (standard error)	Model 2: Coefficient (standard error)	Model 3: Coefficient (standard error)	Model 4: Coefficient (standard error)
Democracy in 1944	1.626*** (.518)	1.659*** (.518)	1.628*** (.518)	1.578** (.525)
Military intervention	.001 (.003)		−.009* (.005)	−.003 (.006)
Proliberalization		.942* (.531)	2.015** (.871)	2.502** (1.033)
Oppose government				−1.907* (.924)
International war				−.150 (.419)
Civil war				−1.304** (.445)
Constant	1.504** (.519)	1.419** (.519)	1.437** (.519)	1.845*** (.557)
−2 log likelihood	196.375	193.041	189.761	171.278
Model chi-square	24.206*** (2 df)	27.540*** (2 df)	30.819*** (3 df)	49.302*** (6 df)
Correctly predicted	59.38%	63.13%	63.75%	70.00%
N	160	160	160	160

*p. < .05; **p. < .01; ***p. < .001; one-tailed tests.

several different ways of classifying the data to determine whether alternative classification schemes change the statistical results noted above. Table 7.4 addresses three types of potential biases against finding a positive relationship between U.S. military intervention and democracy and/or in favor of finding a positive relationship between American-sponsored proliberalization policies and democracy. First, while I have argued above that the U.S. occupations of the Axis powers after World War II should be considered cases of military intervention, some might question this coding decision. Since all of the Axis cases are coded as involving the successful application of proliberalization policies, their inclusion in the analysis might bias the results. The "No Axis Cases" model in Table 7.4 codes the German, Austrian,

Italian, and Japanese cases as involving no U.S. military intervention and no American-sponsored proliberalization policies, and reestimates the fully specified model. The results are similar to those found in Table 7.3, with the exception that the proliberalization variable is significant at the .05 rather than .01 level. This suggests that the inclusion of the occupations of the Axis powers has a slight impact on the results but does not introduce significant bias into the analysis.[10]

Second, this study evaluates the impact of U.S. military interventions that took place between 1945 and 1992 on democracy in 1993. Some will question whether the very different time lags between early Cold War interventions and more recent cases introduces bias into the results. I have argued above that the continuity in the democratic status of target states from one to ten years after U.S. intervention makes it possible to make these kinds of comparisons. There are five states, however, which were not democracies for the full ten-year period after their experience with U.S. intervention, but which had become democracies by 1993. Counting these five cases (South Korea, the Dominican Republic, Thailand, Taiwan, and Guyana) as experiences where U.S. intervention led to democracy could insert a positive bias into the results. While the United States may have helped produce democracy in some of these countries, others clearly became democratic for reasons completely unrelated to American military intervention.[11] The "No Cases > 10" model in Table 7.4 recodes each of these five cases as not involving U.S. military intervention or American-sponsored proliberalization policies.

10. I also estimated the model by excluding the four Axis cases from the analysis rather than by recoding them. The results were almost identical to those in Table 7.4.

11. The dispatch of U.S. aircraft carrier task forces to the Taiwan Straits during the Tachen Islands and Quemoy and Matsu crises during the 1950s clearly did not cause the recent transition to democracy in Taiwan. Similarly, the American intervention in Guyana in the context of the Jonestown Massacre clearly had no relationship with the recent transition to democracy in that country. One could argue that the United States played some positive role in the three other 1993 democracies that were not democracies immediately after U.S. intervention. The regular elections experienced in the Dominican Republic after the withdrawal of U.S. forces in 1966 masked the dictatorship of Joaquin Balaguer that emerged from the intervention. When the opposition won the presidential elections in 1978, however, the diplomatic efforts of the Carter administration helped ensure that the Dominican military would not overturn the results, thus allowing the Dominican Republic to make its transition to democracy (Hartlyn 1991). As noted above, South Korea experienced one year of democracy in the ten years following the Korean War. In addition, Pearson and Baumann code the U.S.-led United Nations intervention in South Korea as continuous from 1950 through 1984. If this study had used Pearson and Baumann's coding decision rather than Tillema's more cautious assessment, the recent South Korean transition to democracy would have occurred within ten years of the end of U.S. intervention. The Thai case has been discussed above.

Recoding these cases does not change the results found in the fully specified model, suggesting that the presence of long lag times does not produce a significant bias in the analysis.[12]

Third, short-term, limited interventions may not provide suitable opportunities for the United States to have a significant impact on the political regimes of target states. The "No Short" interventions model in Table 7.4 recodes all cases that experienced less than twelve months of U.S. military intervention between 1945 and 1992 as involving zero months of intervention. This model indicates that U.S. military intervention broadly conceived still has no statistically significant impact on democracy in target states. American-sponsored proliberalization policies during a military intervention continues to have a positive and statistically significant relationship on democracy. Civil war has an even more significant negative impact on democracy than in Table 7.3. Eliminating short-term interventions also rendered the "oppose government" variable statistically insignificant. This result indicates that many of America's short-term interventions were launched against the governments of non-democratic regimes.

I also test the model using the three major data sets consulted in creating the comprehensive list of military interventions examined in this study.[13] These results, shown in Table 7.5, indicate that the proliberalization variable remains statistically significant in the examination of Pearson and Baumann's and Meernik's data, but not in the analysis of Tillema's data. The divergent results in Table 7.5 illustrate one of the central points raised above about the different emphases of quantitative and qualitative studies of U.S. military intervention. Qualitative studies have placed greater emphasis on America's indirect interventions on the side of governments in proxy wars. I argued above that such efforts are often more likely to involve American sponsorship of proliberalization policies than are the short-term direct applications of

---

12. I also estimated the model by excluding these five cases from the analysis rather than by recoding them. Removing these cases did change the results slightly, with the proliberalization variable significant at the .05 level instead of the .01 level.

13. As in the analyses of Tables 7.3 and 7.4, the military intervention variable is coded for the Pearson and Baumann and Tillema data sets as the number of months in which the United States intervened between 1945 and 1992, as reported by their data. Intervention is coded as a dichotomous variable for Meernik because the 1996 article from which his data were taken listed only the year in which the intervention took place. The other variables are coded using the same procedures noted above for the specific intervention cases included in the three data sets. The statistical insignificance of the oppose-government variable in these tests, especially in the examination of Tillema's data, reflects the fact that they do not include the few cases like Nicaragua during the late 1980s in which regimes opposed by the United States during its military interventions became democracies.

Table 7.4   Assessing the impact of different coding decisions

Variable	No axis cases: Coefficient (standard error)	No cases > 10: Coefficient (standard error)	No short: Coefficient (standard error)
Democracy in 1944	1.551** (.525)	1.551** (.524)	1.616*** (.526)
Military intervention	−.003 (.006)	−.007 (.007)	−.003 (.006)
Proliberalization	2.260* (1.077)	2.758** (1.125)	2.362** (1.007)
Oppose government	−1.841* (.912)	−1.813* (.927)	−1.213 (1.078)
International war	−.136 (.414)	−.053 (.410)	−.265 (.409)
Civil war	−1.328** (.445)	−1.188** (.433)	−1.352*** (.444)
Constant	1.883*** (.557)	1.794*** (.554)	1.880*** (.558)
−2 log likelihood	175.127	172.440	176.278
Model chi-square	45.454*** (6 df)	48.141*** (6 df)	44.303*** (6 df)
Correctly predicted	69.38%	70.63%	70.00%
N	160	160	160

*p. < .05; **p. < .01; ***p. < .001; one-tailed tests.

military force more likely to be captured by the quantitative literature. This expectation is borne out by the results in Table 7.5. Pearson and Baumann include substantially more of these proxy wars, like the Philippines in the 1950s and El Salvador during the 1980s, than do the other data sets. They, therefore, also capture more of the cases in which the United States adopted proliberalization policies. In contrast, Tillema's data only includes eight of the twenty post–World War II interventions that involved the adoption of proliberalization policies, according to the data in Table 7.2. Meernik's data set lies between Pearson and Baumann and Tillema on this dimension. The examination of his data showed a statistically significant relationship between proliberalization policies and democracy, although not as strong as that found in the analysis of Pearson and Baumann's data. The test using Pearson and Baumann's data just falls short of statistical significance at the .01 level, while Meernik's data is significant almost precisely at the .05 level.

Elections, Demilitarization, and the Successful Promotion of Democracy

The evidence presented here shows that target states have rarely democratized if the United States failed to adopt proliberalization policies during its interventions, while a majority of states where the United States adopted

Table 7.5   Examining different data sets

Variable	Pearson: Coefficient (standard error)	Meernik: Coefficient (standard error)	Tillema: Coefficient (standard error)
Democracy in 1944	1.614** (.527)	1.691*** (.530)	1.616** (.526)
Military intervention	−.003 (.010)	−.219 (.717)	.006 (.012)
Proliberalization	2.388* (1.067)	1.683* (1.009)	.302 (.991)
Oppose government	−1.927 (1.228)	.044 (1.430)	−6.810 (16.146)
International war	−.163 (.413)	−.199 (.387)	−.064 (.397)
Civil war	−1.320*** (.425)	−1.332*** (.408)	−1.193** (.410)
Constant	1.930*** (.563)	1.996*** (.569)	1.926*** (.562)
−2 log likelihood	175.374	181.940	180.644
Model chi-square	45.206*** (6 df)	38.641*** (6 df)	39.937*** (6 df)
Correctly predicted	69.38%	68.75%	68.13%
N	160	160	160

*p. < .05; **p. < .01; ***p. < .001; one-tailed tests.

such policies became democracies. Furthermore, states that have experienced proliberalization policies are significantly more likely to be democracies than states that have not shared this experience. Proliberalization policies have, therefore, often had a profound transformative impact on the political regimes of target states. Since all cases of the adoption of proliberalization policies involve support for free and fair elections, these results suggest that elections are a crucial part of the explanation. These results do not, however, provide a definitive answer to the question of which elements of the proliberalization package or which combination of elements are most crucial for successful democratization. A brief examination of the outcomes in the cases included in this book provide some preliminary insights about the relationship between American-sponsored elections and demilitarization policies (or the lack thereof).

South Vietnam provides one of the most profound examples of the potential incompatibilities between pro-electoral policies and strong support for the local military. The United States government helped topple the civilian dictatorship of Ngo Dinh Diem, in part, because it viewed his regime as too repressive and narrowly based to win the popular support necessary to win the war. In 1967 the United States compelled General Nguyen Van Thieu, the leader of the military junta that governed the country at that time, to run for the presidency in relatively free and fair elections in which he won only 38 percent of the vote. There can be no doubt, however, that these limited proliberalization policies were overwhelmed by America's strong alliance with the Army of the Republic of Vietnam (ARVN). The United States created the ARVN during the 1950s and bankrolled its entire budget throughout its brief history. It was to officers of the ARVN that America turned when it was convinced that Diem had to be replaced. The United States strongly supported the subsequent military governments that ruled the country for the next dozen years. It pushed the ARVN to adopt political-military tactics—like the Strategic Hamlet and Phoenix programs and the repression of Buddhist and other neutralist groups—that fundamentally limited democratic liberties in South Vietnam (Karnow 1983; Herring 1986; Kahin 1986; Shafer 1988). South Vietnam represents one of the greatest failures of American efforts to promote democracy during a military intervention. The existence of a civil war in South Vietnam explains part of this failure. The liberalizing impact of American-sponsored reforms was also fundamentally undermined by other aspects of U.S. policy.

The Cuban experience also exhibited some of this tension between U.S. support for free and fair elections and efforts to strengthen local allied military institutions. This case was more ambiguous, however, than the

Vietnamese case, or the experiences of Nicaragua and the Dominican Republic during the early twentieth century, where the leaders of the "non-partisan constabularies" created by American occupation authorities overthrew presidents selected in American-sponsored elections. Indeed, the United States disarmed the Cuban Liberating Army and did not create a new Cuban army to replace it in the immediate aftermath of the Spanish-American War. When opposition parties threatened insurrection against President Estrada Palma's efforts to arrange for a second term through electoral fraud, U.S. troops returned for a second occupation of Cuba from 1906 to 1909. This time, in addition to rewriting the electoral law to ensure that the next presidential elections would not be subject to fraud, American occupation authorities created a new Cuban army that would be friendly to U.S. interests. After two decades of unstable, partially democratic rule, the Cuban army helped sustain the Machado dictatorship of the late 1920s and early 1930s. Then, in the wake of the Cuban Revolution of 1933, U.S. envoy Sumner Welles helped propel Fulgencio Batista, the leader of a sergeant's revolt within the U.S.-trained army, into power (Pérez 1986). Therefore, there was an ongoing tension between U.S. support for free and fair elections and for the U.S.-trained Cuban army. The military elements of U.S. intervention, however, did not undermine Cuban democracy in the same direct way that it did in Vietnam.

The immediate impact of the McKinley administration's colonial policies in the Philippines was antidemocratic. By the end of the subsequent Roosevelt administration, however, American colonial authorities had begun to implant democratic institutions in the Philippines. In the immediate aftermath of World War II, the democratic regime bequeathed to the Filipinos after nearly half a century of U.S. colonial rule was corrupted by the presidencies of Manuel Roxas and Elipidio Quirino. The U.S.-trained Philippine army was not the principal impediment to democracy. Instead, the Philippine landed elite, which had been strengthened by U.S. economic policies during the colonial era, was the principal actor that undermined Filipino democracy during the 1940s (Smith 1994:37–59). The subsequent U.S. indirect intervention in support of the charismatic Defense Minister Ramon Magsaysay provides one of the paradigmatic successes of the promotion of democracy as a strategy to win a counterinsurgency war (MacDonald 1992). When Magsaysay cleaned up human rights abuses among military units fighting the Huk rebellion and then guaranteed the integrity of the 1951 elections, he succeeded in reducing popular support for the rebels. By the time Magsaysay was elected president in 1953, the rebellion had been ended and the Philippines had become a democracy, at least for the next fifteen years. The Philippines, therefore, provides an example of how strengthening the local military need not be incompatible with promoting democracy.

Such examples are rare, however. More often than not, the combination of free and fair elections and strengthening local militaries leads at best to liberalized autocracies or limited and unstable democracy. The U.S. intervention in El Salvador during the 1980s and early 1990s illustrates how free and fair elections can help create regimes that surpass the minimum procedural requirements to be considered democracies, but a comprehensive set of proliberalization policies may be needed for a more complete democratization of a target state. The American-sponsored elections for a Constituent Assembly in 1982 were clearly insufficient to turn El Salvador into a full-fledged democracy. American-sponsored elections for the presidency in 1984, combined with congressional efforts to condition U.S. military assistance on the human rights record of the Salvadoran armed forces, led to the inauguration of an elected government that met the minimum standards to be considered a democracy according to the Polity III data set. Despite these real successes, Salvadoran democracy during the 1980s was fundamentally limited by the extraordinary power of the armed forces relative to civilian political leaders and the intense repression meted out against any left-of-center political movements (Stanley 1996). El Salvador achieved a more genuine democratization only with the resolution of that country's decade-long civil war. American support for U.N.-mediated peace accords, which led to the full incorporation of the left into the electoral process and a substantial reduction in the political power of the Salvadoran armed forces, helped deepen democracy in that country (Stanley 1995).

In the Salvadoran case, as in many others, American support for free and fair elections may be sufficient to push target states over the minimum threshold to become democracies, but a comprehensive set of proliberalization policies, including American-sponsored demilitarization, may be needed to deepen and consolidate that democracy. Indeed, when one examines the list of cases from Table 7.2, in which U.S. proliberalization policies have been followed by successful democratization, what is striking is that virtually all of the cases of successful democratization have occurred in two time periods, the immediate post–World War II era and the end of the Cold War. What do the experiences of the defeated Axis powers after World War II have in common with the small Central American states during the 1990s? In both sets of cases, the United States pursued a comprehensive set of proliberalization policies that included both the adoption of pro-electoral policies and the demilitarization of target states. Thus, the United States pursued the strategies most likely to democratize target states at precisely the times when the permissive character of the international balance of power led it to act most like a liberal state.

The Axis powers experienced some of the most far-reaching efforts on the part of the United States to impose democracy. Although domestic factors played an important role in the subsequent democratization of these countries, the forceful imposition of liberal reforms by the victorious allies clearly played a decisive role (Herz 1982; Smith 1994). It is difficult to see how Nazi Germany or Imperial Japan would have become democracies without having been defeated and then occupied by powers intent on liberalizing their polities. In the contemporary era, the U.S. invasion of Panama led to the democratization of that country in a rather direct fashion (Scranton 1991). The United States supported elections and centrist political parties and interest groups in each of these cases and purged public institutions of at least some suspected war criminals. The military institutions of Germany and Japan were systematically dismantled and U.S. occupation authorities imposed a pacifist constitution on Japan. In Panama the United States not only defeated the Panamanian Defense Forces, it arrested the leader of the PDF and put him in a Miami jail cell. In Honduras and Nicaragua, as in El Salvador, U.S. support for democracy and demilitarization as central to the resolution of the region's civil wars played an important role in the strengthening of democratic institutions.

Today, the public debate on U.S. efforts to promote democracy in Haiti and Bosnia suggests an almost unrelieved pessimism about the likelihood of the success of U.S. efforts. The evidence presented in this chapter suggests that despite the enormous domestic impediments to democratization in these countries, there is reason for hope. This is especially true for the Haitian case in which the United States has not only supported free and fair elections, but also a comprehensive set of proliberalization policies eventually including the elimination of the Haitian military, which had been the principal obstacle to democratization in that country over the previous decade. Even in Bosnia, where ethnic hatred and polarization convince many that genuine democratization is impossible, this study suggests that the electoral process imposed by the United States has a greater chance of taking root than many analysts expect. By combining support for free and fair elections with a substantial effort to enhance the power of an allied military, however, the United States may find that one of the principal obstacles to turning the Bosnian electoral process into a real exercise in democracy might be its allies in the Bosnian military.

8

Leader of the Free World

"Leader of the free world." Countless U.S. presidents and policymakers have described America's global role with this phrase. Countless analysts and scholars have dismissed this label as cynical rhetoric. Yet no phrase better captures the essence of America's distinctive identity as a world power. American leaders have consistently identified other liberal states as America's principal allies in the international system. They have viewed the spread of liberal capitalist democracy as central to ensuring America's security and prosperity. Rather than act as equal partners in the liberal pacific union, however, American leaders have striven to make the United States the undisputed leader of the world's liberal states. America has been the dominant, and often domineering, leader of the liberal alliances against illiberal powers like Nazi Germany, the Soviet Union, and Iraq. It has acquired unrivaled military and economic capabilities, which it uses at times to "encourage" its liberal allies to pursue policies that serve the power and security interests of the United States.

The United States need not have pursued this course. From a realist perspective, the United States could have reached for global domination—

to become leader of the entire world, free and unfree. Or, it could have taken on Great Britain's nineteenth-century role as a global balancer, joining whichever coalition of states was most threatened at any given time in order to maintain equilibrium in the balance of power. From a liberal perspective, the United States could have adhered to the liberal ideal of genuine equal partnership with like-minded states. Alternately, institutional constraints could have persuaded American leaders to pursue a consistent strategy of isolationism.

Instead, American policymakers have engaged in a relentless struggle to reconcile realist imperatives with American liberalism. Equally important has been the ongoing effort to reconcile conflicts within the American liberal tradition between crusading American ideals and constraining institutions. Over the past century, leaders of the United States have forged an American identity as leader of the free world in an attempt to bring these potentially contradictory elements together into a grand synthesis. Thus, the United States asserts its hegemony over other states but infuses its foreign policy with liberal purpose.

The promotion of democracy during military interventions is one of the most distinctive behaviors flowing from America's unique character as a world power. Indeed, this behavior has also played a crucial role in shaping that character. The practice of U.S. military interventions does not conform to the expectations of either the liberal or realist arguments. Liberals do not expect democracies to go to war so easily or so often. Democracies should not violate the fundamental liberal tenet that states should have the right to determine their own political destinies. Realists are surprised that the United States would expend considerable resources and accept significant risks to its security interests in the unwise promotion of its liberal values. What each school of thought fails to grasp fully is that it is through the promotion of democracy that the United States legitimates, to both domestic and foreign audiences, its use of military force abroad. Promoting democracy during military interventions is a crucial part of what it means for the United States to be leader of the free world.

This practice and identity did not emerge in a simple and straightforward way. It evolved over a century of political conflict and trial and error. Lessons about the utility of the promotion of democracy for the legitimation of American power had to be relearned on several occasions since it was first discovered in the "liberation" of Cuba from Spanish tyranny in 1898. The most crucial source of this synthesis has been the constant struggle between Congress and the president to shape American foreign policy.

The mix of realist and domestic liberal political dynamics in the promotion of democracy during U.S. military interventions varies significantly depending on whether presidents adopt proliberalization policies on their own initiative or in response to congressional pressure. Presidents' initial choices are shaped most by realist concerns because their unique institutional role as commander in chief compels presidents to pay greater attention to America's security interests than is true of members of Congress. Chapter 2 framed this argument mostly in terms of constraints and opportunities offered by the global and local balances of power. Presidents were less likely initially to promote liberal reforms during an intervention if they faced a threatening international environment or war in the target country, and if they intervened in opposition to the target regime. Presidents were more likely to adopt proliberalization policies if they faced a less threatening international environment and no war in the target state, and if the United States was allied with the target regime.

The case studies emphasized a different aspect of the realist argument, that presidents adopted liberal reforms because they believed democratic regimes would make stronger and more stable allies in target states. Presidents failed to adopt such policies when they believed that allied autocratic regimes would better serve America's security goals or that promoting liberal reforms could undermine friendly governments. Thus, the McKinley administration initially did not wish to promote democracy in either Cuba or the Philippines because it feared that the Cubans and Filipinos would fail to create stable pro-American regimes. The Reagan administration supported a repressive military-led junta in El Salvador because it believed that junta capable of defeating the leftist insurgents of the FMLN and feared that pressuring it about its human rights performance or democratic standards might destabilize that regime and hurt the war effort.

On the other side of the equation, the Kennedy administration pressured the Diem regime to adopt liberal reforms in South Vietnam because it believed the Vietnamese government to be too repressive, narrowly based, and inefficient to defeat the Viet Cong. The Vietnamese case also demonstrates the flexibility expected by the realist approach as Kennedy alternately pushed for or backed away from liberal reforms based on short-term calculations of the security consequences of his policies. Once it intervened, the Clinton administration maintained a consistent emphasis on proliberalization policies in Haiti because it believed that a democratic regime would be more stable and friendly to the United States and less likely to generate thousands of political refugees headed for Florida. Clinton promoted democracy in Bosnia because he believed that a tolerant multiethnic democracy would provide the type of political regime most likely to resolve the ethnic hatreds that had spawned the Bosnian war.

The domestic liberal argument also plays an important, though lesser, role in the presidential path to the adoption of proliberalization policies. The results in Chapter 2 showed that Democratic presidents were initially somewhat more likely to adopt proliberalization policies than were Republicans. This finding was born out in the case studies as well. Both John F. Kennedy and Bill Clinton were predisposed to the promotion of democracy during their interventions, although the presidential nomination process played the greater role in shaping Kennedy's initial policies while the general election campaign played a more significant role in Clinton's case.

The domestic liberal theoretical argument about the presidential path emphasizes that the constraints imposed on presidents by the electoral process are limited and fleeting. In practice, however, the case studies provided substantial evidence that the predisposition to the promotion of democracy among Democratic presidents lasted longer than expected by the institutional constraints argument. Because Kennedy and Clinton were presidential candidates selected by a party that valued liberal internationalist ideals, they regularly returned to those liberal values in their foreign policies. They did so because they shared the perspectives of those who selected them and appointed like-minded advisers. As presidents, they reconciled their response to realist imperatives and their liberal ideas through a hard-nosed emphasis on the security benefits associated with the promotion of democracy.

The congressional path to the promotion of democracy adheres more closely to the domestic liberal argument. Members of Congress have more freedom than presidents to push for the abandonment of interventions or for a greater commitment to the promotion of liberal values during those interventions, regardless of the security consequences for the United States. The evidence in Chapter 2 shows that congressional pressure does a better job of explaining final presidential choices than the realist variables, with the partial exception of the level of threat faced by the United States in the global balance of power.

The case studies also provide convincing evidence that congressional pressure can compel presidents to adopt proliberalization policies even when they think such policies might damage U.S. security interests. The Teller Amendment to the declaration of war against Spain and the subsequent congressional action on Cuba pushed the McKinley administration to support free and fair elections for that island even though occupation authorities believed the Cubans to be unprepared for self-government and unlikely to elect advocates of American domination of the island. Congressional reductions in military assistance to El Salvador and its conditioning of U.S. aid on the democratic status and human rights record of the Salvadoran government forced the Reagan administration to adopt a series of proliberalization policies during its indirect intervention there. Pressure from the Black Congressional Caucus helped push Clinton to intervene to restore democracy in Haiti, while liberal attacks from Republican members of Congress helped sustain Clinton's commitment to proliberalization policies in Bosnia.

The congressional path also possesses a strong realist component because presidents often promote democracy to encourage Congress to fund interventions undertaken for realist reasons. This was most clearly the case in El Salvador, where Reagan administration officials were concerned that Congress was failing to provide the minimum financial resources necessary for the Salvadoran armed forces to turn the tide against the FMLN, let alone to maintain the military stalemate of the early 1980s. The political dynamics were somewhat different in the Clinton administration cases, where congressional pressure reinforced the initial policies of the president rather than bringing about a change in presidential policy.

These two paths end at the same destination, as presidents attempt to reconcile realism and liberalism by using the promotion of democracy to serve U.S. security interests. This synthesis helps build a domestic consensus in favor of an active foreign policy by tapping into America's liberal ideals. The promotion of democracy thus helps ensure that presidents possess the domestic backing and resources necessary to maintain American power in the international system.

Internationally, the promotion of democracy serves American security interests in the broadest terms. By shaping the character of the political regimes of other states, policymakers believe they can create a world order under American leadership in which the United States can feel secure and prosper. The promotion of democracy can create regimes whose citizens and leaders see the United States as the leader of a community of peace-loving states sharing the same values and interests, rather than as an imperial power imposing its will on others. If other liberal states view the United States as the leader of the free world, they are more likely to serve the interests of the United States without having to be coerced into doing so. For these reasons, the creation of a liberal pacific union under American leadership has been at the core of American grand strategy.

In specific interventions, if the United States is able to convince the people of target states that it comes as a liberator rather than as an oppressor, it is more likely to encourage the creation of friendly allied regimes in these states. The purest and most successful expression of this strategy came with the U.S. occupations of Japan and Germany after World War II. The United States convinced large numbers of Japanese and German citizens that it occupied their countries as liberators, not conquerors. The American occupation governments worked from the premise that a magnanimous policy designed to create prosperous liberal capitalist democracies would encourage these countries to be willing partners of the United States in the postwar order. Indeed, these two countries did become crucial allies of the United States in the free-world coalition against the Soviet Union.

This strategy never worked quite as well in U.S. military interventions in Third World nations. The first expression of this strategy was Leonard Wood's efforts to win "annexation by acclamation" in Cuba. While Cubans accepted U.S. domination more readily than their Filipino counterparts, Wood's strategy was only a qualified success in that opponents of annexation won the U.S.-sponsored elections. El Salvador was also a qualified success in that anti-American actors on both sides of the political scene moderated their stances and accepted democratic rules of the game. However, the political party in El Salvador most tied to the United States, the Christian Democratic Party, has been thoroughly discredited. These cases look like extraordinary success stories when compared to the complete failure of the Kennedy administration's efforts to win the "hearts and minds" of the Vietnamese people.

Despite these shortcomings, Chapter 7 has shown that the United States has often had a positive impact on democracy in target states. While many of these states have not fully embraced the United States as the leader of the free world, most have at least grudgingly accepted American leadership of the liberal community. Grudging acceptance or wary toleration of American power may not be the enthusiastic endorsement that American policymakers hope for, but it is much preferred over the open hostility that has greeted many great powers in the past. With the end of the Cold War, if America's leadership of the liberal community exhibits an increasing emphasis on the domestic liberal component of this synthesis, the credibility of America's claim to be leader of the free world is likely to be enhanced.

Thus, the fears of many realist analysts that the contemporary era of American hegemony will inevitably generate a balancing coalition of the other great powers against the United States are probably misplaced. Japan and the countries of the European Union are not likely to join in opposition to the United States. The United States also appears to have been relatively successful thus far in convincing the Russians that liberal capitalist democracy represents the liberation of the Russian people, not their domination by the victor of the Cold War. Illiberal China could very well become the United States's principal adversary in the global balance of power, but it is highly unlikely that the Chinese will make common cause with the Germans and Japanese against the United States.

This does not mean that we have reached Kant's "perpetual peace," however. A crucial implication of this book is that we should not view the liberal pacific union as a phenomenon that emerges solely from the domestic politics of like-minded states. The liberal peace cannot be fully understood without an appreciation of the central role of American power in constructing and sustaining the pacific union. Perhaps a dozen of today's participants in the "democratic peace," including great powers like Germany and Japan, became democracies in the context of American military intervention. As the Haitian and Bosnian cases indicate, the expansion of the global community of liberal states continues to depend, at least in part, on the military power of the United States. Furthermore, as part of its grand strategy, the United States has played the central role in creating much of the international institutional infrastructure that binds liberal states together in the contemporary era. Institutions like the UN, IMF, NATO, and OAS still rely, often uneasily, on the United States for their continued success.

As long as the liberal peace depends in part on the often illiberal, interest-driven behavior of the world's dominant power, we cannot rest assured that we have indeed reached the "end of history." On the one hand, an increasingly assertive policy, in which liberal rhetoric supplies only the flimsiest of covers for the pursuit of America's material interests, could threaten the cohesion of the liberal community by encouraging some liberal states to challenge U.S. domination. On the other hand, one of the greatest threats to the "world's community of market democracies" could be a breakdown of the domestic consensus in favor of an active liberal internationalist foreign policy within the United States, as isolationists in the U.S. Congress increasingly question why the United States should pay any significant costs in lives and treasure to fight for liberal values abroad. The record of the past century suggests that U.S. presidents in the twenty-first century will consistently return to the promotion of democracy as a way to avoid these extremes and try to sustain America's preferred status as leader of the free world.

References

Albright, Madeleine (1993a). "Yes, There Is a Reason to Be in Somalia." *New York Times*, August 10, 1993.

——— (1993b). "Use of Force in a Post–Cold War World." Address at the National War College, National Defense University, Fort McNair, Washington, D.C., September 23, 1993. *U.S. Department of State Dispatch* 4 (39).

Aldrich, John, John Sullivan, and Eugene Borgida (1989). "Foreign Affairs and Issue Voting: Do Presidential Candidates 'Waltz Before a Blind Audience'?" *American Political Science Review* 83 (1): 123–41.

America's Watch and National Coalition for Refugees (1994). "Letter to the President Regarding Policy Toward Haiti." Unpublished document.

Apple, R. W. (1995a). "U.S. Urges Air Raids in Bosnia: Rejects Past Reinforcement Plan." *New York Times*, July 20, 1995.

——— (1995b). "Flimsy Bosnia Mandate." *New York Times*, December 14, 1995.

Arnson, Cynthia (1989). *Crossroads: Congress, the Reagan Administration, and Central America*. New York: Pantheon.

——— (1993). *Crossroads: Congress, the President, and Central America, 1976–1993*. 2d ed. University Park: The Pennsylvania State University Press.

Atkins, Edward (1926). *Sixty Years in Cuba: Reminiscences*. Cambridge, Mass.: Riverside Press.

Auerswald, David, and Peter Cowhey (1997). "Ballotbox Diplomacy: The War Powers Resolution and the Use of Force." *International Studies Quarterly* 41 (3): 505–28.

Ball, George (1982). *The Past Has Another Pattern: Memoirs*. New York: W. W. Norton.

Baloyra, Enrique (1982). *El Salvador in Transition*. Chapel Hill: University of North Carolina Press.

Barnet, Richard (1968). *Intervention and Revolution: The United States in the Third World*. New York: World.

Beisner, Robert (1968). *Twelve Against Empire: The Anti-Imperialists, 1898–1900*. New York: McGraw-Hill.

Bemis, Samuel Flagg (1943). *The Latin American Policy of the United States*. New York: Harcourt, Brace.

Bernstein, R., and W. Anthony (1991). "The ABM Issue in the Senate, 1968–1970: The Importance of Ideology." In *To Advise and Consent: The U.S. Congress and Foreign Policy in the Twentieth Century*, edited by J. Silbey, vol. 2, 465–74. Brooklyn: Carlson Publishing.

Blaufarb, Douglas (1977). *The Counterinsurgency Era: U.S. Doctrine and Performance, 1950 to the Present*. New York: Free Press.

Blechman, Barry, and Stephen Kaplan (1978). *Force Without War*. Washington, D.C.: Brookings Institution.

Bonner, Raymond (1984). *Weakness and Deceit: U.S. Policy and El Salvador*. New York: Times Books.

Boutros-Ghali, Boutros (1995). "Report of U.N. Secretary-General to the U.N. Security Council, May 30, 1995." New York: United Nations.

Bowles, Chester (1971). *Promises to Keep: My Years in Public Life, 1941–1969*. New York: Harper & Row.

Brady, David (1973). *Congressional Voting in a Partisan Era: A Study of the McKinley Houses and a Comparison to the Modern House of Representatives*. Lawrence: University of Kansas Press.

Brady, David, Richard Brody, and D. Epstein (1991). "Heterogeneous Parties and Political Organization: The U.S. Senate, 1880–1920." In *The United States Congress in a Nation Transformed, 1896–1963*, edited by J. Silbey, vol. 3, 117–36. Brooklyn: Carlson Publishing.

Brinkley, Douglas (1997). "Democratic Enlargement: The Clinton Doctrine." *Foreign Policy* (106): 111–27.

Bryan, William Jennings (1976). "Mr. Bryan's Address on Imperialism, August 18, 1900." In *American Anti-Imperialism, 1895–1901*, edited by G. Markowitz, 43–47. New York: Garland Publishing.

Buchanan, Paul (1991). "The Impact of U.S. Labor." In *Exporting Democracy: Themes and Issues*, edited by A. Lowenthal, 155–90. Baltimore: Johns Hopkins University Press.

Bueno de Mesquita, Bruce, and Randolph Siverson (1995). "War and the Survival of Political Leaders: A Comparative Study of Regime Types and Political Accountability." *American Political Science Review* 89 (4): 841–55.

Burnham, Walter Dean (1970). *Critical Elections and the Mainsprings of American Politics*. New York: W. W. Norton.

Cable, Larry (1986). *Conflict of Myths: The Development of American Counterinsurgency Doctrine and the Vietnam War*. New York: New York University Press.

Carothers, Thomas (1991). *In the Name of Democracy: U.S. Policy Toward Latin America in the Reagan Years*. Berkeley and Los Angeles: University of California Press.

Christopher, Warren (1993a). "New Steps Toward Conflict Resolution in the Former Yugoslavia." Opening Statement at a News Conference, Washington, D.C., February 10, 1993. *U.S. Department of State Dispatch* 4 (7).

———— (1993b). "Building Peace in the Middle East." Address at Columbia University, co-sponsored by the Council on Foreign Relations, New York City, September 20, 1993. *U.S. Department of State Dispatch* 4 (39).

——— (1995). "Remarks by U.S. Secretary of State Warren Christopher at the Initialing of the Balkan Proximity Peace Talks Agreement in Dayton, Ohio, November 21, 1995." Washington, D.C., www.state.gov Bosnia Link.

CISPES (1981). *El Salvador Alert.* Berkeley, Calif.: Committee in Solidarity with the People of El Salvador.

——— (1983–84). "Two Challenges of the Kissinger Commission." *El Salvador Alert.* Berkeley, Calif.: Committee in Solidarity with the People of El Salvador.

Clinton, Bill (1992a). "Excerpts from the Acceptance Speech of Governor Bill Clinton at the Democratic National Convention." *New York Times,* July 17, 1992.

——— (1992b). "American Foreign Policy and the Democratic Ideal: Remarks by Governor Bill Clinton at the Pabst Theater in Milwaukee, Wisconsin on October 1, 1992." Unpublished document, Clinton Campaign Headquarters.

——— (1993a). "Statement by President Bill Clinton." *Foreign Policy Bulletin* 3 (4–5).

——— (1993b). "Confronting the Challenges of a Broader World: Address to the U.N. General Assembly, New York City, September 27, 1993." *U.S. Department of State Dispatch* 4 (39).

——— (1994a). "The President's Oval Office Address to the Nation." *U.S. Department of State Dispatch* 5 (38).

——— (1994b). "Statement of the President, September 17, 1994." *U.S. Department of State Dispatch* 5 (38).

——— (1995). "Statement by President Bill Clinton." Washington, D.C., White House Press Release.

——— (1996). "Statement by the President, November 27, 1995." *Foreign Policy Bulletin,* January/February.

Cohen, Roger (1994). "U.S. and Russia to Back Bosnia Pact Jointly." *New York Times,* June 21, 1994.

Commission on U.S.-Latin American Relations (1975). *The Americas in a Changing World.* Chicago: Quadrangle Books.

——— (1976). *The United States and Latin America: Next Steps.* New York: Center for Inter-American Relations.

Congressional Black Caucus (1994). "Letter to the President Regarding Policy Toward Haiti." Unpublished document.

Crabb, Cecil, Jr., and Pat Holt (1989). *Invitation to Struggle: Congress, the President, and Foreign Policy.* 3rd ed. Washington, D.C.: Congressional Quarterly Press.

Cumings, Bruce (1981). *The Origins of the Korean War, volume 1: Liberation and the Emergence of Separate Regimes, 1945–1947.* Princeton: Princeton University Press.

——— (1990). *The Origins of the Korean War, volume 2: The Roaring of the Cataract, 1947–1950.* Princeton: Princeton University Press.

Dahl, Robert (1971). *Polyarchy.* New Haven: Yale University Press.

Dennison, Elizabeth (1943). *The Senate Foreign Relations Committee.* Stanford, Calif.: Stanford University Press.

Diamond, Larry, Juan Linz, and Seymour Martin Lipset (1989). *Democracy in Developing Countries.* 3 volumes. Boulder, Colo.: Lynne Rienner.

Dietz, Terry (1986). *Republicans and Vietnam, 1961–1968.* New York: Greenwood Press.

DiGiovanni, Cleto, and Roger Fontaine (1980). "Castro's Specter." *Washington Quarterly* (autumn): 3–27.

Divine, Robert (1974). *Foreign Policy and U.S. Presidential Elections, 1952–1960.* New York: New Viewpoints.

Dixon, William (1994). "Democracy and the Peaceful Settlement of Disputes." *American Political Science Review* 88 (1): 14–32.

Downs, Anthony (1957). *An Economic Theory of Democracy.* New York: Harper & Row.

Doyle, Michael (1983a). "Kant, Liberal Legacies, and Foreign Affairs, Part 1." *Philosophy and Public Affairs* 12 (3): 205–35.

——— (1983b). "Kant, Liberal Legacies, and Foreign Affairs, Part 2." *Philosophy and Public Affairs* 12 (4): 323–53.

Drake, Paul (1991). "From Good Men to Good Neighbors: 1912–1932." In *Exporting Democracy: Themes and Issues,* edited by A. Lowenthal, 3–40. Baltimore: Johns Hopkins University Press.

Drew, Elizabeth (1994). *On the Edge: The Clinton Presidency.* New York: Simon & Schuster.

Duarte, José Napoleón (1986). *Duarte: My Story.* New York: Putnam & Sons.

Dupuy, Alex (1997). *Haiti in the New World Order: The Limits of the Democratic Revolution.* Boulder, Colo.: Westview Press.

ECA (1982). *Estudios Centroamericanos* 37 (May–June).

Ellsberg, Daniel (1971). "The Quagmire Myth and the Stalemate Machine." *Public Policy* 19 (2): 217–74.

Engelberg, Stephen (1993). "What to Do in Bosnia? Three Hard Choices." *New York Times,* April 29, 1993.

Farber, Henry, and Joanne Gowa (1995). "Polities and Peace." *International Security* 20 (2): 123–46.

Fenno, Richard (1973). *Congressmen in Committees.* Boston: Little, Brown.

——— (1978). *Home Style: House Members in Their Districts.* Boston: Little, Brown.

Ferguson, Yale (1972). "The United States and Political Development in Latin America: A Retrospect and Prescription." In *Contemporary Interamerican Relations: A Reader in Theory and Issues,* edited by Y. Ferguson, 348–91. Englewood Cliffs, N.J.: Prentice-Hall.

Fisher, Louis (1995). *Presidential War Power.* Lawrence: University of Kansas Press.

Foner, Philip (1972). *The Spanish-Cuban-American War and the Birth of U.S. Imperialism, 1895–1902.* New York: Monthly Review Press.

Forsythe, David (1988). *Human Rights and U.S. Foreign Policy: Congress Reconsidered.* Gainesville: University of Florida Press.

——— (1992). "Democracy, War, and Covert Action." *Journal of Peace Research* 29 (4): 385–95.

Franck, Thomas, and Edward Weisband (1979). *Foreign Policy by Congress.* New York: Oxford University Press.

French, Howard (1993). "Haitians' Advocates Admit Some Feeling of Betrayal." *New York Times,* January 15, 1993.

——— (1994). "U.S. Tells Aristide to Bend on Plan." *New York Times,* February 23, 1994.

Friedman, Thomas (1993a). "Dole Plans Bill to Bar the Use of GIs in Haiti." *New York Times*, October 18, 1993.

—— (1993b). "Clinton Neutral on Geneva Plan." *New York Times*, February 4, 1993.

Gaddis, John Lewis (1982). *Strategies of Containment: A Critical Appraisal of Postwar American National Security Policy*. New York: Oxford University Press.

Gaubatz, Kurt (1991). "Election Cycles and War." *Journal of Conflict Resolution* 35 (2): 212–44.

George, Alexander (1979). "Case Studies and Theory Development: The Method of Structured-Focused Comparison." In *Diplomacy: New Approaches in History, Theory, and Policy*, edited by P. G. Lauren, 43–68. New York: Free Press.

—— (1980). "Domestic Policy Constraints on Regime Change in U.S. Foreign Policy: The Need for Policy Legitimacy." In *Change in the International System*, edited by O. Holsti, R. Siverson, and A. George, 233–62. Boulder, Colo.: Westview Press.

Gibbons, William (1986). *The U.S. Government and the Vietnam War: Executive and Legislative Roles and Relationships, part 2: 1961–1964*. Princeton: Princeton University Press.

Girling, John (1981). *Thailand: Society and Politics*. Ithaca, N.Y.: Cornell University Press.

Gleditsch, Kristian, and Michael Ward (1997). "Double Take: A Re-Examination of Democracy and Autocracy in Modern Polities." *Journal of Conflict Resolution* 41 (3): 361–83.

Gleditsch, Nils Petter, and Håvard Hegre (1997). "Peace and Democracy: Three Levels of Analysis." *Journal of Conflict Resolution* 41 (2): 283–310.

Gordon, Michael (1993). "State Department Aide in Bosnia Resigns on Partition Issue." *New York Times*, August 5, 1993.

Gould, Lewis (1980). *The Presidency of William McKinley*. Lawrence: Regents Press of Kansas.

Gray, William (1994). "Statement by the President's Special Envoy to Haiti." *Foreign Policy Bulletin*, September–October.

Greenhouse, Steven (1994a). "U.S. Supports New Haiti Plan and Faults Aristide for Balking at It." *New York Times*, February 15, 1994.

—— (1994b). "October Deadline Is Cited to End Bosnian Arms Embargo." *New York Times*, August 12, 1994.

Gutman, Roy (1988). *Banana Diplomacy: The Making of American Policy in Nicaragua, 1981–1987*. New York: Simon & Schuster.

Hagedorn, Hermann (1931). *Leonard Wood: A Biography*. New York: Harper & Brothers.

Haig, Alexander (1984). *Caveat: Realism, Reagan, and Foreign Policy*. New York: Macmillan.

Halberstam, David (1965). *The Making of a Quagmire*. New York: Random House.

—— (1969). *The Best and the Brightest*. New York: Random House.

Hammer, Ellen (1987). *A Death in November: America in Vietnam, 1963*. New York: Dutton.

Harper, Steven (1985). "Central America." In *Congress and Foreign Policy, 1984: A*

Report of the House Foreign Affairs Committee. Washington, D.C.: Government Printing Office.

Hartlyn, Jonathan (1991). "The Dominican Republic." In *Exporting Democracy: Cases*, edited by A. Lowenthal, 53–92. Baltimore: Johns Hopkins University Press.

Hartz, Louis (1955). *The Liberal Tradition in America: An Interpretation of American Political Thought Since the Revolution*. New York: Harcourt Brace Jovanovich.

Healy, David (1963). *The United States in Cuba, 1898–1902: Generals, Politicians, and the Search for Policy*. Madison: University of Wisconsin Press.

Herman, Edward, and Frank Brodhead (1984). *Demonstration Elections: U.S.-Staged Elections in the Dominican Republic, Vietnam, and El Salvador*. Boston: South End Press.

Hermann, Margaret, and Charles Kegley (1996). "Ballots: A Barrier Against the Use of Bullets and Bombs." *Journal of Conflict Resolution* 40 (3): 436–60.

——— (1998). "The U.S. Use of Military Intervention to Promote Democracy: Evaluating the Record." *International Interactions* 24 (2) 91–114.

Herring, George (1986). *America's Longest War: The United States and Vietnam, 1950–1975*. 2nd ed. New York: Alfred A. Knopf.

Herz, John, ed. (1982). *From Dictatorship to Democracy: Coping with the Legacies of Authoritarianism and Totalitarianism*. Westport, Conn.: Greenwood Press.

Hilsman, Roger (1967). *To Move a Nation: The Politics of Foreign Policy in the Administration of John F. Kennedy*. Garden City, N.Y.: Doubleday.

Hunt, Michael (1987). *Ideology and U.S. Foreign Policy*. New Haven: Yale University Press.

Huntington, Samuel (1981). *American Politics: The Promise of Disharmony*. Cambridge, Mass.: Belknap Press of Harvard University.

——— (1982). "American Ideals vs. American Institutions." *Political Science Quarterly* 97 (1): 1–37.

——— (1984). "Will More Countries Become Democratic?" *Political Science Quarterly* 99 (2): 193–218.

——— (1991). *The Third Wave: Democratization in the Late Twentieth Century*. Norman: University of Oklahoma Press.

Jaggers, Keith, and Ted Robert Gurr (1995). "Tracking Democracy's Third Wave with the Polity III Data." *Journal of Peace Research* 32 (4): 469–82.

Kahin, George McT. (1986). *Intervention: How America Became Involved in Vietnam*. New York: Alfred A. Knopf.

Kant, Immanuel (1795–1983). "To Perpetual Peace: A Philosophical Sketch." In *Perpetual Peace and Other Essays on Politics, History, and Morals*, 107–43. Translated by Ted Humphrey. Indianapolis: Hackett.

Karl, Terry Lynn (1985). "After La Palma: The Prospects for Democratization in El Salvador." *World Policy Journal*, Spring, 305–30.

——— (1986). "Imposing Consent? Electoralism vs. Democratization in El Salvador." In *Elections and Democratization in Latin America, 1980–1985*, edited by P. Drake and E. Silva, 9–36. La Jolla: Center for Iberian and Latin American Studies, University of California.

———— (1990). "Dilemmas of Democratization in Latin America." *Comparative Politics* 23 (1): 1–22.

Karnow, Stanley (1983). *Vietnam: A History*. New York: Viking Press.

Kattenburg, Paul (1980). *The Vietnam Trauma in American Foreign Policy, 1945–1975*. New Brunswick, N.J.: Transaction Books.

Katzman, Robert (1990). "War Powers: Toward a New Accommodation." In *A Question of Balance: The President, the Congress, and Foreign Policy*, edited by T. Mann, 35–69. Washington, D.C.: Brookings Institution.

Kern, Montague, Patricia Levering, and Ralph Levering (1983). *The Kennedy Crises: The Press, the Presidency, and Foreign Policy*. Chapel Hill: University of North Carolina Press.

Kirkpatrick, Jeane (1979). "Dictatorships and Double Standards." *Commentary* 68 (November): 34–45.

———— (1984). "U.S. Security and Latin America." In *Rift and Revolution: The Central American Imbroglio*, edited by H. Wiarda, 329–59. Washington, D.C.: American Enterprise Institute.

Kissinger, Henry (1984). *Report of the President's Bi-Partisan Commission on Central America*. New York: Macmillan.

Klare, Michael, and Peter Kornbluh (1988). *Low Intensity Warfare: Counterinsurgency, Proinsurgency, and Antiterrorism in the Eighties*. New York: Pantheon.

Koh, Harold Hongchu (1990). *The National Security Constitution: Sharing Power After the Iran-Contra Affair*. New Haven: Yale University Press.

Krasner, Stephen (1978). *Defending the National Interest: Raw Materials Investments and U.S. Foreign Policy*. Princeton: Princeton University Press.

Krauss, Clifford (1993). "Many in Congress, Citing Vietnam, Oppose Attacks." *New York Times*, May 7, 1993.

Lake, Anthony (1993). "From Containment to Enlargement: Address at the School of Advanced International Studies, Johns Hopkins University, Washington, D.C., September 21, 1993." *U.S. Department of State Dispatch* 4 (39).

Lake, David (1992). "Powerful Pacifists: Democratic States and War." *American Political Science Review* 86 (1): 24–37.

Langley, Lester (1983). *The Banana Wars: An Inner History of American Empire*. Lexington: University Press of Kentucky.

Layne, Christopher (1994). "Kant or Cant: The Myth of the Democratic Peace." *International Security* 19 (2): 5–49.

Leech, Margaret (1959). *In the Days of McKinley*. New York: Harper.

Levinson, Jerome, and Juan de Onis (1970). *The Alliance That Lost Its Way: A Critical Report on the Alliance for Progress*. Chicago: Quadrangle Books.

Lewis, Anthony (1993). "The Two Clintons." *New York Times*, February 22, 1993.

Linderman, Gerald (1974). *The Mirror of War: American Society and the Spanish-American War*. Ann Arbor: University of Michigan Press.

Lindsay, James (1990). "Parochialism, Policy, and Constituency Constraints: Congressional Voting on Strategic Weapons Systems." *American Journal of Political Science* 34 (4): 936–60.

———— (1994). "Congress and Foreign Policy: Avenues of Influence." In *The Domestic Sources of American Foreign Policy: Insights and Evidence*, edited by E. Wittkopf, 191–207. New York: St. Martin's Press.

Lipset, Seymour Martin (1981). *Political Man: The Social Bases of Politics.* Baltimore: Johns Hopkins University Press.

Lodge, Henry Cabot (1973). *The Storm Has Many Eyes: A Personal Narrative.* New York: W. W. Norton.

Londregan, John, and Keith Poole (1996). "Does High Income Promote Democracy?" *World Politics* 49 (1): 1–30.

Lowenthal, Abraham (1991). "The United States and Latin American Democracy: Learning from History." In *Exporting Democracy: Themes and Issues,* edited by A. Lowenthal, 243–65. Baltimore: Johns Hopkins University Press.

MacDonald, Douglas (1992). *Adventures in Chaos: American Intervention for Reform in the Third World.* Cambridge, Mass.: Harvard University Press.

Mansfield, Edward, and Jack Snyder (1995). "Democratization and the Danger of War." *International Security* 20 (1): 5–38.

May, Ernest (1961). *Imperial Democracy: The Emergence of America as a Great Power.* New York: Harcourt, Brace.

Mayhew, David (1974). *Congress: The Electoral Connection.* New Haven: Yale University Press.

McCormick, James, and Eugene Wittkopf (1990). "Bi-partisanship, Partisanship, and Ideology in Congressional-Executive Foreign Policy Relations, 1947–1988." *Journal of Politics* 52 (November): 1077–1100.

McCubbins, Matthew, and Thomas Schwartz (1987). "Congressional Oversight Overlooked: Police Patrols vs. Fire Alarms." In *Congress: Structure and Policy,* edited by M. McCubbins and T. Sullivan, 426–40. New York: Cambridge University Press.

McGillon, Chris (1993). "Haiti Must Be Freed from Military's Grip." *Christian Science Monitor,* April 14, 1993.

McNamara, Robert (1995). *In Retrospect: The Tragedy and Lessons of Vietnam.* New York: Random House.

Mearsheimer, John (1990). "Back to the Future." *International Security* 15 (1): 5–56.

Mecklin, John (1965). *Mission in Torment: An Intimate Account of the U.S. Role in Vietnam.* Garden City, N.Y.: Doubleday.

Meernik, James (1996). "United States Military Intervention and the Promotion of Democracy." *Journal of Peace Research* 33 (4): 391–402.

Melanson, Richard (1991). *Reconstructing Consensus: American Foreign Policy Since the Vietnam War.* New York: St. Martin's Press.

Menges, Constantine (1988). *Inside the National Security Council: The True Story of the Making and Unmaking of Reagan's Foreign Policy.* New York: Simon & Schuster.

Millett, Robert (1977). *Guardians of the Dynasty.* Maryknoll, N.Y.: Orbis Books.

Montgomery, Tommie Sue (1982). *Revolution in El Salvador: Origins and Evolution.* Boulder, Colo.: Westview Press.

Morgan, H. Wayne (1965). *America's Road to Empire: The War with Spain and Overseas Expansion.* New York: John Wiley & Sons.

Morgan, T. Clifton, and Sally Campbell (1991). "Domestic Structure, Decisional Constraints, and War: So Why Kant Democracies Fight?" *Journal of Conflict Resolution* 35 (2): 187–211.

Mueller, John (1973). *War, Presidents, and Public Opinion.* New York: John Wiley & Sons.

Munro, Dana Gardner (1964). *Intervention and Dollar Diplomacy in the Caribbean, 1900–1921.* Princeton: Princeton University Press.

——— (1974). *The United States and the Caribbean Republics, 1921–1933.* Princeton: Princeton University Press.

Muravchik, Joshua (1991). *Exporting Democracy: Fulfilling America's Destiny.* Washington, D.C.: American Enterprise Institute Press.

National Security Archives. Collections. Washington, D.C.

Newman, John (1992). *JFK and Vietnam: Deception, Intrigue, and the Struggle for Power.* New York: Warner Books.

Nincic, Miroslav (1992). *Democracy and Foreign Policy: The Fallacy of Political Realism.* New York: Columbia University Press.

Nolting, Frederick (1988). *From Trust to Tragedy: The Political Memoirs of Frederick Nolting, Kennedy's Ambassador to Diem's Vietnam.* New York: Praeger.

O'Donnell, Guillermo, Philippe Schmitter, and Laurence Whitehead (1986). *Transitions from Authoritarian Rule: Prospects for Democracy.* 4 vols. Baltimore: Johns Hopkins University Press.

O'Donnell, Guillermo, and Philippe Schmitter (1986). *Transitions from Authoritarian Rule: Volume Four: Tentative Conclusions about Uncertain Democracies.* Baltimore: Johns Hopkins University Press.

O'Donnell, Kenneth, David Powers, and Joe McCarthy (1970). *Johnny, We Hardly Knew Ye: Memories of John Fitzgerald Kennedy.* Boston: Little, Brown.

Offner, John Layser (1992). *An Unwanted War: The Diplomacy of the United States and Spain Over Cuba, 1895–1898.* Chapel Hill: University of North Carolina Press.

Ostertag, Bob (1983). *Third Anniversary Special.* CISPES El Salvador Alert. Berkeley, Calif.: Committee in Solidarity with the People of El Salvador.

Owen, John (1994). "How Liberalism Produces Democratic Peace." *International Security* 19 (2): 87–125.

Packenham, Robert (1973). *Liberal America in the Third World: Political Development Ideas in Foreign Aid and Social Science.* Princeton: Princeton University Press.

Pastor, Robert (1984). "Continuity and Change in U.S. Foreign Policy: Carter and Reagan on El Salvador." *Journal of Policy Analysis and Management* 3 (Winter): 175–90.

——— (1987). *Condemned to Repetition: The United States and Nicaragua.* Princeton: Princeton University Press.

——— (1992). *Whirlpool: U.S. Foreign Policy Toward Latin America and the Caribbean.* Princeton: Princeton University Press.

Pearson, Frederic, Robert Baumann, and Jeffrey Pickering (1994). "Military Intervention and Realpolitik." In *Reconstructin Realpolitik*, edited by F. Wayman and P. Diehl. Ann Arbor: University of Michigan Press.

Peceny, Mark (1995). "Two Paths to the Promotion of Democracy During U.S. Military Interventions." *International Studies Quarterly* 39 (3): 371–401.

Pérez, Louis (1983). *Cuba Between Empires, 1878–1902.* Pittsburgh: University of Pittsburgh Press.

———— (1986). *Cuba Under the Platt Amendment, 1902–1934*. Pittsburgh: University of Pittsburgh Press.

Pipes, Daniel, and Adam Garfinkle, eds. (1991). *Friendly Tyrants: An American Dilemma*. New York: St. Martin's.

Prosterman, Roy (1981). "El Salvador's Land Reform: The Real Facts and the True Alternatives." In *El Salvador in the New Cold War*, edited by M. Gettleman, 170–78. New York: Grove Press.

Przeworski, Adam (1986). "Some Problems in the Study of the Transition to Democracy." In *Transitions from Authoritarian Rule: Comparative Perspectives*, edited by G. O'Donnell, P. Schmitter, and L. Whitehead, vol. 3: 47–63. Baltimore: Johns Hopkins University Press.

Przeworski, Adam, Michael Alvarez, and José Antonio Cheibub and Fernando Limongi. (1996). "What Makes Democracies Endure?" *Journal of Democracy* 7 (1): 39–55.

Przeworski, Adam, and Fernando Limongi (1997). "Modernization: Theories and Facts." *World Politics* 49 (2): 155–83.

Quester, George (1982). *American Foreign Policy: The Lost Consensus*. New York: Praeger.

Ray, James Lee (1993). "Wars Between Democracies: Rare or Non-Existent?" *International Interactions* 18 (3): 251–76.

———— (1995). *Democracy and International Conflict: An Evaluation of the Democratic Peace Proposition*. Columbia: University of South Carolina Press.

Remmer, Karen (1995). "New Theoretical Perspectives on Democratization." *Comparative Politics* 28 (1): 103–22.

Robinson, William (1996). *Promoting Polyarchy: Globalization, U.S. Intervention, and Hegemony*. New York: Cambridge University Press.

Rosenau, James (1969). "Intervention as a Scientific Concept." *Journal of Conflict Resolution* 12 (2): 149–71.

Rostow, Walt (1972). *The Diffusion of Power: An Essay in Recent History*. New York: Macmillan.

Rubens, Horatio (1932). *Liberty: The Story of Cuba*. New York: Warren & Putnam.

Rueschemeyer, Dietrich, Evelyne Huber Stephens, and John D. Stephens (1992). *Capitalist Development and Democracy*. Chicago: University of Chicago Press.

Ruggie, John Gerard (1997). "The Past as Prologue? Interests, Identity, and American Foreign Policy." *International Security* 21 (4): 89–125.

Russett, Bruce (1993). *Grasping the Democratic Peace: Principles for a Post–Cold War World*. Princeton: Princeton University Press.

Russett, Bruce, and John O'Neal (1997). "The Classical Liberals Were Right: Democracy, Interdependence, and Conflict, 1950–1985." *International Studies Quarterly* 41 (2): 267–94.

Rust, William (1985). *Kennedy in Vietnam*. New York: Scribner's.

Schlesinger, Arthur, Jr. (1965). *A Thousand Days: John F. Kennedy in the White House*. Boston: Houghton Mifflin.

————. (1973). *The Imperial Presidency*. Boston: Houghton Mifflin.

Schmidt, Hans (1971). *The United States Occupation of Haiti, 1915–1934*. New Brunswick, N.J.: Rutgers University Press.

Schneider, William (1983). "Conservatism, Not Interventionism." In *Eagle Defiant:*

United States Foreign Policy in the 1980s, edited by Kenneth A. Oye, Robert J. Lieber, and Donald Rothchild. Boston: Little, Brown.

Schoultz, Lars (1981). *Human Rights and U.S. Policy Toward Latin America*. Princeton: Princeton University Press.

——— (1987). *National Security and U.S. Foreign Policy Toward Latin America*. Princeton: Princeton University Press.

Schraeder, Peter, ed. (1992a). *Intervention into the 1990s: U.S. Foreign Policy in the Third World*. 2nd ed. Boulder, Colo.: Lynne Rienner.

——— (1992b). "Paramilitary Intervention." In *Intervention into the 1990s: U.S. Foreign Policy in the Third World*, 2nd ed., edited by Peter Schraeder. Boulder, Colo.: Lynn Rienner.

Sciolino, Elaine (1993a). "Christopher Casts Doubt on Efforts for Bosnian Peace." *New York Times*, January 22, 1993.

——— (1993b). "Christopher Explains the Conditions for Bosnia Peace." *New York Times*, April 28, 1993.

——— (1993c). "Bosnia Impasse: How U.S. Search for Unity with Allies Unraveled." *New York Times*, May 12, 1993.

——— (1995). "Clinton Makes His Case to Congress for Putting U.S. Troops in Bosnia." *New York Times*, November 15, 1995.

Scranton, Margaret (1991). *The Noriega Years: U.S.-Panamanian Relations, 1981–1990*. Boulder, Colo.: Lynne Rienner.

Seelye, Katherine (1995). "Clinton Gives Republicans Pledge on Arming Bosnians." *New York Times*, December 13, 1995.

Seligson, Mitchell, and Edward Muller (1994). "Civic Culture and Democracy: The Question of Causal Relationships." *American Political Science Review* 88 (3): 635–52.

Shafer, D. Michael (1988). *Deadly Paradigms: The Failure of U.S. Counterinsurgency Policy*. Princeton: Princeton University Press.

Sheehan, Neil (1988). *A Bright Shining Lie: John Paul Vann and America in Vietnam*. New York: Random House.

Shultz, George (1993). *Turmoil and Triumph: My Years as Secretary of State*. New York: Charles Scribner's.

Singer, J. David, and Melvin Small (1982). *Resort to Arms: International and Civil Wars, 1816–1980*. Beverly Hills: Sage.

——— (1994). *Correlates of War Project: International and Civil War Data, 1816–1992*. Computer File. Ann Arbor, Mich., Inter-University Consortium for Political and Social Research, ICPSR 9905.

Smith, Tony (1994). *America's Mission: The United States and the Worldwide Struggle for Democracy in the Twentieth Century*. Princeton: Princeton University Press.

Sorensen, Theodore (1965). *Kennedy*. New York: Harper & Row.

Spiro, David (1994). "The Insignificance of the Liberal Peace." *International Security* 19 (2): 50–86.

Stanley, William (1995). "International Tutelage and Domestic Political Will: Building a New Civilian Police Force in El Salvador." *Studies in Comparative International Development* 30 (1): 132–54.

——— (1996). *The Protection Racket State*. Philadelphia: Temple University Press.

Steinmetz, Sara (1994). *Democratic Transition and Human Rights: Perspectives on U.S. Foreign Policy*. Albany: State University of New York Press.

Stepan, Alfred (1988). *Rethinking Military Politics: Brazil and the Southern Core*. Princeton: Princeton University Press.

Storrs, K. Larry (1983). "Central America." In *Congress and Foreign Policy: 1982*. Washington, D.C.: Government Printing Office.

—— (1984). "Central America." In *Congress and Foreign Policy, 1983*. Washington, D.C.: Government Printing Office.

Sullivan, Shawn (1995). "The State Department and Moderation of the Reagan Administration's Policies in El Salvador." Master's thesis, University of New Mexico.

Tambs, Lewis, ed. (1980). *A New Interamerican Policy for the Eighties: A Report of the Committee of Santa Fe*. Washington, D.C.: Council for Interamerican Security.

Taylor, Maxwell (1972). *Swords and Plowshares*. New York: W. W. Norton.

Thompson, William (1996). "Democracy and Peace." *International Organization 50* (1): 141–74.

Thompson, William, and Richard Tucker (1997). "A Tale of Two Democratic Peace Critiques." *Journal of Conflict Resolution 41* (3): 428–54.

Thomson, James (1968). "How Could Vietnam Happen?" *Atlantic Monthly 221* (4): 47–53.

Tillema, Herbert (1973). *Appeal to Force: American Military Intervention in the Age of Containment*. New York: Thomas Crowell.

—— (1989). "Foreign Overt Military Intervention in the Nuclear Age." *Journal of Peace Research 26* (2): 179–95.

—— (1994). "Cold War Alliance and Overt Military Intervention, 1945–1991." *International Interactions 20* (3): 249–78.

Tompkins, E. Berkeley (1970). *Anti-Imperialism in the United States: The Great Debate, 1890–1920*. Philadelphia: University of Pennsylvania Press.

Trask, David (1981). *The War with Spain in 1898*. New York: Macmillan.

Tregaskis, Richard (1963). *Vietnam Diary*. New York: Popular Library.

Treverton, Gregory (1990). "Intelligence: Welcome to the American Government." In *A Question of Balance: The President, the Congress, and Foreign Policy*, edited by T. Mann, 70–108. Washington, D.C.: Brookings Institution.

U.S. Agency for International Development (1963–1992). *U.S. Overseas Loans and Grants*.

U.S. Arms Control and Disarmament Agency (1963–1992). *World Military Expenditures and Arms Transfers*.

U.S. Congress (1896a). *Congressional Record*, 54th Cong., 1st sess.

—— (1896b). *Congressional Record*, 54th Cong., 2d sess.

—— (1897). *Congressional Record*, 55th Cong., 1st sess.

—— (1898). *Congressional Record*, 55th Cong., 2d sess.

—— (1899). *Congressional Record*, 55th Cong., 3d sess.

—— (1901). *Congressional Record*, 56th Cong., 2d sess.

—— (1963). *Vietnam and Southeast Asia: A Report of Senators Mike Mansfield (D-Mont.), J. Caleb Boggs (D-Del.), Claiborne Pell (D-R.I.), and Benjamin Smith (D-Mass.) to the Senate Foreign Relations Committee*.

—————— (1977). *Religious Persecution in El Salvador: Hearings Before the House Foreign Affairs Committee, Subcommittee on International Organizations*, 95th Cong., 1st sess., July 21 and 29.

—————— (1980). *Foreign Assistance and Related Programs Appropriations for 1981: House Appropriations Committee, Subcommittee on Foreign Operations*, 96th Cong., 2d sess., April 1.

—————— (1981a). *Central America, 1981: Report by Representatives Gerry Studds (D-Mass.), Barbara Mikulski (D-Md.), and Robert Edgar (D-Pa.)*, 97th Cong., 1st sess., March.

—————— (1981b). *Foreign Assistance and Related Programs for Fiscal Year 1982: Hearings Before the House Appropriations Committee, Subcommittee on Foreign Operations*, 97th Cong., 1st sess., February 25.

—————— (1981c). *U.S. Policy Toward El Salvador: Hearings Before the House Foreign Affairs Committee, Subcommittee on Interamerican Affairs*, 97th Cong., 1st sess., March 5 and 11.

—————— (1981d). *Foreign Assistance Authorization for Fiscal Year 1982: Hearings Before the Senate Foreign Relations Committee*, 97th Cong., 1st sess., March 19.

—————— (1981e). *Foreign Assistance Legislation for Fiscal Year 1982, part 9: Markup, House Foreign Affairs Committee*, 97th Cong., 1st sess., April 28–30, May 5–7, and 12–13.

—————— (1982a). *Presidential Certification on El Salvador: Hearings Before the House Foreign Affairs Committee, Subcommittees on Human Rights and International Organizations and Interamerican Affairs*, 97th Cong., 2d sess., February 2, 23, 25, and March 2.

—————— (1982b). *Report of the Official Observer Mission to the El Salvador Constituent Assembly Elections of March 28, 1982, by Senator Nancy Landon Kassebaum to the Senate Foreign Relations Committee.*

—————— (1984). *Congressional Record*, 98th Cong., 2d sess.

—————— (1993a). *Congressional Record*, 103d Cong., 1st sess.

—————— (1993b). *Department of Defense Appropriations for Fiscal Year 1994, part 1: Hearings Before the Senate Committee on Appropriations*, 103d Cong., 1st sess., April 20–22, 28–29.

—————— (1993c). *To Stand Against Aggression: Milosevic, the Bosnian Republic, and the Conscience of the West: A Report of the Subcommittee on European Affairs of the Senate Foreign Relations Committee*, April.

—————— (1994a). *Congressional Record*, 103d Cong., 2d sess.

—————— (1994b). *Impact of a Unilateral United States Lifting of the Arms Embargo on the Government of Bosnia-Herzegovina: Hearings Before the Senate Committee on Armed Services*, 103d Cong., 2d sess., June 23.

—————— (1994c). *The Situation in Haiti: Hearings Before the Senate Armed Services Committee*, 103d Cong., 2d sess., September 28.

—————— (1995a). *Congressional Record*, 104th Cong., 1st sess.

—————— (1995b). *Legislative and Municipal Elections in Haiti: Hearings Before the Senate Subcommittee on Western Hemisphere and Peace Corps Affairs of the Committee on Foreign Relations*, 104th Cong., 1st sess., July 12.

—————— (1996a). *Haiti, The Situation After the Departure of the U.S. Contingent from UNMH: Hearings Before the Subcommittee on the Western Hemisphere* of the House Committee on International Relations, 104th Cong., 2d sess., February 28.

——— (1996b). *Prospects for Free and Fair Elections in Bosnia: Hearings Before the Committee on International Relations of the House of Representatives*, 104th Cong., 2d sess., June 11.

——— (1997a). *Bosnian Elections, A Postmortem: Hearing Before the House Committee on International Relations*, 104th Cong., 2d sess., September 19, 1996.

——— (1997b). *Bosnia Peace Process: Hearings Before the Subcommittee on European Affairs of the Senate Foreign Relations Committee*, 104th Cong., 2d sess., September 10 and October 1, 1996.

U.S. Department of Commerce (1955). *Foreign Aid by the United States Government, 1940–1951.*

U.S. Department of Defense (1971). *The Pentagon Papers: Senator Gravel Edition.* Boston: Beacon Press.

——— (1983). *Remarks Prepared for Delivery by the Honorable Fred Ikle, Under Secretary of Defense for Policy, Before the Baltimore Council on Foreign Affairs,* September 12.

U.S. Department of State (1898). *Foreign Relations of the United States, 1897.*

——— (1900–1901). *Report of the Philippine Commission.*

——— (1901). *Foreign Relations of the United States, 1898.*

——— (1902). *Correspondence Relating to the War with Spain: April 15, 1898–July 30, 1902,* vol. 1.

——— (1904). *Correspondence Relating to the War with Spain: April 15, 1898–July 30, 1902,* vol. 2.

——— (1981). *Communist Interference in El Salvador: State Department White Paper,* February 23.

——— (1982). *American Foreign Policy: Current Documents, 1981.*

——— (1983). *American Foreign Policy: Current Documents, 1982.*

——— (1984). *American Foreign Policy: Current Documents, 1983.*

——— (1986). *Foreign Relations of the United States, 1958–1960: Vietnam.*

——— (1988). *Foreign Relations of the United States, 1961: Vietnam.*

——— (1991a). *Foreign Relations of the United States, 1961–1963: Vietnam: January–August 1963.*

——— (1991b). *Foreign Relations of the United States, 1961–1963: Vietnam: August–December 1963.*

——— (1993). "The Governor's Island Accords." *Foreign Policy Bulletin* 4 (2).

——— (1995). *Text of the Dayton Accords: Annex Three: Elections.* Washington, D.C., www.state.gov (Bosnia link).

U.S. War Department (1904). *Annual Reports of the Secretary of War, 1899–1903.*

Vaky, Viron (1987). "Central America at the Crossroads: Testimony Before the House Foreign Affairs Committee by Under-Secretary of State Vaky." In *Central America Crisis Reader,* edited by R. Leiken and B. Rubin, 493–500. New York: Summit Books.

Walker, Thomas (1987). *Reagan vs. the Sandinistas: The Undeclared War on Nicaragua.* Boulder, Colo.: Westview Press.

Walt, Stephen (1987). *The Origins of Alliances.* Ithaca, N.Y.: Cornell University Press.

Weinberger, Caspar (1990). *Fighting for Peace: Seven Critical Years in the Pentagon.* New York: Warner Books.

Welch, Richard (1979). *Response to Imperialism: The United States and the Philippine-American War, 1899–1902.* Chapel Hill: University of North Carolina Press.

White, Theodore (1961). *The Making of the President, 1960.* New York: Athenaeum House.

Whitehead, Laurence (1991). "The Imposition of Democracy." In *Exporting Democracy: Themes and Issues,* edited by A. Lowenthal, 216–42. Baltimore: Johns Hopkins University Press.

Winslow, Erving (1976). "The Anti-Imperialist League." In *American Anti-Imperialism, May 18, 1899,* edited by G. Markowitz, 29–32. New York: Garland.

Wisan, Joseph (1934). *The Cuban Crisis as Reflected in the New York Press, 1895–1898.* New York: Columbia University Press.

Woodward, Bob (1987). *Veil: The Secret Wars of the CIA, 1981–1987.* New York: Simon & Schuster.

——— (1994). *The Agenda: Inside the Clinton White House.* New York: Simon & Schuster.

Wright, Theodore (1964). *American Support for Free Elections Abroad.* Washington, D.C.: Public Affairs Press.

Zaroulis, Nancy, and Gerald Sullivan (1984). *Who Spoke Up? American Protest Against the War in Vietnam, 1963–1975.* Garden City, N.Y.: Doubleday.

Index